Martyn Whittock read Politics at the University of Bristol and has taught history for 27 years. He is currently the Director of the Humanities Faculty and Head of History in a Wiltshire secondary school. The author of numerous history textbooks and articles, his specialist interests include medieval and early medieval history, the early development of the Arthurian legends and 'signs and marvels' as recorded in medieval chronicles. He has acted as an historical and educational consultant to BBC radio, the National Trust and English Heritage. He is also a Methodist Lay Preacher and an Anglican Lay Minister. He lives in Bradford on Avon, Wiltshire, within the ten mile radius in which his direct ancestors have lived since the Middle Ages.

Titles available in the Brief History series

A BRIEF HISTORY OF

LIFE IN
THE MIDDLE AGES

MARTYN WHITTOCK

ROBINSON

RUNNING PRESS
PHILADELPHIA · LONDON

ROBINSON

First published in the UK by Robinson, an imprint of Constable & Robinson, 2009

Reprinted by Robinson in 2017

9 10 8

Copyright © Martyn Whittock, 2009

The moral right of the author has been asserted.

A CIP catalogue record for this book
is available from the British Library.

UK ISBN: 978-1-84529-685-8

Robinson
An imprint of
Little, Brown Book Group
Carmelite House
50 Victoria Embankment
London EC4Y 0DZ

An Hachette UK Company
www.hachette.co.uk

www.littlebrown.co.uk

First published in the United States in 2009 by Running Press Book Publishers
A member of the Perseus Books Group

Books published by Running Press are available at special discounts for bulk purchases in the
United States by corporations, institutions and other organizations. For more information, please
contact the Special Markets Department at the Perseus Books Group, 2300 Chestnut Street, Suite 200,
Philadelphia, PA 19103, or call (800) 810-4145, ext. 5000, or email special.markets@perseusbooks.com.

US Library of Congress number: 2009920963
US ISBN 978-0-7624-3712-2

10 9 8 7 6 5 4 3 2 1
Digit on the right indicates the number of this printing

Running Press Book Publishers
2300 Chestnut Street
Philadelphia, PA 19103-4371
Visit us on the web!
www.runningpress.com

Printed and bound in Great Britain by CPI Group (UK) Ltd., Croydon CR0 4YY

Papers used by Robinson are from well-managed forests and other responsible sources

MIX
Paper from
responsible sources
FSC® C104740

In memory of William Wyttok, burgess of Langport,
Somerset in 1327; the first recorded medieval Whittock.
And for John Howard, John Worth and Fiona Holland:
good friends who share with me a love of the past.

CONTENTS

ACKNOWLEDGEMENTS

I am grateful for assistance and advice from the following people while I was carrying out research into this book. Professor Chris Brooks, Durham University; Professor Eamon Duffy, Cambridge University; Professor Chris Dyer, Leicester University; Professor Mark Jackson, Exeter University; Dr Leonard Schwarz and Dr Chris Callow, Birmingham University; Marika Sherwood, Institute of Commonwealth Studies; Dr Brendan Smith, Bristol University; Professor Thorlac Turville-Petre, Nottingham University; Professor Chris Wickham, Oxford University; Professor Barbara Yorke, Winchester University; Wiltshire County Library Service and my friends at Bradford on Avon library. It goes without saying that all errors are my own.

As always my wife, Christine, and our daughters, Hannah and Esther, supported me with their love, advice and encouragement. They know how precious they are to me. In particular I am grateful to Christine and Hannah for reading and commenting on a number of chapters. My good friend John Worth also provided valuable advice and comments.

Martyn Whittock
St Simeon's Day, 2008

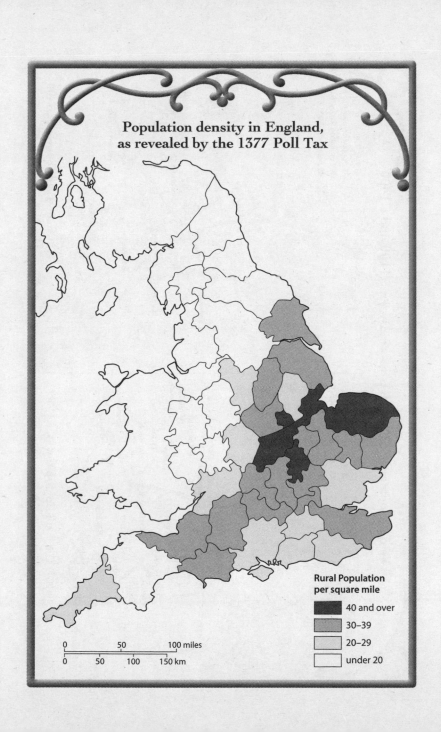

Population density in England,
as revealed by the 1377 Poll Tax

Rural Population
per square mile

40 and over

30–39

20–29

under 20

0   50   100 miles

0   50   100   150 km

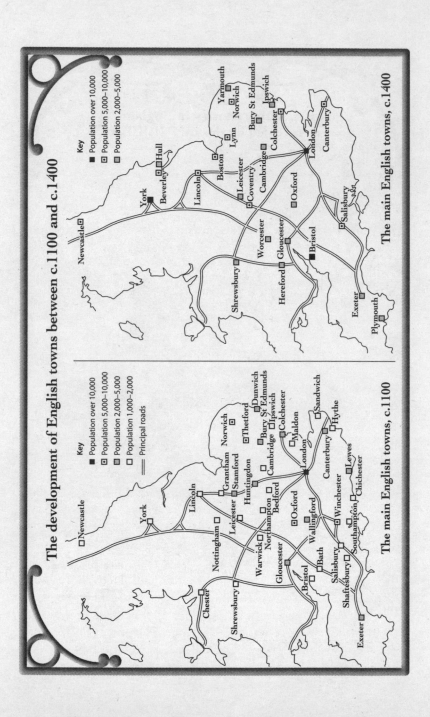

The development of English towns between c.1100 and c.1400

Key

- ■ Population over 10,000
- ▣ Population 5,000–10,000
- ▨ Population 2,000–5,000
- □ Population 1,000–2,000
- ━━ Principal roads

The main English towns, c.1100

Newcastle □
York □
Chester □
Shrewsbury □
Nottingham □
Lincoln □
Grantham □
Stamford ▨
Leicester □
Huntingdon □
Warwick □
Northampton □
Bedford □
Gloucester ▨
Oxford □
Wallingford □
Bath ▨
Bristol ▨
Salisbury □
Shaftesbury ▨
Southampton □
Winchester ▨
Chichester □
Lewes ▨
Canterbury ▨
London ■
Norwich ▣
Thetford □
Dunwich ▨
Bury St Edmunds ▨
Cambridge □
Ipswich ▨
Colchester □
Maldon □
Sandwich □
Hythe □
Exeter ▨

Key

- ■ Population over 10,000
- ▣ Population 5,000–10,000
- ▨ Population 2,000–5,000

The main English towns, c.1400

Newcastle ▣
York ■
Hull ▣
Beverley ▣
Lincoln ▣
Boston ▣
Leicester ▨
Coventry ▣
Shrewsbury ▨
Worcester ▨
Hereford ▨
Gloucester ▨
Bristol ■
Exeter ▨
Plymouth ▨
Salisbury ▣
Cambridge ▨
Oxford ▨
London ■
Canterbury ▣
Colchester ▣
Ipswich ▨
Bury St Edmunds ▨
Norwich ▣
Lynn ▣
Yarmouth ▣

INTRODUCTION

The time frame of the Middle Ages is traditionally built around two apparent watersheds. In England the boundaries have frequently been set at 1066 and 1485. This time frame is therefore formed from two political events: the first date being the Norman Conquest and the second being the battle of Bosworth and the start of the Tudor dynasty.

These were highly significant events but their role as 'boundary points' can be challenged from a number of angles. While 1066 can be demonstrated to have been a *political* watershed, ending the Anglo-Saxon political era and bringing in a new Norman dynasty which had an immense impact on England and its political culture, in *social* terms the date has far less meaning. Many aspects of society continued relatively uninterrupted from the middle and late Saxon periods into and beyond the Norman period. Developments in the Church, while accelerated by the arrival of new leadership, built on long-established trends; the language of the majority of the population remained English (albeit with a large infusion of Norman-French terms and social downgrading of English); trends in urbanization and taxation continued under 'new management' without major dislocation; industrial production of key consumer items, such as pottery, did not reflect the seismic changes happening at the top of the social hierarchy; the penny in the pocket of the average consumer in 1070 not only looked the same as under King Harold (and was minted by exactly the same moneyer within the same system of coinage) but it also bought pretty much the same products as it had done in the 1050s and 1060s. In addition, many of the key features which we associate with the 'Norman period' (such as manorialization, the feudal system and nucleated villages) can be seen as part of a process of development which straddles the mid-eleventh century and which has roots going back at least a hundred years before William the Conqueror took the throne.

Therefore the Middle Ages in England should really be considered to start around the year 900 with the start of the West Saxon re-conquest of the *Danelaw* (the area of the East Midlands, East Anglia and northern England conquered by the Vikings), following the first great phase of Viking invasions and conquest in the mid-ninth century. In fact, key features of society at this point have roots that could push the boundary back another century. And even this would be late for many historians and archaeologists: the British Museum's Anglo-Saxon collection being placed in its 'Early Medieval Room'. If the Sutton Hoo treasures (dating from c.625) are 'Early Medieval' then the events of 1066 are in the middle of 'the Middle Ages', not at its start! However, in the overview of events which form the focus of this book the boundary will *not* be pushed back this far – but it is clear that 1066 comes too late in the process to be the starting point of the exploration.

At the other end of the period, the year 1485 offers even less of a social watershed and, even politically, its usefulness as a defining moment has been questioned. Alternative political watershed dates have been persuasively suggested: One is 1461, since there seems to be significant continuity between the rule of Edward IV and Richard III and that of Henry VII. Or perhaps 1483 is the political watershed? In this case Richard III's royal coup in that year created the real break with the past and set in motion forces which would soon lead to the downfall of the Yorkist dynasty. However, whatever the merits of these political watershed dates, in social terms the date 1485 is without meaning since it led to no significant changes in the lives of ordinary people. A much stronger case can be made that it is with the rigorous Protestant Reformation of Edward VI's reign (and the destruction of the Catholic 'ritual year') that the old medieval world came to an end for many ordinary people. It was this – accompanied by the spread of new ideas made possible by the accelerating pace of printing – which fundamentally changed the texture of life for most people. As we shall see, this was accompanied by demographic and other changes which made the experience of life significantly different from what it had been for much of the fifteenth century and the early sixteenth century. For this reason the social-history focus of this book will be from about 900 to about 1553.

The range of evidence which can be used to piece together the lives of men and women from the English Middle Ages are many and varied. Archaeological evidence is giving us an increasingly intimate picture of the layout of rural houses and their relationship to the farmed landscape. Excavations, such as those at Wharram Percy (Yorkshire) and more recently at St Mary Spital, in London, are providing us with a large set of data regarding health and nutrition, as well as changing fashions in burial practice. Excavations on urban sites have given us greater insights into the relationship between living, producing and consuming in the growing towns; evidence for regional and international trade broadens our understanding of the variety of human experiences.

Written records are as varied. The rolls of manor courts, for example, show us the rural community in all its complexity: cooperation on the yearly round of agricultural practices; the financial demands on villagers for brewing, baking, marrying and even dying; the emergence of hereditary surnames in the thirteenth and fourteenth centuries; traditional customs and changing times. When we read about Richard Rawdon, fined 40 pence at Yeadon (Yorkshire) in 1452 for having a dog reputed to be a 'sheep worrier', or his neighbour, John Wryght, fined 2 pence because he 'allowed oxen to run amok'[1] we are privileged to gain a glimpse into the intimate world of the Middle Ages.

While so much documentation is lost, remarkable survivals such as the Paston Letters open up a window into the ambitions and conflicts of family and neighbours. Court records and coroners' accounts provide information about crime and deviance, as well as about community policing and values. When analysis of legal records shows us that fourteenth century East Anglia had a homicide rate greater than modern New York we can be sure that this will not be the only evidence which challenges our expectations. Sometimes the evidence is highly revealing but sparse, such as that providing information about the actual wealth of individuals within the population. After the 1334 tax subsidy, the next comprehensive assessment of actual wealth has to wait until that of Henry VIII in 1524–5. On the other hand it is often possible to combine information from different classes of evidence in order to build a bigger picture of an aspect of life. For example, complementary evidence from both changing church architecture expressed in chantries and the literary evidence provided by the fifteenth-century *Books of Hours* gives us insights into the personal spirituality of the fifteenth century.

And sometimes, even when records are lost, we occasionally catch a glimpse of how the loss occurred and at times we can link the events in one small location with events happening on a national scale. In this way the manor court roll at Great Bromley (Essex), in 1382, records why earlier records were no longer in existence, because in the previous year the unfree tenants of the manor had: 'assaulted Lady Anna in her hall and threatened her, and illegally took all court rolls . . . pertaining to this manor . . . against the peace of the lord king and against the will of the said Anna, and carried them away in contempt of this lordship, and burned all the said rolls feloniously'.[2] In this way the Peasants' Revolt affected one Essex community.

However, there is a caveat. As with all periods of the past the rich, powerful and famous leave more evidence behind than the poor and powerless. This is almost a truism but needs stating. The semi-free villager of the late eleventh century left no more to his or her heirs than the struggling peasant farmer of a modern LEDC (less economically developed country) today. And the handful of cooking utensils and agricultural tools which formed such a vital legacy to the next generation are often not even mentioned in the surviving documentation. With less to leave, these people had less to be remembered by and were more easily forgotten. Yet to those inheriting these few valuables they represented the careful accumulation of a lifetime. When such evidence *does* survive it is as vital as the more abundant and varied evidence for the life and values of wealthier neighbours. This is because, if we are to attempt a real understanding of life in the Middle Ages, we must take account of those untold millions who left so little information about the beliefs, work and worries of their lives. Such a person was Joan Symkynwoman in Yorkshire in 1366, whose court statement records that she owned 'almost nothing in goods save her clothing for body and bed, and a small brass pot.' She would not have been alone in her poverty.

Finally, it may be helpful to explain something of the approach of this book. Social history must put us firmly in touch with the lives of people in the past and the issues they faced. The examination of the evidence available to us makes the personal experiences of those in the past more accessible, as well as outlining the wider processes and developments which acted on individuals. In order to assist in this balance each chapter makes frequent references to the experiences of individuals as wider issues are explored.

A key point that should be remembered while reading this book is that the Middle Ages were not a static period but rather were a time of dynamic change and development. This involved both progress and regression. The pace of change was faster in some areas than in others. Some processes were stimulated 'from below' while others were the result of the decisions and ambitions of elites. Some changes were largely caused by activities and actions within Britain; others were triggered by events which were played out on a European, or even a global scale.

Some changes affected the mundane aspects of life, while others changed the spiritual and mental outlook of those affected.

What is clear is that, in this complex mosaic of events (from the local to the regional and the national), the lives of men and women reflected and responded to a wide range of issues, processes and developments. Whether it was a Northumbrian tenant of a great monastic estate dying, in 1349, from a disease which had its origins in central Asia, or a Jew abandoned to drown on a sandbar of the river Thames by an unscrupulous ship owner during the expulsion of the Jews from England in 1290, members of English medieval society lived their lives in the context of issues linking them to a wider world. These issues also linked them to questions which are very real and engaging to a reader in the twenty-first century. The common issues of our shared humanity across the ages are at least as striking as the great differences in outlook and experience.

Chapter 1

THE CHARACTER OF LATE ANGLO-SAXON SOCIETY

An Anglo-Saxon conversation. Written by Master Aelfric (between 989 and 1002) for his students in the monastic school at Cerne Abbas (Dorset), the following conversation gives an insight into the life and thoughts of the 'unfree' in late Anglo-Saxon England.

Master: 'What have you to say, ploughman? Tell me how you go about your work.'

Ploughman: 'Oh I work very hard indeed sir. Every day at the crack of dawn I have to drive the oxen out to the field and yoke them to the plough. I would never dare scive at home, no matter how bad the winter weather: I'm too frightened of my landlord for that. No, once I've yoked the oxen and fastened the share and coulter to the plough, I must plough a full acre or more every day.'

Master: 'What else have you to do in a day?'

Ploughman: 'Oh, there's a lot more than that, you know. I've got to fill all the oxen's bins with hay, give them water, muck them out.'

Master: 'Oh, my: it sounds like hard work.'

Ploughman: 'It's hard work alright, sir, because I am not free.'[1]

The Middle Ages did not spring into being in 1066, and many aspects of society were not immediately changed by the Norman Conquest. In fact, many characteristics of life in the second half of the eleventh century had their roots deep in Anglo-Saxon history and would continue to influence the development of people's lives long after the final arrows had fallen around the broken shield-wall of the last Anglo-Saxon king on Saturday 14 October 1066. It is therefore important to gain an overview of the structure and dynamics of late Anglo-Saxon society. Only in this way can we trace the great trends and issues that would dominate the lives of medieval people.

So what was it like to live in England around the year 1000, at the turn of the first millennium since the birth of Christ? Despite a century and a half of social and political upheaval since the Viking 'Great Army' had first overwintered in England in 851–2, England was generally within borders we would recognize today (except for the much-disputed northern border with the Scots). Furthermore, since the over-throw of the last Viking king of York (Eric 'Bloodaxe', in 954), it was ruled by one king who was descended from King Alfred and whose ability to tax and keep order was impressive by any standard. The old kingdoms (Wessex, Northumbria, Mercia, East Anglia), which had characterized England at the beginning of the ninth century, had long gone and it was now possible to call the country 'England' and its dominant culture 'English' (both terms derived from the tribal name 'Angle').

Wealth and economy
England in the eleventh century was a wealthy country in which the ability of the government to raise huge taxes during

the Viking wars had revealed just how dynamic and productive society was, despite the upheaval. These taxes drew on the resources of a well-organized rural society which, during the tenth and eleventh centuries, was taking on many of the characteristics of the medieval countryside: stone churches acting like an anchor slowing down settlement shift; more nucleated villages; new field systems. Many of these developments were influenced by powerful local landowners capable of reorganizing the landscape and its people and maximizing the surpluses of a prosperous farming system.

In 1018 a *geld* (tax) introduced by Cnut, the new ruler of both England and Denmark, raised £82,500. This vast tax was in addition to the £112,000 which had been raised in Danegelds since 991. All of this money paid to the government (and then to Viking marauders) was in addition to any other payments that ordinary people habitually made to local landowners and royal officials. To give this some sense of scale, in the mid-tenth century a fully grown pig cost 6 pence (with 240 pennies in each £1). In the 1060s the four mills of the Abbey of Ely at Hatfield turned in a combined yearly profit of £2, 6 shillings and 4 pence. The combined value of all the estates of Glastonbury – the wealthiest abbey in 1066 – was in the region of £820. So great was the output of tenth-century urban craftspeople that some historians have gone so far as to talk of the tenth century witnessing the 'First English Industrial Revolution'.[2] England was a well managed and wealthy community. Only such a wealthy community was capable of paying the huge Danegelds in the years up to 1018. Consequently, it is no surprise to discover that modern archaeologists have found Anglo-Saxon silver pennies (the everyday English coin for much of the Middle Ages) as far afield as Russia.[3] This trading network which linked England to Russia was no temporary connection, since the 4,600 coins discovered to date span a period from 852 to 1272. English farmers and craftspeople were part of a Europe-wide manufacturing and trading system, importing wine, spices, silk and pottery from Northern France and the

Rhineland, whetstones and querns from the Eiffel mountains, and exporting slaves, linen, horses and weaponry.

An ethnically divided nation?

Was England of the year 1000 a united national community? Or was it a community divided between native Anglo-Saxons and immigrant Danes who had seized land in eastern England (the Danelaw) before this was reconquered by Anglo-Saxon kings in the tenth century? At first glance it might seem more like the latter. The chronicler Ethelweard (who died about 998) described the Danes living in England in the late tenth century as 'sprung up in this island, like poisonous weeds among the wheat.' And it is easy to see how, when a second phase of Viking attacks began in the 980s and eventually culminated in the conquest of England by the Danish King Cnut, in 1016, this could be assisted by an immigrant community who 'cheered' for Denmark rather than for England. When the Anglo-Saxon King Ethelred II ('the Unready') ordered a slaughter of the Danish population in England on St Brice's Day, 13 November 1002, the terrible echoes of modern ethnic cleansing seem to resonate powerfully with the idea of a profoundly divided nation. But is this a reasonable assumption?

In assessing the significance of some 13,500 metal-detector finds of Viking and Anglo-Scandinavian metalwork discovered up to 2004, the picture is emerging of a lower-class immigration of peasant farmers (into Lincolnshire at least), not just the arrival of higher-status warrior-landlords.[4] In addition, comparisons of skeleton evidence from Wharram Percy (from 950 onwards), on the Yorkshire Wolds, and medieval cemeteries from York (about 20 miles away) suggests skull types at Wharram Percy and York in the *later* medieval period are broadly similar, whereas in the *early* medieval period York skulls are similar to ones from Oslo. This suggests that York in the 'Viking Age' was heavily settled by incoming Vikings, while outlying country areas were not. But, as migration from outlying areas into York occurred over the medieval period, the Viking genetic difference 'was diluted and eventually dissolved'.[5]

All of this sharpens the question: how did these people regard themselves? It is this question that we need to address if we are to come anywhere near deciding how united England was in the decades before 1066. Clearly, those who spoke English regarded themselves as the descendants of Anglo-Saxon settlers who had migrated from north-western Europe in the fifth and sixth centuries (whether they really were, or were actually British people who had adopted Anglo-Saxon culture, speech and dress, is another question). But what of the descendants of Vikings – how did they regard themselves? Was England on the eve of the Norman Conquest a culturally divided nation, or one which was basically united from a fusion of Anglo-Saxons and the descendants of Vikings?

Evidence for major changes brought to English life and culture by the Viking invasions includes the following. Many new place names in eastern England (e.g. *by* and *thorp*); new words in the language; new personal names; evidence of a new class of independent farmers known as *sokemen* (enjoying greater freedom than their English counterparts); new units of tax assessment (*wapentakes* and *sulungs* in Danish areas, instead of *hundreds* and *hides* used to organize areas for tax purposes in Anglo-Saxon areas); new titles for the nobility (e.g. *jarl* or *earl*); and new administrative areas (e.g. the *Ridings* of Yorkshire and Lincolnshire). In addition, the Danish settlement involved the dispossession of English landlords of their estates. Alongside these changes, the aftermath of the first phase of Viking invasions saw a huge increase in industrial production: wheel-thrown and glazed pottery; increased marketing and trade; mass-produced metalwork. While the Vikings did not create this tenth-century 'Industrial Revolution', their trading skills meant it developed dramatically. This mass of evidence can leave one assuming that those areas which experienced the greatest concentration of these changes (the Danelaw) must have had a culture and a sense of community very different from that in other areas of England.

However, this may be too simple a view. What probably mattered to most people by 1000 was allegiance to local lords, rather than whether their ancestors were Anglo-Saxons, Britons, Danes or Norwegians.[6] This formed a mosaic of local loyalties within a community that now recognized itself as England. An alternative view, then, rejects this degree of national unity in favour of older, regional, kingdom identities but still insists that there was no great cultural and ethnic divide between Anglo-Saxons and Danes. It was these old regional loyalties which affected how people viewed themselves, and it seems that the incoming Danes had adopted the regional loyalties of the areas in which they had settled.[7]

Similarly, virtually no Scandinavian-style buildings have been found by archaeologists in England. The shops and houses excavated in the 1970s in Coppergate, in Viking Jorvik (York), are identical in style to English ones. There is in fact no 'ethnic signal' from these buildings. Furthermore, it was the English language which triumphed in the Danelaw – albeit with borrowings from Danish – and the use of the Viking runic alphabet soon disappeared. It is surely significant that the Scandinavian language was extinct on the Isle of Man by 1200. So, if it survived only 200 years here, where the Scandinavian culture was dominant, it probably did not last beyond the third generation of settlement where Scandinavian settlement was less intense on mainland England.[8]

A recent re-examination of the archaeological evidence for Scandinavian burials in northern England has concluded that there were many more than have previously been considered; however, the assimilation of the immigrants was rapid. This was a process accelerated by English rulers from Athelstan to Edgar who, even as they were including Scandinavians at court and recognizing Scandinavian practices in law codes, were enforcing their own authority across all England.[9] Under Ethelred II, the 997 'Wantage law code', with much Scandinavian terminology (contrasting with the contemporary 'Woodstock law code'), might suggest an ethnically divided realm but probably simply recognized the need for separate legislation in the north, while enforcing West Saxon authority there. As such, it was produced more to placate the north in the face of renewed Viking attacks than as a result of the ethnic separateness of the region due to earlier immigration.[10] In the same way, Swein Forkbeard's activities in the north in 1013 were probably due to the area's 'distance from the heartlands of the English kings and the dissatisfaction of northern nobles with King Ethelred, rather than the expectation of being able to draw upon latent feelings of ethnic allegiance.'[11] Revealingly, under Cnut, the Scandinavian *Urnes* and *Ringerike* styles of artwork are rare in the north and east Midlands, where they might be expected to have been popular, and instead are found more in East Anglia and southern England. Clearly this says more about the attraction of fashions associated with royalty than the ethnic origins of art patrons, and indicates that even the presence of Scandinavian kings as rulers of England from 1016 until 1042 'did not have the effect of renewing a sense of Scandinavian solidarity amongst the inhabitants of those regions settled by earlier generations of Scandinavians.'[12] Social status was more important than ethnic identity.

A Christian nation?

A key piece of evidence supporting the idea of Scandinavian newcomers quickly adapting to the culture they found in England comes from religion. Late Anglo-Saxon England was a deeply Christian community. There were two main forms in which the Church was organized in Anglo-Saxon England. The first was the monastery (*monasterium*). This was a community of monks and/or nuns. Their vows involved celibacy and rejection of private property (whereas lower orders of clergy were allowed to marry). The second group was made up of secular clergy (priests) leading services and preaching but not following a monastic way of life, although at times they could be found living in a kind of community –

large churches called *minsters*. Local Church administration was probably first centred on minsters at royal estate centres, which sometimes preserve this origin in a modern place name (e.g. Warminster, Wiltshire) with a large *parochia* (area of responsibility) which was later subdivided into parishes where Church work was financed from compulsory tithes.

In addition, there were other Church communities. These included bishops' households of priests and other clerics, and married priests and married clerks in lower orders living in their own households. The evidence for clerical families, married deacons and priests suggests that some of those responsible for preaching and teaching were not living in religious communities (in monasteries or minsters) but were in family units and possibly staffing village churches which had been set up as part of the sub-dividing of large areas once administered by minsters.

Local landowners could remove their lands from royal taxation by setting up a monastic church, administered by a family member. This was clearly not in the spirit of how monasteries should be established and such monasteries were more of a tax loophole than a statement of individual piety. In a similar way, estate-churches were often set up near a lord's hall and administered by the landowner, who appointed the priest. This provided a focus for the local community under aristocratic control. This trend increased under Viking influence in northern England and revealed itself in the dissolution of some monasteries, a huge increase in carved personal stone monuments in the tenth century, and an increase in estate-churches. This does not necessarily mean that the new Danish lords were unsympathetic to Christianity. It may simply mean that they wanted both to give gifts to the church *and* yet keep a close control over how this land was used and its resources distributed.[13]

The extent to which the Viking raids and eventual settlement affected the spiritual state of later Anglo-Saxon England is complex. The Viking influx was clearly an invasion of pagans. Evidence of this is seen in the destruction of monasteries, in pagan carvings (e.g. from Kirk Andreas, Isle of Man), in animal sacrifices (e.g. from Skerne, Yorkshire, on the River Hull), an increase in idol worship (e.g. Archbishop Wulfstan of York's criticism of this in 1000), possible human sacrifice on the Isle of Man and the destruction of Christian graves on the Isle of Man (e.g. Viking boat graves at Balladoole show no respect for an earlier Christian cemetery). But this impact of paganism should not be overstressed. In 869 Vikings martyred King (St) Edmund of East Anglia but, by 890, their descendants were minting coins with his name on them. Attacks on monasteries were not attempts to destroy Christianity but were targeting sources of wealth. By 1000 most northern pagans had become Christians and the Viking King of England and Denmark – Cnut – made Archbishop Wulfstan's attacks on idol worship into law in 1020. There are very few pagan Viking burials (those on the Isle of Man are exceptional). Finally, some grave-stones show Scandinavian art *but* in a Christian context. In short, the Vikings were cultural chameleons and rapidly adopted the lifestyle and beliefs of the advanced and numeri-cally dominant community they had conquered in eastern and northern England.

When we think of Viking attacks on England it is the destruction of monasteries which often provide the most striking visual image of their impact. There is sometimes an assumption that the seventh and eighth centuries were a 'golden age' of monasticism, which was disrupted by Viking invasions then reformed in the tenth and eleventh centuries – this reform being necessary due to a dilution of the once-rigorous system which had been monastic and celibate but had grown lax and worldly during the disruption of the Viking wars. However, many of the issues which were 'live issues' to tenth-century reformers of the English Church were also 'live issues' in the earlier eighth century too.

None was more pressing than sex. Celibacy was a crucial characteristic of the tenth century monastic reforms. This, for reformers, was the mark of difference between a monk and other clergy. Canon law forbade the marriage of bishops, priests and deacons, although men who were already married might be ordained to these higher posts but not if they had remarried after being widowed. Married priests and deacons had to be celibate after ordination (rulings varied as to whether husband and wife should live as brother and sister, or should separate). Minor orders (acolytes, exorcists, readers) could marry and continue sexual relations. That *any* clergy should be married was a scandal to reformers of the Church in the tenth century. It was not resolved then, however, and remained a live issue after 1066 too.

Overall, the Christian Church had a great impact on society. It assisted in record keeping and history making; it was vital for royal administration; it increased the role of women (giving them considerable responsibilities as abbesses); it pioneered building in stone. By 1066 about one-sixth of the land in England was in Church ownership. This provided settled and continuous control of estates, since church land did not change owners on the death of a landholder as secular estates did, making it easier to manage the land, invest in it and develop it. This also encouraged the development of fixed and nucleated settlements. These were focused on churches and monasteries as central places, were generally on lower ground, and were less likely to be on marginal/wilder land which no longer carried as much settlement as it once had. Thus landscape and people's daily experiences were deeply affected by the Church, which produced 'a Christianised way of ordering the landscape which put the church at the centre of settled fields, surrounded by the boundary zone of uncultivated land'.[14]

Churches, then, by the later Anglo-Saxon period, were at the centre of all community life. By 850 cemetery burial near churches was becoming the norm for most people[15], though royalty had been doing this since the 680s. Dispersed lay cemeteries away from churches had vanished by 900, and Church cemetery burial was by then standard practice. And churches were a common feature in the landscape. By 1014 law codes

recognized the existence of a hierarchy of churches ranging from
'head minsters' (cathedrals), to 'rather smaller minsters' (the
usual class of minsters), to 'one still smaller' (in a law code of
1020 defined as having a graveyard) and finally to 'field
churches' (by 1020 defined as a church without a graveyard). In
the period 1070–1120 there was a huge expansion of church
building but it built on the later Anglo-Saxon system and distribution. In Domesday Book (1086) about 2,000 churches are
listed and the assumption is clearly that every village has its
church and its priest. While this was not actually achieved before
1066, the development was well on the way. This process, from
the tenth century onwards, was increasingly associated with
stone church building, the creation of church cemeteries for all
burials and – especially during the eleventh century – the
appearance of fixed stone fonts to welcome babies into the
Christian community. The critical 'period of shift' in this development seems to have been between about 1030 and 1080.[16]

In their architectural styles Anglo-Saxon churches revealed
their formative influences. Early – *Romanesque* – churches
(sixth and seventh century) copied Roman Mediterranean
models: brick construction, relatively short proportions,
eastern apses and side rooms reached from the nave.[17]
However, eighth- and ninth-century churches copied
Carolingian building styles of the new western Holy Roman
Empire: stone rather than brick, towers and transepts, east-end
crypts holding relics, galleries and towers called *westworks*,
and cloisters. From the westwork a second choir added to the
drama of the liturgy, while increased church length allowed for
more processions.[18] The style of German churches continued
to influence English church architecture during the tenth
century[19] and can be seen in examples such as the cathedral
plans of Canterbury, Sherborne and Winchester, and in smaller
churches such as Brixworth (Northamptonshire) and Odda's
chapel at Deerhurst (Gloucestershire).

So, what impact did a second wave of Viking invasions
around the year 1000 have on this well-established Christian

community, which had already absorbed an earlier wave of pagan immigrants? The answer appears to have been: very little impact indeed. The appearance of pagan symbols on carvings from the eleventh century should not be interpreted as a revival of paganism. The overall evidence instead suggests that pagan motifs in art and poetry, dating from the reign of Cnut, constitute aspects of what might be called 'cultural paganism' – that is, not necessarily active pagan belief but references to cultural and artistic images which signalled the different origins of the new arrivals in eleventh-century England. This gave a 'light pagan colouring' to aspects of later Anglo-Saxon society but not to a revival of paganism.[20]

Altogether, then – counter-intuitively and in the face of the massacre of St Brice's Day – it is clear that England in the eleventh century was not a nation of sharply divided ethnic groups. Rather, it was united around a distinct set of Christian values and a sense of an English identity. The fact that there were strong regional identities as well – and that a Scandinavian influx into eastern England had maybe increased these – should not cause us to doubt this basic unity. Indeed, the fact that from 1016 until 1042 the English throne was occupied by a king of a united England and Denmark probably played a major part in unifying the nation and in closing any 'social fault lines' which had opened up during the second phase of Viking attacks around the year 1000. And, whatever the impact of that event on St Brice's Day, the Anglo-Saxon authorities simply did not have the organization and resources (let alone the reason and will) to exterminate all the descendants of Scandinavian immigrants. Dreadful as it was, that massacre probably targeted only a small minority of high-profile foreigners who seemed closely associated with the most recent phase of invasions. Finally, by the time the experiment in Anglo-Danish kingship was over in 1042, the terrible 'ethnic cleansing' of 1002 had been superseded by 26 years (1016–42) of Anglo-Danish cooperation and was a distant memory from another generation. Unity had triumphed over the forces of disintegration and ethnic division.

Life on the land

For about 90 per cent of the English population, regardless of their ethnic origins, life was lived on the land. The Anglo-Saxons had brought no new farming technology or practices to England[21] and the most striking farming practices which emerged by the end of Anglo-Saxon England were developed in this country.[22] Farming continued a pattern which had existed since the Bronze Age of a fully exploited landscape, with the heavier soils of valley floors being as actively worked as the better-drained higher land. On Exmoor, for example, pollen analysis suggests that there was no change caused by the end of Roman rule. In the period 400–600 there was no return to woodland and no alteration to a rural economy which on Exmoor was based on raising livestock. The big change (with increased cereal production) occurred between 600 and 800, and practices then stayed the same until the period 1500–1750.[23]

The Exmoor example is consistent with evidence from across England which suggests that the later Anglo-Saxon period saw great changes in the countryside. In this period were the beginnings of many developments which would be features of the rural scene for much of the Middle Ages. Evidence from the 1990s excavations of an extensive landscape tract at Yarnton (on the Thames valley gravels, north of Oxford) suggests that the earliest Anglo-Saxons settled in a landscape apparently abandoned by the Romano-British for perhaps several generations. The farms they built were scattered across the landscape. But in the 700s (and especially in the 800s) this pattern was replaced by one with more buildings, including timber halls, in more nucleated patterns and with a wider variety of crops grown, along with the creation of riverside hay meadows. This probably indicates the start of nucleated villages and the beginnings of open field farming, and reveals the mobility of settlement patterns which were arrested in the later Anglo-Saxon period.[24]

This raises the question of how much this system of rural communities was affected by the Viking invasions of the ninth and tenth centuries. Why were there so many new place names if other evidence suggests continuity of population? The answers are varied. Many new place names were probably applied to old settlements, since some sites such as Whitby (Yorkshire) and Osbournby (Lincolnshire) show continued occupation. New owners may have simply legitimized their ownership with a new place name without having any impact on those living there. Some new place names may date from a second wave of colonists who moved into previously unused and less-desirable land – the mapping of 'Danish place names' does suggest they are found on the least desirable land and slotted into 'gaps' between Anglo-Saxon villages which continued to be occupied. Mapping of place names suggests that where *by* is used in Yorkshire it indicates Anglo-Saxon settlements taken over as going concerns, and a similar inter-pretation of 'tun-hybrids' (such as the place name Grimston) shows the same pattern. The word *thorp* indicates settlements established on the outskirts of existing villages, whereas *thveit* indicates a woodland clearing and an area of primary culti-vation and settlement by Danes. In addition, evidence in north-west England and the central lowlands of Scotland (and the Isle of Man in some cases) shows that Scandinavian place-name forming elements were still being used long after the Viking Age by people who no longer spoke, or understood, Scandinavian languages.[25] All this suggests that modern place-name experts would no longer use Scandinavian place names as evidence of a massive dislocation of the countryside in the ninth and tenth centuries, even if it accompanied large-scale Scandinavian immigration. Similarly, current research stresses continuity of the parish structure and of estate boundaries in the Danelaw. The Vikings seem to have caused nothing which might be remotely thought to resemble a revolution in the countryside.[26]

But what of the villages themselves? Settlements in even the Middle Anglo-Saxon period do not constitute the start of villages, since most were rarely more than farmsteads. Many of these were abandoned in the later Anglo-Saxon period, and those which survived tended to do so as corners within later villages. This suggests that villages were products more of the Late than the Middle Anglo-Saxon period. This later change was possibly due to a greater degree of estate management by landlords out to maximize profits, the break-up of large so-called multiple estates, church building in stone, and the change from a pattern of dispersed hamlets and farms to more nucleated settlements with a greater degree of property demarcation within and around them.[27] From 700 onwards settlements show increasing stability, with more enclosures accompanied by larger post-hole-built buildings. This trend accelerated in the ninth century, with nucleated villages developing c.850–1200. England on the eve of the Norman Conquest was in the midst of a major formative period in the layout and organization of the countryside.

Associated with these developments was open-field farming, in which large areas of the countryside were divided into communally farmed arable strips, within great open fields. Open-field farming was probably a Middle to Late Anglo-Saxon reorganization designed to maximize efficiency due to population increase. Experiments with modern cereals have produced 5,183 dietary kilocalories per hectare by this method, compared with 884 for milk and 312 for beef.[28] This process of adopting open fields and increasing reliance on arable farming was not completed until after 1066. It was probably stimulated by the break-up of earlier 'multiple estates' which caused an emphasis on self-sufficiency of the new smaller estates (since they could no longer rely on the mixed resources of the larger units) and saw the emergence of a class of local lords, called *thegns*. This *manorialization* of the countryside was an Anglo-Saxon, not a Norman, invention. So, it was the period after 700 which saw manor-estate construction and ambitious landscape (often monastic) management, producing the 'typical Anglo-Saxon landscape'. Detailed local studies, such as that of the Bourn valley south-west of Cambridge, reinforce this impression that it was in the period 700–900 that systematic planning laid out the first open fields in central England.[29]

By the 1060s about 30 per cent of the landscape was employed in arable farming and about 15 per cent as managed woodland; the remaining 55 per cent supported pastoral farming, or was too poor to be used (with a small but unspecified area in urban use). By comparison, early twenty-first-century figures for England are: arable 40 per cent, woodland 9 per cent, pastoral 25 per cent. The remaining 26 per cent of the modern landscape is mostly within urban areas.

Early Medieval towns

If the vast majority of people lived in the countryside in the year 1000, a very important minority (about 10 per cent) lived in towns. This proportion was comparable with Roman Britain at its peak. During the eighth century, after a period in which there had been no true urban settlements in England, places began to appear which had features resembling towns. Archaeologists call these early trading centres *wics* or *emporia*. For example, Lundenwic was a huge 120-acre (48.5-hectare) town to the west of Roman London under what is now the area named Aldwych. Hamwic lay under modern Southampton. Gippeswic (Ipswich) was in Suffolk and another settlement was probably located at York. Some of these early trading centres appear to have been occupied on a temporary basis only. There also existed so-called 'productive sites'.[30] On these there is no surviving evidence of permanent structures but there is evidence of production and trade. These sites, when excavated, tend to produce large quantities of worked artefacts.[31]

These *emporia* were probably products of direct political intervention. Evidence for this is that they appear at a similar time and there was one per kingdom. Wessex had Hamwic, Mercia had London, East Anglia had Ipswich and Northumbria had York. This is important because it reminds us of an important feature of towns in the Middle Ages – they rarely grew up of their own accord but were usually encouraged by a powerful local member of the elite who gained from the increased trade opportunities. They quickly stimulated more elaborate patterns of exchange across wider regions, and this is particularly apparent in eastern England from the Tyne to the Thames. For example, wheel-thrown Ipswich Ware pottery has been found on monastic sites as far away as the north-east of England.[32]

By the ninth century these early semi-urban sites had developed into what are recognizably towns. A number of factors encouraged this further development. Firstly, they provided defended places, or *burhs*, which were particularly important as Viking attacks escalated from the mid-ninth century. However, burhs were not simply a response to invasion, since the Mercian King Offa (758–96) set up burhs at Bedford, Hereford, Oxford and Stamford, and these were clearly part of early state-building. Secondly, the Vikings themselves may have increased opportunities for trade, since they had wide-ranging trading connections. The Harrogate Hoard of coins, a gold arm ring and scrap silver (discovered in 2007 and probably deposited in the 930s) contained items from as far apart as Afghanistan, the Middle East, Russia, Scandinavia, Ireland, France and England. Thirdly, both the Church and local elites may have created semi-urban sites to encourage trade. There is an ongoing debate as to whether the most influential encouragement for the development of towns was provided by the Church, or by royalty and local elites. In other words: was a royal palace built near a pre-existing minster church, or was a minster church built near a pre-existing royal palace? This in turn can colour how archaeologists interpret what they find at these early urban centres. Was the stone building at Northampton a palace, or a minster refectory? Was the palace at Cheddar the centre of the site, or simply added to a pre-existing minster? Since hundreds of minsters are associated with small towns these are important questions. On balance the evidence suggests that royal centres were located near minsters and that by about 850 monastic towns had become 'progressively more urban, progressively less monastic'.[33] Fourthly, increasing sophistication in government meant that towns were useful places in which to place royal administration, justice and trade. As a consequence, where towns grew up around minsters, elite laity patronized them, benefited from them and eventually took them over.[34] Fifthly, the re-emergence of a money economy by the eighth century encouraged the growth of trading centres. The main difference between Middle Saxon *wics/emporia* and tenth-century towns are that the towns, unlike the earlier *wics*, had many functions – providing regional market centres, centres of craft production and places in which coins were minted. Any medieval townsperson would have recognized them.

From the tenth century onwards the growth of urban centres reduced the range of craft specialization on rural sites. Clearly, by this time towns had become places where most items were *made* as well as *sold*. From the ninth to the twelfth century it was town-based pottery kilns that produced the so-called 'Saxo-Norman pottery' (such as Stamford, Thetford and St Neots Ware) which was used across the country. Other examples include weapons, which were produced on a commercial basis. By 996 Winchester had a 'Street of the shield-makers' and London in 1016 reputedly contained 24,000 mail-coats which had clearly been made by local crafts-people. And any suggestion that the Vikings were the main cause of urban growth – from about twelve towns in the 850s to over a hundred in 1066 – must be rejected. Town expansion happened in non-Viking areas too and it is clear that towns were not a Viking invention but a general trend. On the Isle of Man, where Vikings dominated, there were no towns. In Ireland, Viking towns copied Anglo-Saxon forms.

A feature of early eleventh-century towns, which mirrored the situation after 1066, was the predominance of London (with its population of about 15,000). It was significantly above the next tier of towns (York, Winchester, Norwich, Lincoln, Oxford, Thetford), with populations each of

5–10,000. The *ealdormen* of London began to play a role in the succession of kings, which was something unheard-of a century earlier. A sign of this growing importance of London lies in the fact that Cnut garrisoned Danish military units there to secure its loyalty. This was necessary as London had earlier loyally supported Ethelred II and Edmund Ironside against Cnut. So Cnut, ever the tough pragmatist, had to enforce the loyalty which he celebrated as being his by right!

Social classes

What kinds of social classes existed in the two centuries before 1066? The simple answer is that Anglo-Saxon England was not a society of 'free-born Englishmen'. Instead, it was a clearly hierarchical society and a slave-owning one at that. In this last respect it differed from Norman England.

The nobility was a varied group. In the highest stratum were the *earls*, who had authority over regions, such as Northumbria, which had once been independent kingdoms. Below earls lay *ealdormen*. This literally meant 'one senior in age' (a prominent nobleman in the king's service, prominent in the army and royal court, deputizing for the king in law courts). Ealdormen came to have a key role in administering local government in the shires and in overseeing local justice in the *hundred* – local – courts (which are first recorded in the early tenth century). The country gentry of Anglo-Saxon England were the *thegns*. This term covered a huge range, from privileged nobles to retainers. By the 1060s there were about 4,500 of these local landowners, with their estates defined by charters. More powerful nobles – such as the king himself and the bishops – enjoyed a power called *borh*, or personal protection. This gave them special rights to compensation regarding offences on their property, or against their servants, and the power to administer justice. Whereas fines paid to members of the lower classes for crimes against their household went to the king, those with borh took it themselves – and presumably made sure they got it too.

The free Anglo-Saxon peasant farmer was usually described in Old English as a *ceorl*. He could carry weapons, could clear himself of crimes by swearing an oath protesting his innocence and could do the same for others. He could play a full part in the army and in local courts and possessed a share of the village land and flocks. He was responsible (on pain of a fine) for responding to royal commands to fight and attend court. Such freemen (termed *sokemen* in the Danelaw) made up about 15 per cent of the population and appear in large numbers in the eastern counties. Whilst many were little better-off than their semi-free neighbours, the dividing principle was whether a person was free to give (or sell) their land to another. While every man was under a superior lord, freemen could choose their lord. However, it seems that in eastern England lordship was weak. Here the growth of manors and labour service (key features of medieval feudalism), which was already an established part of rural society in other parts of England, seems less developed. By the end of the Anglo-Saxon period a ceorl could attain the rank of thegn by owning five hides of land, a bell house, and a place in the king's hall.

Below free peasants lay the *gebur* (semi-free peasants owing labour service to the local lord in return for their own land). About 70 per cent of the population was made up of these semi-free peasants by the mid-eleventh century, and Domesday Book describes them in a number of hierarchical terms, often later simplified to that of *villein*. This last point reminds us that the feudal system, with its manor courts and its labour service, whereby villagers were forced to provide free labour on the land farmed directly by a lord, had roots which went back long before 1066.

And what of slaves? This class, described by the Old English term *theow*, made up about 10 per cent of the population, had no legal rights other than the expectations in Christian teaching (e.g. a slave forced to work on a Sunday would be freed). Some slaves were victims of defeat in war; some descended from slaves; others were penal slaves such as those enslaved for working on a Sunday, or for some classes of theft. Others might sell themselves into slavery to avoid starvation. Bristol was a port which specialized in the shipping of slaves to Ireland 700 years before its more infamous specialization in the African slave trade to America. The Bristol slave trade with Ireland was fiercely opposed by Wulfstan, bishop of Worcester from 1062 until his death in 1095. From the Viking port of Dublin, Anglo-Saxon slaves shipped from Bristol could be bought for labour in Iceland, Scandinavia or even Arabic Spain. The trade was eventually banned in 1102, at some loss of revenue to the crown which took a 4 pence tax on every slave sold.

As in any society, differences in wealth revealed themselves in personal adornment, quality of weapons and the ability to display wealth and power through methods as diverse as protecting retainers and giving gifts to churches. Curiously, there is a noticeable decline from the mid-tenth century of precious metal in personal adornment (despite discovery of new silver sources in the European Hartz Mountains in the 960s and continuing lavish gifts to churches). The same decline is true of elaborate swords with makers' names inscribed on them. This was clearly not due to poverty, since the large number of coin hoards from the mid 1060s indicate significant portable wealth in the hands of wealthy elites. Instead, something was changing in the patterns of production and consumption. But what it was is not clear. It accompanied other changes in which elites were relying more on urban trade for high-quality goods than on household, or travelling, craftsmen. 'The Germanic world of gift giving, tribute taking and shifting personal relationships had ceded to one in which values could be measured and paid in coin, services commuted and subjects taxed, with social position even more likely to be dependent on birth than on attainment'.[35] There is a very medieval – even modern – flavour to this development.

Population and health

The population of England by the mid-eleventh century was about 2.5 million. To put this into context, the English population in 1541 was probably about the same size (estimated at about 2.7 million) after all the demographic ups and downs of the Middle Ages. Life expectancy was about 35 years for a man and 25 years for a woman. This difference was mostly caused by death in childbirth. In terms of life expectancy, life in early medieval England was comparable with the poorest less economically developed countries (LEDCs) of the twenty-first century. In fact, when the life expectancy for women dropped to 26 years in Sierra Leone in 2002, following a catastrophic civil war which had brought that country to the lowest point on the world rating of LEDCs, it was one year longer than the estimate for women in the early Middle Ages. That same year, the male life expectancy in Burkina Faso was 35.3 years – about the medieval male average. Current projections suggest that in 2021 male life expectancy in Britain will be 74 years and female life expectancy 80 years.

The reasons why England, on the eve of the Norman Conquest, can be compared with a modern LEDC are fairly simple and apply to the whole of the Middle Ages: no knowledge of germ theory and, consequently, poor disease prevention and pre-scientific approaches to treatment of injury and disease. In a period of history before knowledge of anti-sepsis and anaesthetics, death was an everyday reality. This does not mean to say that there was no medical tradition. There certainly was and some medical manuscripts have survived from the later Anglo-Saxon period. Whilst these indicate 'knowledge' available to the most educated, they probably also contain folk traditions used by less literate rural communities.

One of the most famous of these manuscripts is *Bald's Leechbook*, a physician's reference book which describes many illnesses, symptoms and treatments. Dating from c.900–25, this manuscript quotes from a variety of classical works and folk remedies. It contains many formulas and herbal treatments alongside many superstitious ideas about how to apply these herbal medicines. Alongside such ideas as the use of oak bark as an astringent, this leechbook gives over a whole chapter to remedies for elf-shot (diseases caused by elves) and identifies many kinds of elves (including wood elves and water elves) and the diseases they were thought to cause, along with supposed 'remedies'. Remedies are given for ailments as varied as fevers, tumours, snake bites, abscesses, skin diseases, paralysis and wounds.

In *Lacnunga* (a mixed collection of medical texts, mainly in Old English, and probably copied in south-west England, c.1010) are a number of charms which give an insight into Anglo-Saxon popular religion within a Christian culture. Alongside these charms are references to the use of herbs such as mugwort, *waybroad* (plantain), *stime* (watercress), *maythen* (camomile), *wergulu* (nettle), crab apple, chervil and fennel. In addition, as evidence for the survival of some aspects of classical medical knowledge, Anglo-Saxon translations of classical works such as Dioscorides' *Herbal* survive from the tenth century.

Contrary to what might be expected, living standards may actually have risen following the end of the Roman Empire, with a knock-on effect for nutrition and health. The end of imperial taxes and long-distance trade may have meant that many people were living in closer proximity to protein sources in the countryside, and in England – in common with northern Europe generally – there may have been an increase in protein-rich diets which may explain a rise in average height until the early eighth century. The average western European height returned to the lower Late Roman level by 725.[36] In England this coincided with increased reliance on arable farming (along with open fields) in the three centuries up to 1066, which probably accompanied a reduction in protein as a proportion of the average person's diet. However, other evidence suggests that, despite these fluctuations, average height has remained fairly stable for the past 5,000 years, although it must be said that early medieval children's reduced access to protein probably meant that they did not achieve their 'fully grown adult height' until they were in their 20s.[37] By this time, though, their height was comparable with that of modern adults.

Regarding diet on the eve of 1066, the staples were bread wheat and – in wetter areas – rye. Archaeology shows this was supplemented with peas and beans. Barley was used in brewing. The increasing reliance on arable crops was assisted by very favourable climatic conditions in the period between the ninth and twelfth centuries.

The role and status of Late Anglo-Saxon women

Anglo-Saxon women had the power to own property in their own right. At marriage a woman received from her husband a *morgengifu* (morning gift), which could include land and which was hers to sell, or bequeath, as she willed. Within marriage, finances were held to be the property of *both* husband and wife.[38] Women could own substantial estates in their own right, one example being Elfgifu who owned fifteen estates in and around Buckinghamshire in c.970. In the 1060s Eadgifu 'the Fair' held estates amounting to 27,000 acres in eastern England and was an immensely wealthy woman. Revealingly, a significant number of royal land grants are to husband and wife jointly, and over 25 per cent of surviving Anglo-Saxon wills are by women bequeathing their own property. (In contrast, after the Norman Conquest no woman could make a valid will without the consent of her husband.) As well as having the right to sell and exchange land, women had free access to the courts to enforce their rights or to settle disputes. In addition unmarried aristocratic women were highly influential in running abbeys.

Surviving laws and marriage contracts reveal that women had a significant amount of protection within marriage. A woman had to be in agreement with the proposed marriage and was not liable for any actions of her husband. Monogamy seems to have been the norm by the eleventh century, although Viking influences may have challenged this at times. A law of 1008 insisted that widows should remain unmarried for one year and were then free to marry whoever they wished, and that such a widow was entitled to a substantial share of the inheritance. The laws contained severe penalties for sexual

THE CHARACTER OF LATE ANGLO-SAXON SOCIETY

assault and indicate that compensation was paid to a free woman herself if she was a victim. However, a law of Cnut states that any woman guilty of adultery would lose all her property and have her nose and ears cut off. This, however, is unrepresentative of the normal practice, the usual punishment being financial not physical. Overall the evidence suggests that the average Anglo-Saxon wife was valued and respected and had her economic rights safeguarded. Wills show many men leaving valuable property to female relations. With regard to children, the laws suggest that there was no automatic bias in favour of husbands with respect to the custody of children if a husband and wife separated, and no bias in favour of the husband's family in the event of his death.

We know less about the economic activities of women in this period than in the later Middle Ages, but certain manufacturing skills seem associated with women, such as cloth making. This could include the high-status production of gold-embroidered cloth as well as more mundane articles.

Art and ideas

When English drawing led European artistic fashion, in the twelfth and thirteenth centuries, it built on skills established in late Anglo-Saxon England. However, within eleventh-century England there were two competing schools of artistic thought. The *Winchester Style* produced naturalistic art inspired by classical traditions, while the curling tendrils of the decoration found on many objects looked instead to Scandinavia (and to earlier Anglo-Saxon traditions) for its models. Tinted outline drawings within the Winchester tradition gave convincing form and depth to line drawings. Other drawings made greater use of colour. The Winchester Style also influenced sculpture in stone, in examples such as the two stone angels found at the tiny church at Bradford on Avon (Wiltshire). Other examples of such carving are found on ivory.

In stark contrast to these naturalistic forms are Scandinavian *Jellinge Style* animals, with their sinuous double outlines which, around the year 1000, gave way to the *Ringerike Style* in which tendrils of acanthus leaves issue from the stylized bodies of animals. The finest example of Ringerike Style comes from a grave slab found in St Paul's Churchyard, London, dating from around 1035. It was Ringerike which finally gave way to *Urnes Style*, around 1050, in which the tendrils become longer and there is less foliage.[39]

These great traditions of art and of decorated architecture did not end in 1066 but continued to be deployed and to influence developments beyond the Norman Conquest. Even as it was giving way to *Romanesque Style* in the late eleventh and early twelfth centuries, the Winchester Style gave a 'lightness of touch' to English Romanesque drawing.[40] Also, by the 1020s ornate Gospel books, which had once displayed the finest styles of Anglo-Saxon art, were already going out of fashion – to be replaced by books such as the *Hereford Gospels* which were influenced by Romanesque Style. While few such books were produced between the 1050s and the early twelfth century, it was not the Norman Conquest which had weakened the link with the artistic past; the change had already begun before 1066. As with so much of late Anglo-Saxon England, these artistic achievements outlived even the traumas of the 1060s and 1070s and were key elements in the character of the emerging Middle Ages.

Chapter 2

THE CHANGING COUNTRYSIDE

The 20 years between 1066 and the compilation of Domesday Book, in 1086, saw huge changes in the English countryside. A large group of about 4,500 Anglo-Saxon aristocrats was replaced by a new structure of lordship. At the top of this social pyramid were 180 *tenants-in-chief* (or *barons*) who held land directly from the king. Of these, in the mid-1080s, only two were Anglo-Saxon. Below these were 1,400 medium-sized landowners, of whom about 100 were Anglo-Saxon. Under these were 6,000 sub-tenants (including a substantial number of Anglo-Saxons), many of whom leased land they had previously owned in 1066. There can be no doubt that across the English countryside the message was clear – an occupying power had control of the national resources.

The laws of the manor
When historians describe the countryside of the Middle Ages – both before and after 1066 – one word dominates the description; *manor*. But what was a manor? It was certainly

more than simply an estate, or an area of land. The word also describes the way in which these estates were run. The lord of a manor (the overall landowner) had the right to run the land through a manor court administered by his or her officials, and these manor courts both organized the running of the manor and punished those who failed to follow the rules, the fines being paid directly to the lord of the manor. The most powerful lords had rights granted to them by the king which would normally have come within the job description and authority of local royal officials, the sheriffs. These powerful landlords had by the thirteenth century gained the right to have their courts oversee justice regarding theft, crimes punishable by death and the pricing of bread and ale. One such landlord, the bishop of Winchester, also had oversight of a system known as *Frankpledge.* Dating from before the Norman Conquest, this system was one in which groups of ten households (a *tithing*) were bound together and held responsible for one another's behaviour. All males aged over 12 years of age were made members of one of these groups. Each tithing, under a leader known as a tithing-man, was then responsible for producing any man of that tithing suspected of a crime.

Usually, however, manor courts concerned themselves with more mundane matters. They decided the rules of the manor, supervised the election of local officials (e.g. the *reeve*, who oversaw administration, and the *pinder*, who rounded up stray cattle), witnessed transfers of land, oversaw payment of *heriot* – paid to the lord on the death of a tenant (usually the best animal), punished those who let cattle stray on to the lord's pasture or who *assarted* (cleared woodland without permission), and fined villeins who refused labour service on the lord's land (the *demesne*).

During the period 1160–1216 the system of royal justice known as the *Common Law* emerged. One of the key principles of this was that only freemen could take complaints about land to the royal courts; villeins were denied this right and had to rely on the manor courts, which were heavily weighted towards the interests of the lord of the manor. It became a common feature in cases in the royal courts for one side to accuse the other of holding land for which they owed labour service. This meant they would have their claims dismissed. In 1224 the royal court refused William of Pilton (Somerset) the right to plead his case because it was found that he owed ploughing and reaping service to his lord and needed a licence from the lord before his daughter, or sister, could marry.[1]

These manorial estates, which dominate the nature of medieval rural life, were generally divided between so-called demesne land, which was farmed directly for the profit of the lord of the manor, and land either rented for cash or held by villeins in return for unpaid labour on the lord's demesne land. This was not a new system, although it has often been cited as a consequence of the Norman Conquest. In reality many in the Late Anglo-Saxon countryside were semi-free or unfree, and what the Norman Conquest brought was an intensification of this system rather than its introduction. In this sense the abolition of slavery in England in 1102, by the Statute of Westminster, was largely due to the fact that the bottom end of the English rural population was being so effectively exploited there was little need for this institution. The statute itself, presided over by Anselm the Archbishop of Canterbury, decreed: 'Let no one hereafter presume to engage in that nefarious trade in which hitherto in England men were usually sold like brute animals.'[2]

A survey dating from 1120 of a Church estate at Pinbury near Cirencester (Gloucestershire) indicates that here the demesne land came to about 400 acres (161.8 hectares), with the remaining 300 acres (121.4 hectares) being worked by villeins who, in addition to the work required on their own land, were expected to give five days' unpaid work per week.[3] The nuns of Caen, who owned this land, were not alone in making high demands on the villeins of their estate. Earlier, in 1086, Domesday Book records that the estate also had nine slaves. By the 1120s these would have been freed, but it would be interesting to know whether freedom had brought them much reduction in their workload now that they were villeins.

Being forced to provide unpaid labour service was not the only way that villeins were made to pay 'rent' for the land they worked. Another way was for some to have to pay a proportion of their crops and animals – known as *champart* payments. Yet another was to pay money rents. Some peasants had to pay all three types. On the Wiltshire manor of Childehampton in 1315, the villeins owed to Wilton nunnery: 5 shillings a year rent, labour service and each year a cock, three hens and a proportion of the grain harvest. Peasants tended to prefer the second and third forms of payment for the simple reason that it left them free to work only on their own land.[4] On top of labour service there were a whole range of ways in which villeins were targeted to pay cash to the lord of the manor: *merchets*, a payment to allow a daughter to marry; *heriot*, a death duty; *leyrwite*, a fine paid (most often by women) for forbidden sexual activity;[5] *chevages*, permission to leave the manor; *faldagium*, permission to graze animals outside the lord's fold; *entry fines*, when taking on a new piece of land; *tallages*, a land tax; and *suit of mill*, which forced villeins to use the lord's mill at his prices. This last demand was very profitable for lords and, around 1300, the Bishop of Durham took 10 per cent of his annual income from this alone.

In 1293 a Worcestershire man drowned himself in the river Severn rather than be forced to take on land, from the Earl of Gloucester, which would have caused him to be considered a villein. The shame was clearly too great to contemplate. In the period 1066–1200, villeins could be sold by their lords and families split up. But, terrible as the suicide of 1293 was, the situation was changing during the thirteenth century. By 1300, although villeins still resented the restrictions placed on them, they should not be thought of as slaves. They were protected by the custom of the manor – arrangements and practices which had developed on an estate and which established the rights of villeins as well as lords. Furthermore, most lords allowed villeins to make wills and buy and sell land – as long as they met their obligations and paid their heriots. It was especially acceptable if villeins could be forced to pay for permission to carry out these transactions. Also, although in theory villains could be evicted from their land if their lord so decided, this rarely happened in practice. Most villeins passed their farms down through the generations, and such villeins might prosper and become wealthier than their 'free' neighbours. In addition, as the thirteenth century progressed, a growing number of lords were willing to allow villeins to pay cash in order to be free of specific services. Finally, the amount of labour service owed varied from manor to manor. Tenants on the bishop of Worcester's estates in 1299 owed the bishop four or five days' work a week (plus other dues) and were charged three times as much rent for land compared with freemen. On average these villeins paid between 29 per cent and 33 per cent of their net output to the bishop.[6] On other estates the load on villeins was much lighter. As with so much in the Middle Ages, one size did not fit all.

Moreover, there were communities who were actively resisting their status as villeins long before the upheavals following the Black Death in the 1350s. In 1280 the peasants of the village of Mickleover (Derbyshire) appealed to the royal courts insisting that since their manor had once been royal land they could not possibly be villeins. This was because villeinage did not exist on crown lands. They lost the case, however. Nevertheless they were not alone in trying to discover legal loopholes through which they could escape their servile status. In 1278 tenants at Halesowen (Shropshire) lost a long legal challenge similar to that at Mickleover. Other legal challenges took place at Mildenhall (Suffolk) in the 1320s and at Ingatestone (Essex) in 1346.[7] None succeeded, since behind determined landlords lay the power of their class – royal courts, sheriffs and fines. For a reluctant villein, running away was probably a more effective form of resistance.

Others asserted their ambitions in different ways. Some of the villeins of Peterborough Abbey ignored the legal ban on villeins using personal seals and proudly used them when they made agreements with their lord. Over the generations such wealthy villeins increased in number, and it could come as a nasty shock when some rival or enemy tried to bring them down by proving that their villein status barred them from a legal case or a land transaction. As late as 1460 – when villeinage was long in decline – John Paston of Norfolk found himself accused by an enemy of being descended from villeins. This was a common way of attempting to extort money.

What is clear is that, in 1290 (the peak of the population rise in England in the Middle Ages), about 60 per cent of the rural population on arable land was still technically unfree. However, the distribution was uneven. And, high as this figure was, this still left 40 per cent who were free. In Kent, the western Midlands, the south-west and north-west, there were few villeins. Here lords relied on paid labourers and money rents. In East Anglia and southern Cambridgeshire, manors tended to be relatively small and dominated by large numbers of free smallholders. (Exceptions were the great Church estates of Bury and Ely, which contained a large percentage of unfree tenants.) On the other hand, in areas of Oxfordshire villeins made up 80 per cent of the population. Extensive manors, with large numbers of the unfree, were also common in Huntingdonshire. Overall, villeins were found in highest numbers on the great arable estates of the Midlands. In areas where farmland was being carved out of woodland they were rarer, as here lords wanted to attract new tenants and offered land on more attractive terms.

Overall, therefore, by 1290 probably three in five English tenants were unfree and some of those who have usually been considered free were more restricted than has often been assumed. In the Danelaw (the East Midlands, East Anglia and northern England) a class of small farmers called *sokemen* are assumed to have been descended from free Viking colonists in the tenth century and to have guarded their freedoms. There is some truth to this as, even when they owed labour service, it was lighter than that demanded from the average villein. But even sokemen might find themselves classified as unfree by an ambitious landlord.

This last point is a reminder that Church estates included concentrations of both unfree and free communities, depending on where they were located and on their style of organization. The Benedictines, for example, were long-established in England and had many of their estates in arable areas. Here there were many villein tenants. In contrast, the Cistercians, on their great wool-ranges in the north and west, mixed the work amongst both free and unfree labourers. The Templars and Augustinians preferred to rely on money rents from free tenants because these monastic orders tended to own land scattered across a number of villages, which were difficult to organize in the way a great Benedictine house such as Glastonbury might organize its estates.

Trades, crafts, agriculture and industry

Village communities included a range of craftspeople but these are sometimes strangely invisible. For example, Domesday Book records 6,000 mills but only eight millers and over one million sheep but only ten shepherds. In addition, we must add the smiths and foresters, pigmen and beekeepers, fishermen and eel catchers, keepers of vineyards and salt makers, quarrymen and a host of other craft skills which made the rural economy vibrant and active. As the medieval records increase in the twelfth and thirteenth centuries these roles begin to emerge, but they will always have been there. Many of these people, such as the smiths, carpenters, tilers and masons, were directly employed by the lord of the manor. Of these, some would have been labourers and others skilled craftspeople employing other workers themselves. Surnames derived from occupations –and appearing in records from 1280 to 1340 – indicate crafts and skills found on larger manors. These include: comber, draper, dyer, fuller, tailor, weaver (all textile workers); ironmonger, smith, carpenter, cooper, turner (iron and wood workers); baker, brewer, butcher (food and drink production); bailiff, hayward and woodward (manorial administrators). The countryside was also the location of much of the pottery industry, which after 1100 relocated from towns. Like ale brewing, it was carried out by peasants who used it to diversify their income. Other rural-based industries were quarrying, salt making, glass making, iron working and mining (e.g. lead and coal).

Every village also contained landless labourers, so poor they survived on wages paid for work performed on the land of better-off neighbours. However, these landless labourers made up only a small part of the rural population. Most peasants farmed no more than 30 acres (12.1 hectares) and few employed more than one labourer. The English countryside in the Middle Ages was therefore made up of a large number of relatively small farmers. It was a long way from the kind of society which would emerge after 1500, in which a decreasing number of landowners employed a growing number of landless labourers. In 1851, by contrast, 50 per cent of farms covered between 100 and 300 acres (40.4 to 121.4 hectares) and an average of six landless farmhands were employed by each farm.[8] By marrying late and living in nuclear families, peasants in the Middle Ages tried to keep their holdings together and, if possible, to enlarge them from one generation to the next.

Nevertheless, the desire to better themselves was clearly a highly motivating factor in the lives of many peasant farmers. Through manorial records individual life stories give us an insight into what must have been the experiences of many more. In 1277, Hugh Cok was the poorest villager in Codicote (Hertfordshire), but his position started to improve when he rented a stall to sell fish in the market. With the money he earned he bought, or rented, eight small pieces of land. Following this success he rented a strip of land for ten years and another for four years. The income from his land transactions allowed him to buy a further plot and then a new house and an accompanying piece of land. A further plot of land followed, protected by a hedge. Hugh was now rising through the ranks of the village. When the opportunity arose he leased three more plots of land for nine years. After this he leased a further piece of land for twelve years and yet another for three years. Clearly conscious of his growing status, he gained permission to dig a ditch to demarcate one of his land holdings. And his ambitions took him into the brewing trade, since the manorial records show he was fined for brewing bad beer. When Hugh died, in 1306, he left his little empire to Christina, his daughter. In Hugh's life we can see the kinds of small scale wheeler-dealing which dominated village life in the Middle Ages.[9]

But where did the majority of this rural population live? By the late eleventh century East Anglia was the most densely populated area of England (with between 15 and 20 people per square mile), followed by the south coast east of the Solent, Kent and the chalk lands of Hampshire, Wiltshire, Berkshire and Oxfordshire. In contrast, a density closer to five people per square mile prevailed in Cornwall, the Welsh borders and north of the rivers Humber and Mersey.

Whatever the population density of a region, or its manorial structure, the business of the countryside was making money. In order to achieve this its natural resources were to be efficiently exploited in order to maximize the profit of an estate. There was of course nothing new in this; it is the story of farming since the Neolithic era. What marks out the period around the Norman Conquest is the acceleration in commercial exploitation. This was a social, not a political, phenomenon. It owed much to population increase and little to Norman conquerors, since the economic potential of rural resources was being increasingly exploited from the Middle Anglo-Saxon period onwards. In this sense the strategies we see being adopted around 1100 were only the latest developments in a process which had been gathering pace since 800.

From 800 until 1300 arable farming increased in both its area and its intensity in order to feed a growing population. In this period the English population rose from probably just under 2 million to about 5.5 million. Some estimates put it as high as 6.5 million in 1300.[10] This growth increased demand for food and provided opportunities for increased profits from the best-managed estates. The plotting of scatters of pottery, found during field walking at Leckhampstead (Buckinghamshire), shows the dramatic increase in manuring of fields between 1100 and 1400.[11] Similarly, the increased quantities of silts which modern archaeologists find in the valleys of the rivers Thames and Nene point to the intensification of ploughing on land which had fallen out of arable cultivation after the end of the Roman period. The erosion which led to this being swept into the river systems reminds us that economic impacts on the environment are by no means a modern phenomenon. This increased production was assisted by improved agricultural techniques, relative political stability, a growing economy in which towns played a vital part, and climatic improvements.

The last point is one which is often overlooked. Scientists know that a historic global cooling, called the 'Little Ice Age', lasted from about 1450 to 1850 and coincided with two periods of decreased solar activity. But fluctuations in climate had started before this. The so-called 'Medieval Warm Period' was a time of unusually warm weather around 800–1300 and it partially coincided with the peak in solar activity named the 'Medieval Maximum' (about 1100–1250). During the Medieval Warm Period wine grapes were grown in southern England. At the same time, Scandinavian settlers took advantage of ice-free seas to colonize Greenland and other outlying lands of the far north and even reached the eastern coast of North America. The fact that this warming occurred alongside population increase and accelerated agricultural production is no coincidence. Neither is the fact that its ending coincided with population fall and economic stagnation at the end of the Middle Ages. This is not to assume, however, that climate was the single determinant. Other factors strongly influenced the commercial success of vineyards, and the time of the greatest extent of medieval vineyards falls outside the Medieval Warm Period. Nevertheless, climate clearly played a great part in extending the growing season for arable and other crops, and in underpinning medieval expansion.

By 1300 the expanding rural economy was closely integrated, with about 1,500 market towns. With somewhere in the region of 10 million sheep producing 40,000 sacks of wool a year for the international market, these market towns were a key feature in the redistribution network that saw wool bought by merchants and shipped abroad. In turn the cash gained stimulated trade within the towns. The English countryside was dynamic and trade was expanding.

Woodland too was a valuable resource, beyond its obvious use for the supply of timber and coppiced wood. Wood ash was produced in industrial quantities and was an ingredient in a range of different manufacturing processes. The liquid leached out from the burnt ash made an alkaline known as *lye*. When this liquid lye was boiled with lime and evaporated in large iron pots it left a residue known as *pot-ash*. It is from this that the element potassium takes its name. So-called lye pits are identifiable in a number of medieval woodlands. Lye was used as a cleansing agent and was an ingredient in medieval soap. The residue was used in glass making since, when mixed with sand, it lowers the melting point of the sand and makes the molten liquid easier to handle.[12]

What should be made clear, though, is that areas designated as 'forest' in the Middle Ages were not necessarily areas of extensive woodland. Nor were they necessarily areas of poor agricultural land. The Forests of Wychwood (Oxfordshire), Rockingham (Northamptonshire) and Whittlewood (Buckinghamshire/Northamptonshire) were all areas which had been actively worked in the Roman period – although the New Forest (Hampshire) was an area whose soil reduced its agricultural value compared with nearby landscapes. An area designated as 'forest' was, in reality, simply one over which the king, or major lords, had the sole right to keep and to hunt

deer. Within these areas the game animals were protected by –
and human activity restricted by – Forest Laws. Such areas
might include woodland but not exclusively so. In fact, the
word *forest* comes from a Latin word meaning 'outside' and
applied to the exclusive rights over deer in these areas which
were outside usual customs. Since some medieval forests were
also located on the edges of ancient Anglo-Saxon kingdoms, or
blocks of territory, they may have been originally designated as
forest because they were frontier areas as opposed to core terri-
tories. What is clear is that many people living in such forest
areas resented the restrictions placed on them; indeed William I
had apparently cleared areas of the New Forest in order to
reduce its population. Crimes against Forest Law were, in the
early years after the Conquest, severely punished, although
this rapidly gave way to a series of fines designed to deter
encroachment, which were paid to the Crown.

Industries such as quarrying, coal mining and iron working
were obviously located close to the sources of their raw materials. In some places major industries were created in areas so
rural that – after their decline – it is now difficult to imagine the
scale of activity once practised there. In the north of England
examples of local medieval ironworks can be found in
Weardale, which had a large enough output from the 1480s to
displace imports from Spain. From the fifteenth century
improvements in technology increased output as water was
used to power hammers and bellows in the working of iron.
Most of the iron produced was wrought iron, which was
heated and hammered to drive off impurities and to shape the
metal. As blast furnaces were introduced – based on continental models – it became possible to create enough heat to
produce cast iron. Blast furnaces were operating in Sussex from
the mid-1490s.

Medieval coal mining was carried out using shallow *bell-pits*
which were sunk until they reached a coal seam and then
worked outwards. A major source of coal was in the north-east
of England. In 1291 there are records of coal sent by sea from

Newcastle to Corfe Castle (Dorset), and coal was shipped to London from about 1305. By 1334, on the strength of this trade, Newcastle was the fourth wealthiest town in England after London, Bristol and York. While this position did not last, it is an indication of the importance of coal's place within the national economy. In 1378 Newcastle shipped an impressive 15,000 tons of coal. By 1508 this had risen to an annual output of 40,000 tons. As demand for coal increased, so bell-pits gave way to more ambitious *pillar and stall mines* in which larger galleries were opened up and the roof supported by material which was not removed. Such mines were operating in Leicestershire by the late fifteenth century. Deeper mines stretched medieval technology towards its limits but horse-powered pumps were in use around Durham by the 1480s. Recorded productivity shows that individual output at this time was similar to that of mines in the early nineteenth century, before the introduction of the technology made possible by the Industrial Revolution. This is an indication – as in so many areas – of the impressive scale and efficiency of industry in the Middle Ages. It was only the impact of more powerful industrial techniques which allowed the massive leap forward from what was, in many areas, still a fundamentally medieval baseline of efficiency and output.

The quarrying industries of Dorset were also of great importance in the Middle Ages. Purbeck marble from the Isle of Purbeck was in great demand from the thirteenth century, due to its suitability for cathedrals and churches developing Gothic and Early English architectural styles. Archbishop Hugh Walter's decision to use it to build his Archbishop's Palace at Canterbury in 1190 caused it to become the material of high fashion. Purbeck marble was used in the interior of churches at Chichester, Lincoln, Wells, Winchester and York. Salisbury Cathedral (built between 1220 and 1258 in the Early English style) made extensive use of the stone. In the thirteenth century the rebuilding of Westminster Abbey allowed Dorset marblers to penetrate the London stone trade. It is significant that the earliest royal effigy in England (that of King John, 1199–1216, at Worcester) was carved in Purbeck Marble.

Life on the coast and river

Natural resources from rivers, wetland areas and the sea also played a major part in life in the Middle Ages, as a source of food, power and (in the case of wetland areas) fuel and building materials. Fish played a particularly large part in medieval diet due to the frequency of fast days in the Christian calendar. On these days fish could be eaten in place of meat. At Hemington Quarry (Leicestershire) archaeologists have found numerous fish weirs. These consisted of lines of stakes, linked by wattle panels, which funnelled fish into wicker baskets or traps. At the same quarry parallel lines of oak posts and wattle panels were infilled with stones and brushwood to form a probable mill dam, dating from around the 1280s. Part of the housing for a vertical waterwheel was also preserved here.[13] Similar fish weirs, but dating from the seventh to the tenth centuries, have been discovered within the intertidal zone of the Blackwater Estuary (Essex), where a complex network of weirs and traps has been mapped. The effort which went into building these structures, in what must have been a very uncomfortable and, at times, dangerous environment, was considerable. One site in the estuary (Collins Creek) contained over 20,000 stakes.[14] Similar structures harvested the vast quantities of eels and fish in the network of rivers flowing into the Wash and the Somerset Levels, and in the wetlands around these areas.

Fishing as an occupation was, of course, a feature of life on the coast as well as along rivers and in wetland areas. Archaeological excavation between 1996 and 2006 along Townwall Street, leading to the Eastern Docks at Dover (Kent) has revealed evidence for the fishing community of Dover during the Middle Ages. One of the *Cinque Ports* (along with Hastings, Hythe, Romney, Sandwich and later joined by Rye and Winchelsea), Dover provided shipping for the Crown and received various rights and privileges in return. Among these was the right of Cinque Port fishing fleets to fish the great herring shoals of the southern North Sea in autumn and to land their catches – and dry their nets – on the beach at Great Yarmouth (Norfolk). This did not go down at all well with the fishermen of Norfolk but the right to profit from this annual herring fair was jealously guarded by the fishermen of Kent and Sussex.

The amount of fish bones and fish hooks found among the domestic rubbish in simple wooden houses make it clear that these houses along Townwall street were the homes of the Dover fishermen. Here fish was processed, stored and eaten in huge quantities, with sampling producing over 83,000 fish bones. This allowed researchers to identify the sea harvest worked from Dover: herring, cod, whiting, conger eel, thornback ray and mackerel. These probably represent fish caught locally in the English Channel during the winter months. Such fishermen occupied the slack time in their year with ferrying to the continent, long-distance trading, sail, rope and net making, boat building and providing ship service for the king. They probably also farmed smallholdings. Evidence from the site also suggests that they wove their own plied yarns for making cordage and fishing nets, along with small-scale metal working. In short, this community of hardworking fishermen turned its hand to a wide range of activities to support itself.[15]

Food was not the only resource exploited by those living beside water. Around the Wash vast quantities of peat were dug for fuel from carefully managed *turbaries* (the name for such peat-digging places), and this would have been a similar activity in other wetland areas such as the Somerset Levels and south of the Humber. These areas also provided large amounts of reeds, or *lesch*, cut for use in thatching. Islands of meadow provided winter fodder for cattle while water levels were controlled by dykes and sluices as these frontier farmers and fishermen laboured to tame and exploit the wild, wet landscape. What, to the modern eye, might seem to have been marshy wilderness would, in reality, have been valuable areas providing a wide range of resources. No wonder the term *fish silver* was used around Boston (Lincolnshire) in the fourteenth century for the rents paid by tenants who harvested these resources.

Structure of the medieval village

Although, as we have seen, the resources to be exploited were varied, the classic image of the medieval village is of a nucleated settlement, focused on its church and set within open fields, in which the arable and meadow resources of the village were divided into strips. Beyond the arable and meadow was the common land on which tenants grazed their animals and woodland was used for timber, coppiced rods for tools and buildings and *pannage* (an English legal term for the practice of turning out domestic pigs in a wood or forest to feed). In this scenario a village was part of one manor. But this classic image describes only a certain type of medieval village and its landscape, and was not by any means true of the whole of England. It closely fits the arable landscape of the corn-growing belt of the central and west Midlands and extending to the south coast; it could also be found as far north as Durham. In these areas the most regulated open-field farming and the most manorialised areas (with free tenants, plus villeins and labour service) coincided.

In the Midlands perhaps 80 per cent of the available landscape was occupied by this open field arrangement. Such a system of nucleated villages, as opposed to dispersed hamlets and farmsteads, may have had its origins as far back as the ninth and tenth centuries as enterprising lords sought to concentrate human resources in order to more efficiently exploit both arable and pasture at a time of increasing population and the breaking up of large multiple estates. Many of the villages in this landscape show evidence of planning in their layout. At Wharram Percy (Yorkshire), the house plots were carefully laid out and formed two long rows with their fronts on to the main street of the village. The regular appearance of this set-up, plus the very consistent size of the individual house plots, strongly suggests that the village was carefully planned. The available evidence suggests that this was done at some time between the tenth and the twelfth centuries. This seems to have been the case with a large number of villages in the open field landscape.

On the edges of this 'open field and nucleated village system' greater variety occurred. In East Anglia, for instance, one village might contain several manors, and the guiding hand of one landlord on a village's development was replaced by a number of different influences. At Feltwell (Norfolk) there were seven manors. Sometimes one manor had land scattered over several villages. All of this variety had an impact on the way villages and landscapes developed. Field systems became less regular and there might be as many as twelve open fields in contrast to the two, or three, in the classic Midland landscape. Peasant holdings might be grouped in one part of the fields and the pattern was more enclosed. In Kent peasant holdings were grouped, sometimes in hedged fields and sometimes within open fields.

In other parts of England the variety was even more pronounced. The landscape was very different in the far north and the north-west. Here higher rainfall and a more rugged landscape encouraged a pattern of more scattered, smaller, settlements and pastoral farming. A region dominated by free tenants, who paid light rents, it was very different from the classic Midland landscape and manor. In Devon and Cornwall there were fewer open fields and peasant farms were hedged and enclosed, giving the characteristic high banked Devon hedgerows. A large manor might include several different hamlets (*vills* or *townships*). About 35 per cent of the land here was held by free tenants.

Historians and archaeologists no longer accept the once-prevalent view that peasant housing was flimsy and poorly constructed. In fact the evidence suggests that it was timber framed and designed to last for several generations. There has been much study of the *tofts* (house sites) and *crofts* (the small enclosed field or pasture associated with a toft) from medieval villages. Two main forms seem to have existed. Within northern and western England the pastoral economies, based on cattle rearing, accompanied *longhouses*. These were rectangular buildings split between an animal byre and a living area for people. Over time upper chambers were sometimes added to the living space and, during the fifteenth century, chimneys were often built. In southern and eastern England the *hall*, or *courtyard farm*, predominated, which consisted of a house with separate farm buildings and barns. Sometimes these were placed around a central space called a *crew yard*. After the late fourteenth century a large number of these houses were rebuilt, with greater height and more first-floor accommodation. This provided more privacy and more space for live-in servants separated from the family. Poorer members of the village community, however, almost certainly lived in less substantial and more squalid housing. When manor records record *cottages* let at an annual rent of 6 pence, it was probably these which were being referred to.

The larger of these crofts were usually arranged with a narrow end facing the village street and the croft running back from this, behind the toft. In a number of cases a back lane offered further access to the property. Where a village was occupied over centuries, these streets and lanes could be worn down into substantial hollow-ways and these can still be traced between the rectangular crofts on deserted medieval village (DMV) sites in the modern landscape. The size of a plot varied with the social status of its occupying family unit. The similarity of these so-called plot-plans across a number of villages is clear evidence for the planning out of villages by medieval lords. Exactly when this happened varied from place to place. In some areas it was a product of later Anglo-Saxon reorganization of the landscape in the tenth century; in other areas it was a product of enterprising lords seeking to maximize output from their estates in the century after 1200. Work at Wick Dive, Whittlebury and Lillingstone Dayrell (on the Buckinghamshire/Northamptonshire border) appears to confirm this approximate date for planned extensions to existing villages from the early twelfth century.[16] This recent study of Late Medieval manorial centres within this area of the Whittlewood Forest has shown a number of instances where the expansion of a lord's base in the mid-thirteenth century cleared away the earlier peasant tofts to make way for the new buildings. In addition to the lord's residence there would be storage buildings, mills, dovecotes, byres, malthouses, brew-houses and bakehouses. In some cases watermills and wind-mills might also be itemized in accounts.[17]

The fashion for moated manor sites increased in the thir-teenth century in lowland eastern England. Essex has more than any other English county. Some of these were constructed with drainage in mind; others were designed largely for show – to display the wealth of their gentry owners. From the fifteenth century, manor houses became larger but still retained the hall-centred plan of an earlier period. This allowed for more rooms for servants and provided additional quarters to give more privacy to the lord of the manor and family. These rooms were eventually provided with their own fireplaces and chimneys. This shift from a central hearth in the hall, as the focus for the life of the manor house, signals a real change in relationships and is about much more than just a change in architecture. These developments were particularly pronounced in the wealthier wool-producing areas and surviving examples, such as Great Chalfield (Wiltshire), reveal just how grand a gentry house could be on the back of the wool trade.

Changes in the countryside

The rural system, though varied and complex, faced some of its greatest challenges in the fourteenth century. Population increase until the mid-fourteenth century put great pressure on resources in the countryside. This led to large reclamation projects in areas of fen and marshland. In Romney Marsh, Kent, this probably began in the early twelfth century when the land was used for grazing. However, by about 1200 this gave way to more intensive cultivation and occupation. This took the form of pioneering farmsteads pushing on to reclaimed land. During the fourteenth century the number of farmsteads declined and this depopulation continued into the fifteenth and sixteenth centuries. Many of the medieval drainage ditches were infilled at this time. It was a period of settlement retreat.

A number of serious problems afflicted the English countryside at this time. A bad harvest in 1314 was followed by two years of wet weather and crop failure. Another disastrous harvest coincided with disease of cattle and sheep in 1319–21. Wheat and barley prices rose by 300 per cent and starvation became widespread. Some sold their land to buy food while others turned to crime. Many manorial records indicate death rates running at up to 15 per cent of the local population. After 1322 the weather improved and population began to recover – but then, in 1348, the Black Death arrived at Melcombe Regis in Dorset. Taxation figures for 1377 suggest that the population of England had fallen to about 2.5 million, and it would remain at about this level until 1520. This was a human catastrophe – but what was the impact on the rural economy?

In fenland areas of East Anglia, the Sussex and Kent marshes and around the Thames Estuary campaigns of land reclamation slowed down, stopping in many areas. Increased flooding due to climate change accelerated this reversal. A similar retreat from marginal land took place in Cornwall, Devon and Northumberland. Nowhere is this retreat from areas of former activity more obvious than in the case of DMVs. There are at least 3,000 DMVs in England. In a large number of Midland areas former ploughland reverted to pasture leaving the characteristic humps and bumps of deserted crofts and tofts and the corduroy pattern of ridge and furrow. It is common to suggest that these were places in which the plague had wiped out virtually all inhabitants. In fact the DMVs of England occurred over many centuries and for complex and particular reasons peculiar to each site and its economy. Many that failed were already economically marginal units, and many failed only after a long period of decline. Many, no doubt, had run perilously short of the resources such as woodland and pasture which were needed to act as insurance in case of crop failures in the open arable fields.

Nevertheless, the cycles of infectious diseases after 1348 (with the accompanying fall in population) clearly had a significant and negative effect on such communities even if desertion was not solely due to the Black Death. The famous historian of the English countryside, W.G. Hoskins, calculated that in Leicestershire about 18 per cent of villages were abandoned between 1450 and the early seventeenth century. Other settlements were reduced in size. The Whittlewood Forest study found that 'After 1350 signs of contraction can be found in all the villages and hamlets that have been investigated'.[18] What is clear is that the pattern of desertion and shrinkage, though widespread, is not uniform. Some villages grew, no doubt as a result of migration from those settlements which were in decline. In other words there were 'winners' as well as 'losers' in the unsettled period following the trauma of the mid-fourteenth century.

Challenge to the status quo

What seems certain is that the Black Death led to a rise in per-capita wealth through a shortage of labour and – consequently – rising wages. The Bishop of Winchester found that the price of his wheat rose by 6 per cent in the period 1360 to 1380 but, at the same time, the wages he paid his labourers rose by 69 per cent.[19] Standards of living rose as a result. However, this was eroded by the cost of war with France. The rise in prosperity and the ability to challenge a system which had attempted to keep wages down and enforce the continuation of villeinage led to social unrest by men and women who had a new sense of empowerment. These protests against villeinage had occurred since the thirteenth century but they accelerated after the Black Death. In some areas peasants hired lawyers to argue that their particular manor had once been a royal estate, on which all labourers were free from villeinage. Contemporaries watched the changes with excitement, or horror, depending on their prejudices. The poet Langland, in *Piers Plowman*, echoed the view of the wealthy and powerful when he unkindly suggested that 'When hunger was their master none complained', with the clear implication that what was needed was a dose of famine to put such pretentious villeins in their places.

Attempts by the authorities to arrest these developments could not stop the tide of change. However, at the time the efforts to protect the status quo were seen in a number of areas. The Ordinance of Labourers in 1349 and the Statute of Labourers in 1351 made it illegal to demand pay higher than that given before 1348. This legislation banned alms giving to beggars and made it a criminal offence for a labourer to refuse a work contract if offered. This aimed to prevent workers from negotiating short-term contracts and then leaving for a better-paid job if the first contract was not renewed on terms the labourer thought were favourable. Justices of the Peace (selected from the landowning knightly class) were empowered to enforce this legislation which, of course, worked to their economic advantage. It was blatant class legislation. Similarly, in 1363, *sumptuary laws* were passed, which attempted to define what different classes of society were allowed to wear. It was clear that people should not merely know their social rank, they should look it too. Such legislation was, of course, bound to fail and was indicative of a government trying to arrest processes beyond its control.

In the summer of 1381 the simmering resentment boiled over into the Peasants' Revolt. As with so much of the Middle Ages this was not what it seemed. It was by no means confined to peasants but involved a wide range of groups: villeins, *hedge-priests* (priests unfrocked for breaking Church laws), better-off townspeople and rival members of London guilds. The key factor which motivated most of these different groups was resentment at legal and social restrictions which hampered their economic activities, freedoms and ambitions. They were less 'desperate and starving' and more 'ambitious and frustrated'. The chronicler Thomas Walsingham, in his *Historia Anglicana*, later recorded a speech supposed to have been made by the hedge-priest John Ball. In part of it he spoke the famous words:

> When Adam delved [dug], and Eve span, who was then a gentleman? From the beginning all men were created equal by nature, for servitude was introduced by the unjust and evil oppression of men, against the will of God, who, if it had pleased Him to create serfs, surely in the beginning of the world would have appointed who should be a serf and who a lord.[20]

The trigger event causing the revolt was the activities of tax commissioners pursuing evaders of the heaviest of three recent poll taxes (1377, 1379 and 1381). This one was set at 3 groats each (12 pennies, or one shilling) which would be about a week's wages for a labourer. All those over the age of 15 were to pay. Contemporary chroniclers mention two petitions made in response to the last of these poll taxes. One called for freedom from serfdom and a standard rent of 4 pence per acre. The second called for abolition of villeinage and lordship and the redistribution of Church property. Passive resistance grew, and somewhere in the region of 450,000 people who had paid tax in 1377 evaded it in 1381.

Later demands of the rebels pointed up many of the features of English life which so antagonized ordinary people: an end to villeinage; a ceiling of 4 pence an acre rent on land; opening up of all markets to traders who would no longer have to pay for the right to sell their goods; abolition of outlawry; all rabbit warrens, fisheries, deer parks and woods to become common property. But the key to understanding the explosion of violence lies in the sense of outrage against the rising level of taxation, accusations of government incompetence and failures in the war against France. Between 1371 and 1381 the government tax burden stood at £380,000 and over half of this had been raised in the four years since 1377. Contemporary accounts suggest that many rebels claimed they were acting on behalf of the young king to save him – and them – from his 'corrupt advisers'.

The violence broke out in Essex and Kent, and these outbreaks may have been coordinated. Dissatisfied activists had been encouraging action across a wide area of eastern England. Some of these were hedge-priests, such as John Ball, who had already been punished in the Church courts for preaching the doctrines of John Wycliffe and for his belief in social equality. Ball was thrown into prison on three occasions and also appears to have been excommunicated. He was in the archbishop of Canterbury's prison, at Maidstone, when he was released by the Kentish rebels. Such people had a background in social radicalism and were sparks amongst dry kindling. To what extent there was organization is now hard to assess, but there are clues. The revolt was probably deliberately coincided to fall on the Corpus Christi celebrations (Thursday 13 June 1381), traditionally a day of community activities. And near-contemporary chroniclers refer to cryptic notes, which appear to contain coded references to insurrection, passed between rebellious groups.

Once the revolt exploded into violence, groups rapidly made contact with each other. As the unrest spread it certainly began to show signs of rudimentary coordination, even if only of allied rebels with similar aims. The centralized nature of England gave the protesters an obvious target for their actions: the young king, Richard II, and his royal council. There was particular antagonism towards the king's uncle, John of Gaunt, and officials associated with the latest poll tax. In addition, when the rebels entered London they were assisted by fishmongers engaged in inter-guild disputes with more prosperous Londoners.

The revolt collapsed when, during a tense stand-off with the young king at Smithfield, the Mayor of London, Walworth, stabbed Wat Tyler the rebel leader. Seizing the opportunity, Richard led the leaderless rebels away and they were swiftly surrounded by armed troops. A few days later the king withdrew promises to end villeinage made under duress. It seemed that the forces of reaction had triumphed. Shortly after this John Ball was arrested in Coventry and executed in the presence of the 14-year-old king.

One clear target of the 1381 revolt had been the villeinage system. But villeinage was already crumbling due to economic and demographic pressures which no amount of resistance could hold back. The increased economic 'muscle' of peasants after the Black Death meant they could demand higher wages whatever the Statute of Labourers vainly demanded. And manorial lords, desperate to get a return from their land, would accept incoming labour without asking too many questions about whether these were free farmers or villeins escaping the constraints of a neighbouring manor. This had been happening even before the traumas of the 1350s. As early as 1305 over 10 per cent of the tenants in Stoneleigh (Worcestershire) had originated outside the shire. It is unknown how many were villeins on the run.

Even in the years before the disruptions of the mid-fourteenth century some landowners – keen to increase their cash flow – were willing to accept cash payments instead of villein services. This, of course, was in a period when labour was relatively plentiful. Evidence from counties as far apart as Norfolk and Somerset show villeins paying *chevage* payments, allowing them to live off their native manor: the first step towards escaping villein status entirely. From East Anglia large numbers of immigrants entered London, taking their dialect of English with them and influencing the emerging London version of Middle English. Furthermore, during the late thirteenth century, land was in such short supply (due to population increase) that freemen were willing to take on land which had labour services attached. Another complication was provided by the marriage of free and unfree, which was by no means an uncommon arrangement.

After the Black Death the tide flowed ever more strongly against villeinage. In addition, as traditional social restraints weakened, women seem to have used the opportunity to seek greater economic freedom, often in towns. In Northampton in 1377, 30 per cent of the population was made up of servants and many of them were women. Most of these were probably first-generation town dwellers who had escaped the more restrictive atmosphere of the countryside.

The end of villeinage was also assisted by the increase in the amount of coins available in the English medieval economy from the late fourteenth century. After all, labour service could be replaced by paid labour and the leasing out of demesne land for cash only if sufficient coins were available. When coinage increased in quantity, as it did in the fifteenth century, it coincided with increasing peasant agitation following the Black Death. This increased economic strength led to the loosening of a system which was centuries old. As it declined, a whole outlook passed with it. No longer would manor rolls refer to some of their tenants as 'in bondage'. Instead, they were now simply tenants holding their land according to the custom of the manor and paying cash rents. But the long echo of past social structures would not die away so quickly. Medieval legal terms for unfree peasants still remain in modern English as negative descriptive terms: villain (from *villein*), churlish (from *ceorl*) and boorish (from *gebur*).

During the fifteenth century the countryside continued to experience considerable turbulence. From 1376 grain prices began a downward spiral which would last for almost the rest of the Middle Ages. Between 1430 and 1470 there was a severe agricultural depression and in 1438–39, after three wet summers, a terrible famine occurred. Diseases of cattle and sheep reduced the national herd. A depressed population and low demand meant that grain prices continued to fall after 1440; wool and cloth exports also slumped around 1450. The problems in the cloth trade were particularly acute between 1448 and 1471. Protests in a number of rural areas demanded reduction in land rents, and social unrest was reported in many urban centres. Labour shortages, rising wage bills and the falling price of corn encouraged landlords to reduce their outgoings and enlarge profits by turning to increased wool production and combining (or 'enclosing') landholdings (often accompanied by ejecting peasant farmers as a result of these 'enclosures'). The priest John Rous (died 1491) listed 60 villages in his native Warwickshire that he personally knew to have been abandoned as a result of such actions. Thomas More, in 1516, wrote in his book *Utopia* that sheep had 'developed a raging appetite, and turned into man-eaters. Fields, houses, towns, everything goes down their throats.'[21] More's bitter irony arose from the same concerns which had earlier led Rous to call down God's anger on the landlords he held responsible for rural depopulation. In some areas the retreat from arable farming led to increased exploitation of income from fish farming and rabbit warrens.

Yet the later fifteenth century saw the continuation of the rise in overall standards of living which had marked the later fourteenth century. Real wages continued to increase and villeinage had virtually disappeared. As a result, land was available without the constraints which had restricted freedoms before the 1350s. The purchasing power of the wages of those engaged in agriculture increased by 100 per cent in the period 1350–1450. Better-off farmers – the *yeomen* – exploited the opportunities presented to them and prospered, and the rural cloth trade increased the prosperity of country areas in East Anglia, the Cotswolds and the West Country. There was therefore, unsurprisingly, no uniform experience in the countryside by 1500. The opportunities and aspirations of the wealthier yeomen contrasted with the frustrations of the victims of enclosure. And in the tensions between these two experiences lay the forces of change which would help take the English countryside out of the Middle Ages in the following half-century.

Chapter 3

THE GROWTH AND DECLINE OF TOWNS

Richard Whittington was the third son of a Gloucestershire knightly family. He was by no means impoverished but was not likely to inherit any of the family estates. Relocating to London, he became a successful mercer. This word was derived from the Old French *mercier*, which itself came from the Latin word *merx*, meaning 'goods'. During the Middle Ages the term came to describe a dealer in high-quality textile fabrics, especially silk and other fine materials. Whittington became a very successful trader and was a major supplier to the royal court after about 1388. Between 1392 and 1394 he sold goods to King Richard II worth somewhere in the region of £3,500. He exported woollen cloth and there is evidence that he also began moneylending from the late 1380s. By 1397 he was lending large sums of money to the king. His economic power was rapidly translated into political influence.

In 1384 Whittington had become a member of the council of the City of London and, in 1392, he was one of the city's delegation to King Richard II at Nottingham. By 1393 Richard was an alderman and an influential member of the Mercers' Company. When the current mayor died in June 1397, Whittington was imposed on the city by the king as Lord Mayor of London. As mayor, Whittington successfully negotiated a deal which allowed the city authorities to buy back lost freedoms for the sum of £10,000. He was elected mayor in 1398.

When Richard II was deposed in 1399, Whittington cultivated an equally positive relationship with the new king, Henry IV, and then with his successor, Henry V. Whittington was again elected mayor in 1406 and 1419. In 1416 he became a Member of Parliament. Whittington died in March 1423. His tremendous achievements are recorded in the late rhyme – supposedly relating to a boyhood temptation to leave London and try elsewhere – which he allegedly heard sung out by the bells of London churches: *Turn again Whittington, thou worthy citizen, thrice lord mayor of London*. The reality, though, sheds more light on the powerful economic and political position of town merchants than the pantomime image does.

The career of someone like Whittington would have been impossible without the huge growth in towns and their influence which had occurred since 1066. While this had its roots in late Anglo-Saxon England, it was given fresh impetus by the Norman Conquest. This reveals itself clearly in the case of London, where the Norman impact on London was massive – with a new palace at Westminster and a new St Paul's, as well as the building of fortifications at Baynard's Castle and the Tower of London. In addition, the period following the Conquest saw the building of 11 new monasteries and 100 parish churches. The Conquest also coincided with a leap in London's population. From a figure of about 8,000 in 750, the population of London rose to 25,000 by 1100 and 100,000 in 1300. Incidentally it probably halved around 1350 and had risen to about 120,000 in 1558.

The increased number of new religious houses also had a large impact on the growing city. A huge area outside the City walls was occupied by monasteries: for example, St John Clerkenwell, St Mary Clerkenwell, St Mary Graces, St Mary Spital, Westminster, Bermondsey and Merton. They were each significant economic communities with great effects on their local area, and even their end in the sixteenth century provided a stimulus to the economic growth of London as their property and land passed into private hands.

However, there were other, more destructive, effects of the Norman Conquest on English towns. At Oxford the building of the Norman castle flattened an entire quarter of the town. Lincoln and Warwick each lost 166 houses and 27 were demolished in Cambridge for the same reason. In some towns, such as Southampton and Norwich, new French Quarters were established and, while these may have increased trade, the land for their construction may have been seized from the indigenous population.

The union of Normandy and England acted as a stimulus to long-distance trade and with it the growth of certain key towns. But towns were not a Norman invention. They were a Europe-wide phenomenon and in England their roots lay in the Anglo-Saxon period after 750. Neither was the increasingly rapid growth of towns after 1066 due to a particular Norman set of ingredients. Towns would have increased in number and importance whether the Conquest had happened or not. However, the impact of an aggressive group of arrivistes, keen to make the most of the new financial opportunities brought by the Conquest, can only have added to the cocktail of reasons why town growth accelerated after 1100.

Towns and trade
By 1300 perhaps as many as 20 per cent of the English population lived in urban centres, most of which acted as market centres for their local areas. They provided rural communities with the products they could not individually provide for

themselves, such as clothing and specialist iron tools. They also provided a market for the sale of farming produce from the demesne land of local estates. In this way they enabled local lords to turn the products of their estates into cash. The largest towns had the largest hinterlands, with which they were closely connected. London, for example, relied on grain supplies from about ten different counties. This in turn affected other towns which were part of the supply network connecting farms with the capital. So, Faversham (Kent), Ware (Hertfordshire) and Henley-on-Thames (Oxfordshire) all acted as gathering places for grain which was then transported on to London. The distance involved varied according to ease of transportation and the relationship between effort and eventual profit. Consequently, items such as fuel travelled shorter distances than drovers and their cattle. On a related theme, the concentration of available luxury goods in the largest towns (either imported through them, or produced there) likewise drew in purchasers from considerable distances. So, for example, wax and spices from London and parchment from Oxford were both purchased by the bishop of Hereford – despite both towns being considerable distances from Hereford.[1]

Many towns were established after 1066, while others had a history which stretched back far before the Conquest and some, of course, had been important centres in Roman Britain (although had not been continually urban since then). But many were new towns of the Middle Ages. In these cases ambitious local lords had seen the advantages a town could bring and invested in setting one up to make the most of a town's money-making opportunities. Boston was just such a new town which had, by 1300, become an international port. Some new developments started with very high hopes indeed. When the Knights Templar established Baldock (Hertfordshire) in 1168 its name was derived from *Baldac*, the medieval form of Baghdad in Iraq. Baldock never quite came to rival the famous and ancient Middle Eastern city.

The importance of the establishment of new towns is revealed in the fact that between 1200 and 1300 the number of *boroughs* (originally a defended place but later possessing certain rights, such as self-government) jumped by over 100 per cent, from about 220 to about 500. Of these towns about 25 per cent were directly administered by the Crown. An insight into the Crown's interest in urban development is provided by Edward I. When he wanted to give a gift to the nurse attending to his baby son (the future Edward II) the ideal gift was a *burghal* plot in a town; later, in 1297, he called together the first recorded meeting of English town planners to help rebuild the town of Berwick, and the king himself wheeled a symbolic wheelbarrow of earth as work on the town's defences started. However, important as the input was of the English Crown, this left 75 per cent of towns which had been set up by local lords. The Church too saw the advantages of developing towns on its estates, and 25 per cent of the national total were administered by the Church. The returns to those who established towns, or who invested in them, could be impressive.

Of all the industries located in towns, the largest was the cloth industry. The large number of people living in towns provided a good-sized labour pool for the many different stages involved in the industry, from preparing the wool through to processing the finished cloth. During the thirteenth century the cloth trade was a major source of the prosperity of towns such as Beverley, Lincoln, Stamford and York. Regional specialization meant that certain locations were associated with particular products, including 'Lincoln scarlet' and 'Bristol red'. This high-quality cloth was consumed on the domestic as well as on the international market. Other towns were associated with other trades and products, varying from knives at Thaxted (Essex) to herrings at Great Yarmouth (Norfolk).

The benefits enjoyed by townspeople
Towns also offered a wide range of attractions for those living there. As well as providing new job prospects they also offered

opportunities for escaping villeins to lose themselves in a large population. It was this that caused towns to grow as a proportion of the national population from about 10 per cent in 1086 to perhaps approaching 20 per cent by 1300. This growth was driven by migration from surrounding areas. In fact, the unhealthy state of a town such as London meant that it was only this inward migration which was capable of sustaining its growth through the Middle Ages. Even in a smaller town such as Exeter it seems that about 27 per cent of its inhabitants migrated from up to 40 miles (64 km) away.[2] This movement ranged from poor peasants looking for opportunities to improve their economic situation, to wealthier artisans making the most of the trading opportunities through renting a plot of town land. The immigrants often included a surprising proportion of women.

However, towns were very varied. By 1377, the year of the Poll Tax levy, London – with a population of about 50,000 – was far larger than any other town in England. Far below it were the four towns of Bristol, Coventry, Norwich and York, with populations between 8,000 and 15,000. The next tier of towns, such as Lincoln, had populations ranging from 5,000 to 8,000. The fourth tier consisted of 27 towns, such as Stamford (Lincolnshire), with populations between 2,000 and 5,000. Finally there were some 5,000 towns, such as Grimsby (Lincolnshire) or Stow-on-the-Wold (Gloucestershire) with populations smaller than 2,000.

One clear characteristic of towns was a distinct set of rights (*borough freedoms*) which outsiders did not enjoy. Not that there was one clear and tidy definition of what these were. Instead, there was a typically English set of arrangements which varied from place to place. Some towns, it is true, had been granted *borough charters* by a lord. These laid out the rights and privileges enjoyed by those living there. Others, however, had evolved a series of local customs. Some of these towns later formalized these in a charter, but some did not. Probably the most obvious characteristic of an English medieval town was that the properties within it were rented out at relatively low rent and that those who rented were not liable for any kind of labour service. These plots of land could be freely sold or given as a gift, and none of this needed the agreement of the lord who owned the land. This is technically known as *burgage tenure*. The word *burgage*, like *borough*, is derived from the Old English word *burg* or *burh*, meaning a defended place or town. This burgage tenure was an attractive proposition to a population who were all too familiar with the humiliating restrictions and unpaid workload which often went with renting land in the countryside. The person who rented land in a town had freedoms that a villein in the countryside could only dream of. Furthermore, inflation in the thirteenth century made the cost of renting these urban plots even more attractive.

Towns thrived on trade. Owners of town land had the right to hold fairs and weekly markets and were free from the tolls which had to be paid by outsiders visiting these. The yearly cycle of fairs started for many thirteenth-century continental merchants with Stamford before Easter, through Boston in July, to Winchester in September and on to Northampton in November. Townspeople celebrated their membership of an exclusive club and kept outsiders at a disadvantage. Their freedoms often included the right to transport goods across the kingdom without paying tolls. In some towns these privileges were not enjoyed by all townspeople but were restricted to those traders and craftsmen who were members of the *guild merchant*. We shall return to the guilds shortly, but suffice to say that this arrangement was a device to restrict access to the wealth brought by trade to even smaller numbers. And it was an access worth having. In Southampton members of the guild merchant had the right of first refusal of goods brought into the city; they could run a tavern and buy items such as honey, herrings and salt without being restricted to market days and fairs. At Lynn (Norfolk) 'foreign traders' could not stay in the town longer than 40 days and such restrictions were the norm.

In many towns these freedoms were enjoyed by all the inhabitants. However, as the Middle Ages progressed they became more restricted and a distinction grew up between those traders and manufacturers who had been granted the 'freedom' of the town and the majority of the town population with fewer privileges. This 'freedom' of the town could be gained through inheritance, purchase or apprenticeship; the exact situation varied from town to town. In Norwich in 1415, the town's authorities raised money by forcing all shopkeepers to buy the 'freedom' of the borough. After this anyone owning a shop could trade for two years but then had to buy the freedom of the town, or shut the shop.

Over time, more and more towns enjoyed the benefits of self-government and elected their own mayors and bailiffs. This occurred when the *burgesses* (citizens) of a town clubbed together and paid a fixed fee to the lord who had originally owned the land on which the town lay. The fee compensated the lord for the loss of income from the rents and tolls of the town and meant that these in future belonged to the town itself. This payment was called a *farm*, from the Old French word *ferme* and the medieval Latin word *firma*, meaning a fixed payment. This trend exploded after 1189 because both Richard I and King John were short of cash and found granting charters and selling town rights attractive financial propositions. Urban self-rule therefore grew most swiftly in royal boroughs.

Some private lords tried to resist this trend. Church land-lords, such as those who controlled the towns of Abingdon, Bury, Cirencester, Dunstable, Reading and St Albans, found themselves the targets of resentful townspeople keen to press their rights for more freedom to regulate their own affairs. In 1327 in Bury, townspeople plundered the abbey and imprisoned some of the monks in an attempt to force the abbot to grant them greater self-government. There was trouble here again in 1381 (during the Peasants' Revolt) and it is revealing that Bury was the only town excluded from Richard II's general pardon, issued in December 1381. Only the Reformation, in the 1530s, broke the abbot's control.

In these self-governing towns it was the town authorities who were now responsible for carrying out royal instructions; no longer were they under the authority of the sheriff of the shire. They had come of age as communities. In Beverley (Yorkshire) the present guildhall dates from 1501 and still contains the silver fifteenth-century *waits chains* worn by musicians employed to play on civic occasions. Similar items make up the oldest of the regalia in Exeter, where three of the silver waits chains were made in the fifteenth century. They are believed to be those which records state were remade in 1476–7 at a cost of 14 shillings. These are tangible links to the town privileges and sense of community from the Middle Ages.

In Bristol in 1373, this urban autonomy reached its logical conclusion when the city also became a county in its own right. It was followed in this by other English towns: York (1396), Newcastle (1400), Norwich (1404), Lincoln (1409), Hull (1440) and Chester (1506). Such confident and self-regulating towns had their mayors and councils, seals and seats of government. They frequently excluded 'lesser trades' from occupying these positions. The Somerset city of Wells (albeit a tiny city) excluded butchers from all local offices between 1377 and 1500. In the same way the town governments of Exeter and York in the fifteenth century were dominated by merchants, with only lesser posts open to members of the craft guilds.

Nevertheless, even if such powerful officials looked to their own interests, they were political realists and showed a surprising degree of respect for the traditional customs and expectations of their communities. Real conflict could occur when financial charges were made on the population without respect for traditional rights or consultation with representatives of the wider town community. Towns were certainly not democracies, but they were not run by oligarchies who could afford to ignore the less-wealthy members of the urban community. But when it came to active participation in government, the trend during the fifteenth century was to reduce popular involvement and restrict access to the corridors of power. This meant that Late Medieval town councils were often made up of the wealthiest members of urban society, replacing more open assemblies. Increasingly, those eligible for the post of mayor became restricted to the elite. This state of affairs could become so extreme that the top leadership became self-selecting, such as happened in Bristol in 1499 and Exeter in 1504. This leadership no longer had to fear the violence and disorder which had sometimes occurred at election times.

The guilds

Within these towns, traders and manufacturers were grouped into *guilds*, which administered their *mysteries* (professional knowledge, rules and arrangements). These organizations were made up of three main groups. The first were the *masters*, who owned their own workshops, or shops. They bought in raw materials and owned the tools and equipment of the trade. In addition, they sold on the finished products. Many used the wealth they accumulated to further expand their businesses. As a fifteenth-century rhyme put it: 'money makythe the man'. Most were limited, however, by the small scale of their enterprises. In London in 1456, the largest known workshop employed only eleven apprentices and seven servants. None in York in this period was as large. The second group were the *journeymen*. Having been trained but not yet acquired their own premises, these skilled workers were employed by the masters. They enjoyed higher status than other people employed by the masters because they were on their way to becoming masters too one day, if all went well. Some had their own organizations as a mark of their importance within the town. The third group were the *apprentices*. These provided free labour to the masters, while learning the trade. The expectations on both sides were laid down in *indentures*. There could be a huge gulf between the most wealthy masters and the skilled workers they employed. Some of the wealthiest of the elites in

cities such as London, Bristol and York had little in common
with the other townspeople with whom they did business.
However, many merchants operated on a much smaller scale
and were not much better off than successful craftspeople, even
if these seemed below them on the social scale.

In some trades the skilled masters no longer bought in the
raw materials themselves and instead became employed by
others who controlled the supply of raw materials. Examples
of such powerful suppliers were the wool merchants in some
areas of the textile trade. These elites often determined to
control those who depended on them. In Leicester the weavers
and fullers were excluded from the merchant guild, although it
set the prices for their work. In Winchester the town's
merchants so dominated the politics of the town that weavers
and fullers were banned from selling cloth except to the
merchants, who then sold it on, to their advantage. From 1400
to 1500 the process in which more and more power in the
lucrative textile industry was gathered into fewer and fewer
hands accelerated. In time the wealthy merchants who could
afford to purchase huge quantities of wool dominated all
aspects of the trade and employed large numbers of different
kinds of skilled workers – carders, spinners, weavers, shearmen
and fullers. The merchants then supplied the finished cloth to
drapers, who sold it in their shops. This system of transferring
items from stage to stage in the production process was called
putting out, and these wealthy *clothiers* remained the owners of
the product and the employers of those working on it
throughout all these stages. By the early sixteenth century this
pattern had replaced that of the fourteenth century in which
many independent small-scale producers had existed.

The guild system grew up in English towns mainly during
the fourteenth century, though it was under way in the biggest
towns from the 1280s. Before guilds became so important,
wages and conditions were often decided by the town authorities. And there had been apprentices learning their trades
long before the guilds brought together large numbers of

craftspeople and formalized their arrangements. The guilds, though, were useful in keeping the elites in control of their areas of expertise. By insisting on long apprenticeships they could limit those coming into the trade and so reduce competition. By limiting the number of apprentices a master could take on, they stopped more energetic masters from dominating the trade of a town and forcing other masters out of business. Powerful guildsmen did their best to prevent their journeymen from organizing their own groups to press for higher wages, as happened in London, in 1396. The journeymen saddlers had been attempting to set up a guild in honour of the Virgin Mary but the organizers of the saddlers' craft guild considered this a front for a trade union and clearly felt threatened by this show of independence. Similarly, by fixing prices the craft guilds established cartels which worked to their own mutual benefit. In 1484, when the Coventry town authorities tried to intervene in the setting of prices for bread, the bakers refused to produce any – and so made the point that they alone should fix the prices. Guilds also regulated working hours: banning night work and work on Sundays and other holy days.

During the fifteenth century the guilds in the largest towns gained many functions beyond regulating manufacturing and trade. They took on a religious role by promoting the feasts of their patron saints, they paid for candles and ceremonies in local churches and they organized ceremonies such as the great processions on the celebrations of Corpus Christi and at midsummer. In fact the *Mystery Plays* (see Chapter 8) performed around Corpus Christi took their names from the guilds, or mysteries, who organized them. Indeed it is possible that in some towns it was as crafts organized themselves to pay for these events in the fourteenth century that craft guilds formed in these places. Often different guilds took different parts in a way which promoted their crafts – so the fishmongers provided fish for Gospel scenes by Lake Galilee, goldsmiths made gifts for the Wise Men to bring to the baby

Jesus, and carpenters might build Noah's ark. In York in 1425, when the cooks' guild gave up the selling of fish they stopped their contribution to the play put on by the fishermen. They clearly no longer saw a connection between themselves and this particular part of the play cycle.

The guilds also offered mutual support to their members and assisted widows and organized funerals. At Killingholme (Lincolnshire), guild members each paid a half-penny to support other guild members in need. For many poorer towns-people in the fifteenth century, the support of their guild at time of death was the equivalent of the prayers and Masses said for the souls of wealthier citizens in chantries, which were paid for from richer citizens' more substantial estates.

By the mid-fifteenth century many of the most powerful guilds dominated the government of towns such as Bristol. In this way they operated as 'both judge and jury' in ensuring that towns were run in their interests. Another metaphor might be 'both poachers and gamekeepers', since, by the mid- to late sixteenth century, such powerful merchants evaded royal customs duties to an astonishing degree and persecuted any 'whistleblowers'. This 'white ruff crime' could account for as much as 50 per cent of the export trade of many of Bristol's wealthiest merchants.[3]

Merchant Adventurers and foreign investors

By this time a new kind of trading association was coming to prominence – the Merchant Adventurers. These were different from the traders' guilds of the earlier Middle Ages in their scale, their ambitions and in their commitment to long-distance trade. It was this group which had come to dominate the commercial life of Bristol by the sixteenth century.

Bristol's Merchant Adventurers remind us that a significant amount of trade was conducted over considerable distances. In an excavation of a merchant property in Cuckoo Lane, Southampton, dating from about 1280, a seal from Normandy was found in the rubbish pit.[4] Clearly, Southampton was at the hub of a major trading network – and it was not alone. Some of the goods imported were at the end of a chain of transactions which stretched into Asia. Particularly valuable was the trade in pepper and spices, which commanded huge sums of money. Export goods, however, were less exotic, ranging from English finished cloth to tin (from Cornwall and Devon) and lead (from Wales and the Pennines). What is very clear is that the yearly total value of trade in and out of England was enormous. In 1204 it may have been as high as £75,000 and in 1304 perhaps as much as £500,000.[5]

The importance of international trade was recognized by the Crown, which required payment for granting permission to merchants to trade abroad. In this way William Whittoke was granted his licence to 'pass over the sea' in 1390 and yet another William Whittok faced a royal command to the sheriff of Southampton in 1345 to seize his ship, goods, chattels and lands since he had travelled 'to the parts of Normandy, and has unladed the ship there for the benefit of the king's enemies.'[6]

This growth in international trade provided opportunities for enterprising bankers. By the thirteenth century the head-quarters of the Riccardi merchants of Lucca, Italy, had been established in London, adjacent to the area south-west of The Poultry named Bucklersbury. This was the first financial trading house in the city. After the expulsion of the Jews, in 1290, Lombard bankers financed the crown and other major players in the English economy. By the middle of the four-teenth century the Florentine banking companies of the Bardi, Peruzzi and Frescobaldi had joined the Riccardi in London. In fact the first English gold coin – the *florin* – took its name from these Florentine bankers. Florentine merchants might make a profit up to 15 per cent on their trading in English wool. This was not a very high rate of return and still left plenty of profit to be enjoyed within the English economy. On average, by comparison, the London Grocers' Company between 1450 and 1479 averaged profits of 10 per cent. And English wool merchants might expect a 20-per-cent return on their export of wool to the continent.[7]

Other European players developed a keen interest in English international trade. German merchants of the *Hanseatic* trading league set up a base at the Steelyard near London Bridge and dominated the fourteenth-century London export trade. The German merchants were allowed to have an alderman of their own choice, provided he was a freeman of the City. At first these were foreigners but before the end of the fourteenth century two City aldermen were elected in succession by the merchants to be their alderman, one of them being William Walworth, who killed Wat Tyler at the climax of the Peasants' Revolt in 1381.

Other foreigners were also involved in English trade goods. European cloth workers were encouraged, after 1337, to assist in the development of finished cloth. These skilled newcomers included Flemings, who were bitterly resented by many English textile workers and a number were murdered during the Peasants' Revolt. Until this time the main English woollen exports had been of raw wool. This involvement of skilled continental craftspeople boosted the growing English textile industry, which, despite periodic trade slumps, remained a major exporter throughout the fifteenth century. Exports of raw wool peaked at 46,382 sacks in 1308. However, from 1360 wool exports began to lose ground to the export of finished cloth, and by 1420 more finished cloth was exported than raw wool. This rapid expansion of the textile industry led to towns such as Stamford and Norwich becoming major manufacturing centres of finished cloth. In fact the type of cloth known as *worsted* takes its name from a village close to Norwich. The capital also benefited from these developments, and London's expansion continued as cloth production stimulated the economy. London's dominance was seen in many other fifteenth-century industries too, including gold smithing, bell founding, brass making and the growing market in spices. However, as some towns – and especially London – boomed, ports such as Hull and Yarmouth suffered due to the decline in the export of raw wool.

Cloth production was not the only trade assisted by European involvement. Dutch immigrants brought skills in leather working and gold smithing; they were also at the cutting edge of fifteenth-century technologies such as printing, clock manufacturing, optics and even brick making. Prior to the late fourteenth century few buildings in England were made from bricks; instead construction relied on timber and wattle walls, or stone for the wealthy. By the end of the Middle Ages bricks were increasingly used in major construction projects. Overall the number of so-called 'aliens' in London rose from 1,500 in 1440 to 3,000 in 1501.

Town planning
While the population and organization of towns, which we have examined so far, has been studied for generations it is more recent research which is giving us a clearer insight into the actual layout and physical structure of medieval towns. Typical towns were set out in so-called *burghal plots* – long, rectangular areas of land with frontages giving access to the street. When activities outgrew the town boundaries the town itself might grow as new areas were added; often revealed in surviving suburb names such as *Newland* and *Newtown*. While many inhabitants of towns lived in very cramped conditions, richer citizens could often afford a large enough plot of land with a garden behind the buildings.

In terms of zones within these cities, the most sought-after location was in the centre, in what would today be described as the central business district (CBD). The main difference between the CBD in the Middle Ages and modern urban developments was that this area was also the residential (as well as the trading) area for those able to afford to live there. Only the poorer citizens were zoned on the edges of the town, or beyond its boundaries. Commuting – such as it was – was the experience of the poor, not the rich. Other aspects of zoning occurred in the grouping together of similar trades. Goldsmiths, woodworkers and fishmongers, for example, would often be located in similar areas. This is often reflected in surviving street names such as Fish Row and Butcher Row, and even in such names as Grope Lane, found in a number of cities and revealing areas of medieval prostitution (often close to market areas). When a trade produced particularly unpleasant side effects (such as butchery and tanning) there would often be town ordinances – supported by the energetic efforts of suffering neighbours – to try to ensure that these were located away from prime sites and, if possible, beyond town boundaries.

Excavations in Cambridge have revealed how stable town property boundaries could be over a thousand years of town growth, even when the *use* of these plots has changed greatly. Twentieth-century boundaries often follow the line of sixteenth-, thirteenth- and even eleventh-century boundaries.[8] This was a continuity which, due to insufficient survival of documentary evidence, only archaeology could prove. These plots changed in use as declining trade saw Cambridge reinvent itself as a monastic and then a university town.

Provision of clean water was crucial to survival in the crowded confines of even the smallest town. Excavations in Cambridge revealed that when eleventh-century plots were laid out in a new suburb, south-east of the town's boundary ditch, each property had its own well. Such is the continuity of urban sites that these were the first of a series of wells in each property which continued to be used until the coming of piped water in the nineteenth century. The earliest of these wells (constructed between the eleventh and fourteenth centuries) had wickerwork reinforcing the sides. As a general rule these gave way to constructions lined with timber-planked barrels in the fourteenth and fifteenth centuries, stone-lined ones from the sixteenth century and eventually brick shafts from the seventeenth century. Concerns about the supply of clean water affected all towns. By 1285 the Great Conduit had been built in order to supply London with clean water. Its intact fountain house has been excavated under the modern road of Cheapside.

Despite the way in which medieval towns were represented on contemporary illustrations and maps, only the major towns such as Exeter and York were fully walled. In the case of most other towns their walls and gates were products of civic pride rather than realistic forms of defence. At Beverley (Yorkshire), the early fifteenth-century North Bar Gate was designed to impress visitors, not to repel attackers. Within town boundaries there were many open areas as well as houses and shops. Churches and priories often occupied large areas and the latter had their own open spaces within the urban landscape.

Whether walled or otherwise, these medieval towns relied on the transportation of goods – both raw materials and foodstuffs – *into* towns and finished products *out* of towns. Clearly, the largest towns could not rely on the local market alone for their economic well-being. Connections to markets and suppliers further afield was crucial. Modern research has suggested that transport costs were not a barrier to trade. Figures for transport costs were in the region of about 2 per cent of the selling price of goods sent by road and about 6 per cent of selling costs for bulkier and heavier items sent by ship or barge.[9] Most of the bridges which would support long-distance trade in England until the 1750s were in place by 1300. While there was no national system of road construction and maintenance, many towns and landlords contributed to improvements of their local road system, including bridges.

Over the Middle Ages a shift from ox-drawn to horse-drawn carts speeded up the movement of heavy goods, and lighter goods were carried by packhorse. Inland waterways supplemented the roads and played an important part in the movement of heavy and bulky goods. However, until the canal building of the second half of the eighteenth century, rivers could not provide a comprehensive network. The same limitations of geography applied equally to transport by sea using the heavily built ships known from written sources as *hulks* and *cogs*.

Two steps forward, one step back?

Clearly, the Middle Ages were a period of both progress and regression in the growth and development of towns. For many towns their development was marked by contrasting periods of 'boom and bust'. There certainly was no clear upward trajectory of growth. A classic example is that of Northampton. Its urban life started as a 'frontier town' in the late ninth century on the border of the Danelaw and Mercia (a once-independent kingdom whose remnant was absorbed into Greater Wessex in 918 by Edward the Elder). It was already the site of a minster church with an adjacent Mercian royal palace. Rapid growth took place in the tenth century and this accelerated in the late eleventh and twelfth centuries. By 1200 its walled interior was the third largest in the country after London and Norwich, and it still boasts the largest market place in England. Northampton's walled area grew from 50 acres (20 hectares) to 220 acres (89 hectares). This growth meant that by 1200 it was a major urban centre of national importance. From the twelfth century, suburbs grew up outside the four main gates of the walled town.

However, by the fourteenth century Northampton's growth had stalled and it had fallen back to once again being no more than a middle-ranking county town. Areas which had once seen urban use reverted to gardens and allotments. While the town centre continued to be intensively occupied, its back streets and suburbs showed signs of being 'more sensitive to the ebb and flow of a town's economic fortunes' and this can be demonstrated in other medieval towns too. For Northampton, its medieval history can be told in distinct phases: an eighth-century Mercian church and royal centre; tenth-century growth into a town of regional importance; twelfth-century rapid expansion; fourteenth-century contraction of more marginal sites on its edges and suburbs; and late-fifteenth-century contraction across the whole town, which continued into the sixteenth century. By about 1520 almost the whole south-west quarter of the town was given over to the polluting activities of tanners.[10]

By 1450 a Europe-wide economic depression was at its worst point. Population decline as a result of plague combined with a shortage of precious metals to reduce the volume of international trade. English prices and income from agricultural produce were already low, and this wider reduction in trading activity hit towns hard. The fall in population had begun to affect towns before 1400. This decline in urban numbers meant that there were fewer people to consume products within towns, and these numbers were not made up by inward migration from the country to the town as in the past. This was because, with low rural rents and higher wages (along with a lessening of rural restrictions on villeins), there was less incentive to 'escape' to the town. Problems in the early fifteenth century were aggravated by war in France, which disrupted trade, drained manpower and required a high level of taxation and an outflow of precious metal to finance it. As if this was not bad enough, in northern England heavy rainfall between 1438 and 1440 hit the farming economy, which had further repercussions for town-based trade.

A recovery in the cloth trade later in the fifteenth century assisted recovery in some exporting towns but, since cloth production was now more a rural than an urban industry, this did not arrest urban decay overall – although it did assist in the growth of smaller towns in Essex, Somerset, Suffolk and Wiltshire. Here the close relationship between the spinners, weavers and dyers of the villages, and the larger markets in places such as Exeter and Salisbury was mutually advantageous. A similarly positive picture applied to the capital. However, London's continuing growth (with a population of about 120,000 by 1558) was not representative of many English towns. Indeed, its increasing monopoly of export trade meant that its growth was at the expense of other towns such as Boston and Hull, which had earlier benefited from trade which was lost to London after 1440. These last two ports also suffered due to English merchants being excluded from trade in the Baltic, following hostilities with towns of the north German

Hanseatic League in 1467–74. Many other towns, such as
Bristol, Colchester, Grimsby, Lincoln, Winchester and York
also experienced significant economic decline and falling populations in the fifteenth and early sixteenth centuries, with
massive problems revealed in Coventry in the 1520s. This
degree of change could be dramatic. The populations of Boston,
Lincoln and York fell by about 50 per cent between the 1370s
and the 1520s and there was a significant shrinkage in the built-
up areas of towns such as Beverley, Leicester and Stamford.

It must be admitted though that there were exceptions to
this picture of stagnation after 1400. Norwich and Exeter
remained buoyant, while newer towns such as Taunton grew.
The revival of exports to the continent (most notably the
Netherlands) between 1470 and 1490 assisted some southern
cities such as Bristol, and we have already seen how Exeter and
Salisbury benefited from a close relationship with their local
cloth manufacturers. And those urban merchants and manufacturers who were able to weather the unsettled economic
times might even prosper to a surprising degree. Recent
evidence from New Buckenham (Norfolk), along with tree-
ring dating of timbers from buildings in other towns, suggests
there was a significant rebuilding of urban properties between
1450 and 1530. This was long before the commonly accepted
period of the 'Great Rebuilding', thought to have occurred
c.1570–1640, which may have applied more to rural areas.[11]

Overall, then, the vibrant urban growth of the earlier Middle
Ages had been replaced by a more mixed pattern. Evidence
from taxation returns from the 1520s suggests an urban population of about 18 per cent of the national population. This is
similar to the proportion in the 1370s. So, towns continued to
be a significant part of national life but the trajectory of growth
had flattened off and reached a plateau in a number of cases. It
would not be until the later sixteenth century that the upward
direction would be resumed. But that is another story.

Chapter 4

CHANGING EXPRESSIONS OF CHRISTIAN BELIEF

The Norman conquerors of England were, of course, as Christian as the nation they had conquered. In this vital respect there was no significant change brought by the Norman Conquest to the spiritual fabric of England. But the matter did not end there. This is because the conquerors – including representatives of the great churches and abbeys of Normandy – brought with them both the social condescension of those who had made themselves master in another person's country and a spiritual commitment to 'reform' any areas of the English Church which did not meet current continental norms. Amongst their targets were lesser-known – to Normans – Anglo-Saxon saints, cathedrals in rural settings (the continental pattern located them in towns), purchase of Church positions, royal control over the Church, and married clergy.

By 1080 only one out of 16 bishops was an Anglo-Saxon. This made it easier to pull the Anglo-Saxon Church into line with developments on the continent which had not hitherto been implemented in England. In England many seats of bishops dated from before the development of towns in the ninth and tenth centuries. Centres such as Dorchester-on-Thames (Oxfordshire), Selsey (Sussex) and North Elmham (Norfolk) were not urban centres. However, in Normandy the Mediterranean practice of locating bishops in towns had become the norm. This was a spiritual geography which made the English set-up appear strangely old-fashioned and was rectified by relocating English sees into centres of administration. This served the dual purpose of 'modernizing' the English church structure and coordinating the management of the conquered country in a more consistent way, since the elites of Church and State were now both part of the same imposed Norman social order. In this way North Elmham gave way, first to Thetford and then to Norwich; Selsey gave way to Chichester.

Accompanying this shift was a vast rebuilding programme which saw all the great Anglo-Saxon churches demolished and rebuilt in the latest continental styles. Under Edward the Confessor, Norman influence had already revealed itself in the *Later Romanesque* church of Westminster with its broad transepts and nave. The contrast to the Carolingian style of Canterbury signalled the direction of his political and cultural sympathies. After 1066 this trend accelerated. Galleries over the nave aisles (sometimes linking into the transepts) may have housed additional altars, or been used in processions, as the liturgy became more complex. The great church centres such as Winchester Old Minster and St Augustine's, Canterbury – where history was intertwined with both the origins of English Christianity and kingship – were remade in the image of the new political realities and liturgical trends. It was as if the entire spiritual and cultural heritage of England had been reinvented; as if nothing of worth had existed before. It seemed as if the English Church had been a mere dress rehearsal for the main event, on which only the Norman Conquest had proved capable of raising the curtain. This was spiritual and cultural imperialism of an astonishing kind. Only here and there – at places such as Brixworth and Earl's Barton (Northamptonshire), Deerhurst (Gloucestershire), St Laurence, in Bradford on Avon (Wiltshire) – do we catch glimpses of the ecclesiastical architectural treasures of Anglo-Saxon England. Accompanying these physical changes were organizational reforms. The establishment of local archdeaconries subdivided dioceses and increased the efficiency of Church government, and Canon law cases were taken out of the hands of the hundred courts.

However, it would be wrong to conclude that 'reforms' advocated by the papacy swept all areas of the English Church. Strong royal influence continued; shire courts continued to hear Canon law cases; not all churches adopted the new liturgy pioneered by Lanfranc at Canterbury, and a number, such as Winchester, continued with that used before 1066; the purchase of Church posts and married clergy remained areas slow to change, despite the Norman Conquest.

The Church in medieval society

What is clear is that the Church (despite shortcomings targeted by Norman reformers) played a huge role within society. However, it would be a mistake to assume that full-time paid members of the Church spent all their time on Church business. In reality, as literate members of the nation, often skilled in administration and part of an international community, they were in demand by secular authorities for assistance in government. Since the Church was also a major landowner, those who headed it – bishops, abbots and abbesses – also had to play a major role in running these estates, just like a secular landowner. Before 1400 almost all those involved in the day-to-day running of royal government in its lower levels were drawn from the clergy. They were both paid members of the Church and royal civil servants. This changed during the fifteenth century. In 1388 the chancery was administered almost exclusively by clerics but by 1461 it was dominated by laity.

For the medieval Church virtually all people in England were members of its community; England was a Christian country. The only religious minority after 1066 was the Jews, and they were expelled in 1290. Since Anglo-Saxon times the nation had been divided into parishes, within a diocese overseen by a bishop, within one of the two archdiocese (overseen by an archbishop) of Canterbury and York (with primacy going to the archbishop of Canterbury in Kent). The local unit – the parish – played a huge part in the lives of ordinary people. Its boundaries were usually centuries old and marked each year by a procession at *Rogationtide* (the week before Ascension Day, a feast 40 days after Easter). Everyone living within the parish was expected to attend parish Mass on Sundays and the main festivals of the year (see Chapter 11).

All those living within the parish paid a *tithe* of their income to their parish church. During the later Middle Ages many parishes were granted to monasteries, and income went to the monastery with a vicar appointed for the parish. The stipend paid to him ensured that the bulk of the revenue from the parish went to the monastery. In the case of Augustinian and Premonstratensian monasteries this job was often filled by one of their own *canons* (a priest living in a community, sometimes serving a cathedral or placed in a parish church). The wealthiest abbeys built *tithe barns* to store this income from local parishes. Since the original aim of the parish tithe was to support the local parish priest, the local church and the poor, this creaming off of the tithe could cause local resentment.

Only those ordained to the higher orders of the clergy could carry out the essential sacraments which were believed to bring people into close relationship with God and which led to the forgiveness of their sins. By the late fifteenth century these sacraments were: baptism (of babies), confirmation (often of toddlers), penance, the Eucharist (though only priests drank the wine), marriage, ordination and extreme unction (the final ritual anointing of a dying person). Ordination, whereby a person entered into the clerical orders, could be carried out only by a bishop.

But who were the clergy? Today that might seem an obvious question. They constitute those in paid employment within the Church, who teach and lead worship of the Christian community. In the Middle Ages the matter was much more complex. In the thirteenth and fourteenth century any schoolboy who received a *tonsure* as a mark of his literate status was technically a member of the clergy. This could include boys as young as seven years old. As a result, anyone accused of a crime could claim what was called 'benefit of clergy' if they were literate. This allowed them to be tried in a Church court, where punishments (usually involving penance and without the death penalty) were lighter than in royal courts. The Bible passage used for this test of literacy was Psalm 51: 1, whose words, in Latin, contained this appropriate opening verse: 'Have mercy on me, O God, according to your unfailing love; according to your great compassion blot out my transgressions.'[1] Thus, an illiterate person who had memorized the appropriate Psalm could also claim benefit of clergy, and Psalm 51: 1 became known as the 'neck verse'. A reaction against those avoiding justice by reciting this verse led to restrictions, and by the end of the sixteenth century the crimes of murder, rape, poisoning, petty treason (e.g. a wife's murder of her husband), sacrilege, witchcraft, burglary, theft from churches and pickpocketing went before a secular court. Analysis of those 'clerics' (whose professions can be checked) who successfully pleaded 'benefit of clergy' as recorded in the records of the archbishop of York between 1452 and 1530 show that only 24 per cent were genuine clerics.

Above this category of 'technical clerics' were the ordained four *minor orders* of doorkeeper, lector, exorcist and acolyte. Members of these orders did not have to be celibate. Above these were the three *major (holy) orders* of sub-deacon, deacon and priest. Only priests could consecrate the Eucharist and rise to the higher ranks of the Church such as bishop. Priests had to be at least 24 years old and bishops at least 30 years old (the age when it was believed that Jesus had begun his ministry). There were restrictions on who could enter these orders. Illegitimate men needed a bishop's dispensation to enter minor orders and one from the pope to enter major orders. The same applied to sons of clergymen, since their fathers should have been celibate – a discipline hard to enforce, and as late as 1070 an archbishop of Canterbury had stepped back from demanding it from all clergy. It was only after 1200 that higher clerics in the diocese of Hereford ceased to be married and only shortly after this did hereditary succession to *benefices* (the income a priest had from the church for which he was responsible) cease. However, even as late as 1300 there are examples of married priests amongst the lower clergy.

No villein could be ordained since, as William Langland summed it up in the late fourteenth-century poem *Piers Plowman*, no 'bondmen and bastards and beggars' should be in holy orders. Candidates should have no physical defects. Finally, they should be of appropriate character, with sufficient learning. Once ordained, clerics were supposed to avoid brightly coloured fashionable clothes and had the character-istic haircut, the *tonsure*.

What is clear is that there were a very large number of clerics; perhaps 33,150 in 9,500 parishes in 1250. To this should be added 7,600 monks, 3,900 regular canons and 5,300 friars. These may have made up as much as 5.6 per cent of the adult male population in 1200.[2] In addition, there were about 1,500 men and women working in hospitals as part of a religious order and perhaps as many as 7,000 nuns (though some esti-mates are as low as 3,000). After 1200 financial pressures meant that many monasteries operated a quota system of new recruits to reduce numbers entering the orders. 'It was a drastic reversal of the missionary strategy' from which these orders of monks and nuns had originally emerged.[3]

Grants of land made the Church extremely powerful and in the later Middle Ages at least 20 per cent of land was owned by the Church. Critics as varied as the Peasants' Revolt leader John Ball and the educated lay lords who patronized the writers of literature such as the *Gest of Robyn Hode* supported the redistribution of the vast estates owned by the Church. However, critics of the Church faced opposition from both royal and Church authorities. Between 1250 and 1435 about 16,000 excommunicates were notified to royal authorities; sheriffs were required to arrest all who were not reconciled to the Church within 40 days.

Church architecture and rebuilding

This wealth and influence of the Church was expressed in the many parish churches across England. While these act as physical representations of Christian beliefs, a closer study of these buildings shows that both beliefs and architecture were not as unchanging as they might first appear. Indeed, the ways in which Church architecture changed across the Middle Ages opens a window into the beliefs of men and women and also into ways in which expressing these beliefs changed. There were certain architectural features which applied to most churches in the Middle Ages. First was the graveyard associated with a parish church, since the Church offered the message of salvation and the hope of eternal life through Christian faith. As we saw in Chapter 1, churchyard burial was something which did not immediately happen following the Christian conversions of the Anglo-Saxon kingdoms but, by the eleventh century, it had become well established as the norm. Burial rights were rigorously defended by parish clergy and they brought a significant income to the local church. It was not uncommon for *chapels of ease* to be established elsewhere within a large parish for occasional services but these did not have the status of the parish church with its burial and baptismal role. If these developed into full churches there could often be disputes with the *mother church*. In the fourteenth century, for example, a dispute over burial rights between Sutton-on-Hull (Yorkshire) and its mother church at Waghen led to bodies being exhumed from Sutton and reburied at Waghen.

The principal entry to churches was usually via the south doorway, and near here, inside the church, would be located the font for infant baptisms. Both of these features had symbolic significance. The doorway (often with a covering porch) was the gateway between the secular world and the sacred. It was here that babies were given to the priest for baptism and where weddings were solemnized. The positioning of the font near the door was also significant since it symbolized the point of entry to the medieval Christian community. The main focus of the church building was the altar located at the eastern end, or *chancel*, and particularly associated with the priest. This was the focus for the celebration of the Eucharist, also known as the Mass (Holy Communion); the main body of the church – the *nave* – being occupied by the laity. A physical barrier between these two areas emphasized this internal division of the building. Named from an Old English word for the cross which surmounted it, this was called the *rood screen*. Many churches also contained subsidiary altars in other parts of the building. By the later fourteenth century these were increasingly associated with *chantries*.

The responsibility for the upkeep of the parish church had, by the 1350s, fallen to annually elected members of the parish, the *churchwardens*. They raised money for this from a variety of sources: collections, social events such as *church ales* and *hocking* (requesting gifts from passers-by), income from church-owned animals and leasing out of property.

Church buildings were deeply imbued with meaning. After 1297 the cloisters at Norwich cathedral were rebuilt following severe damage caused by riots in 1272. The masons created a structure in the cloister's East Walk which was capable of 'integrating sculpture, architecture and meaning'. The complex roof bosses of the vaulted corridor were designed to elaborate and extend the meanings of the carvings around the great doorway into the church. Research has decoded the rich imagery of these elaborately carved items and the insight they give us into the Christian world view of the late thirteenth century. These lead through the 'First Judgement' (where a saintly few are admitted to paradise, the rest to purgatory) to the 'Second Judgement' (where those in purgatory are assigned either to heaven or to hell) and finally up the seven ascending steps into the cathedral itself, an earthly symbol of heaven.[4]

Between 1066 and 1230 England might have seemed to have been one vast building site. Indeed, so great was the extent of church construction in the thirteenth century that it has been calculated it was the equivalent, in modern terms (2006), of every family in England paying £500 every year for the whole century![5] From about 1250 many church buildings became more complex, developing from the simple components of nave and chancel. By 1300 many added bell towers, side aisles and porches. This change accelerated between 1300 and 1500. In the decades either side of 1300 many spires were added to existing church towers; the one at Salisbury being so heavy it actually distorted the piers of the crossing beneath. At Old St Paul's in London the amazing height of – reputedly – 500 feet (152.4 metres) was achieved by constructing the spire from timber. Such spires in these *High Gothic* churches seemed to reach towards God, just as the elaborate vaulted roofs below and the light falling through the traceried windows seemed to afford glimpses into heaven. The increasing elaboration and flowing patterns increased in the *Decorated Style.* And then there was a reaction: after about 1330 the more sweeping, vertical lines of the *Perpendicular Style* may have struck a particular chord with a society which, after the Black Death, saw its spirituality more in terms of a personal faith surviving the destruction of earthly confidence and ambition. This was a style which saw little innovation throughout the fifteenth century.[6]

The rebuilding of churches in the fifteenth century was particularly associated with rich wool-producing areas such as the Cotswolds, Somerset, Suffolk and northern Essex. Here, churches such as Huish Episcopi (Somerset), Northleach (Gloucestershire) and Lavenham (Suffolk) are classic examples of this great rebuilding. Other features of church furniture and

decoration also increased in this period: font covers, rood
screens, brass lecterns, images of Jesus and Mary and of saints,
and stone funeral monuments. It was only during this period
that seating, in the form of benches and pews, became
common. Some of these changes were the results of increasing
wealth reflected in gifts to the Church and in social display.
Other changes reflected developments within Church rituals
and beliefs.

From the later fourteenth century and throughout the
fifteenth there was an increase in the building of *chantry
chapels*, where Masses were said for the dead. This dovetailed
into the doctrine of purgatory – which had come to prominence
in Church teaching since the twelfth century. Purgatory, it was
said, was an intermediate state between heaven and hell in
which sins could be purged away. Prayers said for those in
purgatory could lessen time spent there and make it more likely
that they would reach heaven. In the years after the cataclysmic
events of the Black Death a huge investment took place in
building chantry chapels and in leaving money for chantry
priests to celebrate Mass on behalf of the dead benefactors.
Bristol by the late fifteenth century had 18 parish churches,120
temporary chantries and 20 permanent chantries. Since Church
law stopped priests from saying more than one Mass a day, each
of these chantries needed its own priest. Such chantries often
provided employment for clergy who were unable to gain other
appointments. At Ilchester (Somerset) in 1415, seven houses, a
garden and 10 acres (4 hectares) of land were made over to the
priory of Whitehall to support a chaplain to 'celebrate divine
service daily at the high altar in the church of Holy Trinity,
Ilchester, for the souls of Joan, late the wife of John Stourton
and William Whittok and Agnes his wife and their relations and
for the keeping of their anniversaries on Thursday in Easter
week'.[7] Such arrangements multiplied in the fifteenth century,
and accompanying this focus on death were new styles of
tombs illustrating decaying bodies and skeletons. Other developments in society were also reflected in burial practices.

Burial practices and beliefs

The study of chantries indicates the more general ways in which changes in society were reflected in changing burial fashions. This applies across the whole of the Middle Ages and reveals itself in recent archaeological discoveries in medieval grave-yards. There is no evidence that the Church actively attempted to change burial fashions before the tenth and eleventh centuries, but its influence on burial practice increased after this. However, the Norman Conquest itself had no impact on burial fashions. Grave slabs did increase in number in the eleventh century but this had started before 1066. Indeed, the evidence suggests that eleventh-century burial fashions were varied. Late Anglo-Saxon graves from beneath York Minster reveal the use of stone and wooden coffins, two biers, domestic storage cases used as coffins, and a boat. Some graves had stones as pillows and placed on either side of the head; some were lined with stones and tile; some were filled with charcoal (presumably to absorb fluids and smells from decomposing bodies). Many were marked with carved markers and slabs.[8] More insights into late Anglo-Saxon burial fashions have come from the excavation in the 1990s of Raunds Furnells (Northamptonshire). The church here was used from around 900 until about 1100. During this time there appears to have been an increasing zoning of who was buried where, according to gender and age. Babies, for example, were usually buried under the eaves of the church. Interestingly, although the bodies were orientated west–east (and supine), as would be expected in an early Christian cemetery, they were often not truly west–east and were more closely orientated with the church building itself.[9] At the later site of Wharram Percy, babies and a dispro-portionate number of children aged 2–17 years were buried on the north side of the church. This was the traditional side for the unbaptized but this would not have been the case here, so it is uncertain what this positioning signified.

At Raunds Furnells most of the dead were buried in coffins, the highest-status graves having ones made from stone. A number had markers indicating their location. In some cases arrangements of stone slabs protected the body. These were probably related to the social status of the dead. Where later graves disturbed earlier ones it is because the later ones were placed closest to the earliest church, which was probably regarded as especially sacred. What these indicators show us is that the rites which surrounded these burials mattered greatly to the living. As Martin Carver comments: 'A grave is not simply a text, but a text with attitude, a text inflated with emotion . . . In brief, burials have a language'.[10] This 'language' increased in complexity as the Middle Ages progressed, as more elaborate monuments commemorated the burial of wealthy people. In the later Middle Ages the fashion grew for reflecting human mortality in tomb carvings showing the emaciated corpse, or skeleton, of the dead person. Sometimes carvings included the lifelike appearance of the person and beneath it a stone representation of the decaying corpse. As the inscription on the tomb of John Baret at Bury St Edmunds concludes: 'He that will sadly behold me with his eye, may see his own mirror [and] learn for to die.' This call for personal piety in the face of inevitable death, and preparation for 'a good death', is a strong feature of religious attitudes in the late fifteenth century.[11] It is surely no coincidence that one of the first books printed by Caxton in the 1490s was one entitled *Arte and crafte to knowe well to die.* And throughout the Middle Ages the dead and the living were part of a related community: cemeteries were used for processions and parts of Easter services; sermons were preached and fairs held in these same areas; the dead were often publicly displayed before burial; graveside memorials and rituals kept fresh the memory of the dead. While burial in rows in some large cemeteries reduced disturbance of earlier graves, there is plenty of evidence from archaeology and written sources to show this often could not be avoided and the physical presence of the dead was a daily reality.

In a revealing study of about 8,000 graves dating from c.1050–1600, in over 70 cemeteries,[12] a number of changing practices can be identified which are probably reflections of developing ideas about death. From the mid-eleventh century the use of stone lining for graves increased, along with stone head supports and inscribed crosses placed with the dead. This may reflect increased fears that the dead needed defence against demonic attack. At the same time the placing of a pilgrim's staff in a grave may have been part of the increase in commemoration of the character of the dead. By 1100 the burial of chalices and crosses with clergy reflected the increasing distinction of the clergy as a separate (celibate) group. This fashion increased during the twelfth century. The practice of burying personal possessions with the dead had extended to the laity by 1200. This became very noticeable from 1200 to 1300, as rosaries and pilgrim badges were increasingly added to personal items such as jewellery and clothing. This may have accompanied greater emphasis on personal social status and ideas of individuality, as urbanization challenged the traditional social structures and class divisions of medieval society. This presence of personal dress accessories accelerated again from about 1350. Clearly the family (especially women), as well as the Church, were influential in the presentation of the dead for burial. This evidence appears to contradict earlier assumptions that, from the thirteenth century, the clergy almost totally replaced the family as the group responsible for burial rites and practices[13] and that the dead were hidden from view.

Other patterns are also apparent. By 1200 the belief in purgatory was well defined and the dead constituted a distinct group who occupied a place between this world and heaven. The burial of religious objects therefore might have been thought to give comfort to the dead. In addition, during the second half of the fourteenth century burials in coffins became more common. This may have been caused by distress at decaying corpses resulting from the Black Death's impact on both the manner of death and the numbers of the dead – coffins may have been felt to contain this contaminating corruption (both in a physical and a spiritual sense) and to have preserved bodily integrity as the dead awaited the Final Judgement. This seems to have been particularly the case with women, since medieval concepts of sexuality held that women would decay more swiftly than men. This was related to the *Theory of Humours*, which classified female bodies as more changeable, colder, wetter and more liable to decay than male bodies. This heightened anxiety about death increased the value placed on objects such as papal pardons, which were buried with the dead and which may explain the presence of fourteenth-century papal seals in graves. At the same time examples of embalming (added to the established practice of reburial of exposed human remains, or their collection in *charnel* houses or pits), reflects medieval belief in the unity of body and soul (in purgatory) until the very literal bodily resurrection at the Last Judgement. After the Reformation (with the end of the belief in purgatory and a more spiritual definition of the resurrection at the Last Judgement) it became rare to place objects with the dead and charnel houses went out of use, although above-ground monuments became more elaborate.

Religious orders

The increased 'visibility' of the clergy in the burial record as the Middle Ages progressed reminds us again of the central importance of those who felt called to the 'religious life'. In its highest expression this took the form of a commitment to a celibate life as a monk or a nun. This was a process which increased in the central period of the Middle Ages, since in the twelfth and thirteenth centuries there was a huge expansion of *religious houses* of monks and nuns in England. This was the period which saw the growth of such huge houses as Fountains Abbey and Rievaulx (Yorkshire). The largest religious orders in England were the Benedictine, Cistercian, Augustinian, Premonstratensian, Cluniac and Carthusian orders. Military orders included the Knights Templar (suppressed in 1308 and ever since the subject of the wildest of conspiracy theories and fantasies) and the Knights Hospitaller. A continued reaction against over-involvement in worldly affairs led in the four-teenth and fifteenth centuries to the steady growth of Carthusian houses, in which most of the day was spent in – relatively comfortable – isolation: praying, studying and tending the garden attached to each cell.

The oldest of these orders was the Benedictine, which had many of their houses in towns. By contrast, the Cistercians sited their houses away from centres of population and in these areas developed huge sheep ranches. Within these religious houses the head was often the abbot, or abbess, assisted by a prior or prioress. When daughter-houses were founded they came under the authority of the original abbot/abbess. A small number of abbots from the most powerful houses (the so-called *mitred abbots*) sat with the bishops in the House of Lords.

The growth of such houses affected people at all levels of society. Royalty and nobles gave huge grants of money and land; local landowners made donations on a smaller scale; men and women felt called to the religious life (in the earlier period they might be placed there as children by their parents); farm workers were employed as *lay brothers* to do manual work; others were tenants of the great abbey estates; travellers took advantage of the hospitality provided by monastic inns; sick people were given rest and medical care in monastic hospitals. The Crown might pension off loyal retainers to religious houses, as Richard Whitoc was, to the convent of Stanley (Wiltshire) in 1333, since he had been 'butler to the king's household' and had 'long and faithfully served the king'.[14] Others made land grants to abbeys dependent on their receiving support from the house to last their lifetime. As a result of such an arrangement with the abbot of Sherborne (Dorset) in 1374, John and Agnes Whittok received 'two monks' loaves of the largest size and a bottle of the best convent ale and a black loaf' every day for life.[15]

During the thirteenth century a reaction against conven-tional religious houses led to an explosion of a new type of reli-gious expression – the *mendicant orders*, also known as the *friars*. Relying entirely on charitable donations, friars travelled from town to town preaching and administering the sacrament. They were a reaction against what was considered to be the comfort and lack of simplicity of life in the wealthy monastic houses. In this sense the friars attempted to return to Biblical principles of self-denial and to reflect the kind of values which had led to the early monasteries in the first place. In a similar reaction against monasticism, hermits increased in number, living lives of simplicity and prayer away from the world and its activities. There were four main groups of friars which emerged in the twelfth and thirteenth centuries: Franciscans (Friars Minor), Dominicans (Black Friars), Augustinians (Austin Friars), and Carmelites (White Friars). Committed to preaching and teaching, many Dominicans attended the early universities and were trained in theological study and debate. The friars caught popular imagination and enthusiasm and by 1300 there were over 120 Franciscan and Dominican bases in Britain. The land for these was usually held in trust for them by wealthy patrons, since the friars could not own property. Helping to maintain such a friary – with its team of preachers and teachers – became much sought after, as did burial in its grounds. In 1291 the heart of Eleanor of Provence, Queen Consort of King Henry III, was buried in the cemetery of the Grey Friars in London, although she had died in Amesbury (Wiltshire). Such patronage was complex though, as the friars soon found themselves living in – though technically not owning – wealthy properties. This was the very thing they had been reacting against. Henry III, for example donated a key urban site to the friars in York, opposite the castle gate, in 1243. From around 1300 friars were allowed to accept small cash gifts. This was a shift away from their founding idealism, and the friars were beginning to compromise their radical credentials. Soon they were open to the same accusations of wealth that had been levelled at earlier monastic orders.[16]

The impact of the friars is difficult to exaggerate: when most people relied on a poorly educated parish priest the appearance of these trained speakers in urban settings was revolutionary. In addition, there was great appeal in their message that salvation could be fully experienced without entering a monastery. But these activities often led to friction too. Local clergy might resent the popularity of the preaching friars and money paid to maintain friaries was diverted from existing Church giving. In Beverley in 1309, the canons at the minster complained that parishioners were abandoning the minster for the Dominican friary. In Scarborough there was tension when the arrival of Franciscan friars caused the monks of Citeaux (in France) – who had been given the church at Scarborough – to fear they would lose income since the friars were more popular. As a result the friars were granted land well out of the town to try to defuse the crisis.

As more money flowed to the friars they lost their radical edge. The situation was coming full circle. As a result, gifts of money moved away from the friars and instead increased to local parish churches, where clearly people felt they could monitor its use more closely. Similarly, instead of monasteries, or friaries, wealthy benefactors were now more likely to fund a *college* which, as well as saying Masses for the souls of their patrons, often included an educational function or provided homes for the 'deserving poor'. These ranged from magnificent establishments such as King's College, Cambridge to small colleges and almshouses in less prestigious market towns. This was not an abandonment of medieval spiritual enthusiasm but rather a desire to see it carried out more effectively. As with so much of the later Middle Ages, it was complex. What might be presented as an end to old patterns of behaviour can equally be regarded as a refocusing of them. This is connected with the whole debate over whether the later medieval Catholic Church in England was in decline and facing a crisis which was a prelude to the sixteenth-century Reformation, or instead was vibrant and dynamic but developing new expressions of personal religious practice. At the same time the number of hermits, often located in town churches rather than in deserted spots, increased. These *anchorites*, while living in relative isolation were still available for giving spiritual advice and provided an accessible personal 'holy presence' in the middle of busy urban communities.

The friars were not the only ones whose strict rules became more flexible in the later Middle Ages. During the fifteenth and early sixteenth centuries many religious houses saw a development away from communal living and an increase in individual accommodation. At the Augustinian house at Merton, London (founded in 1117), the infirmary was originally an open hall. Later, increased privacy was provided when it was subdivided into a number of small rooms, with wooden partition walls. By the time of the abbey's dissolution in the sixteenth century, even the cloister walk had been divided up into small rooms. This was not an isolated development.

Pilgrimage, spiritual callings and superstition

The support given to the early friars reminds us of the demand for a deeper spiritual experience from amongst the laity. Whatever the compromises which occurred as a result of the earthly power of the medieval Church, the desire for a closer communion with God was always fundamental to the medieval Christian experience. This revealed itself in the popularity of pilgrimage. The custom of visiting a place closely associated with the Christian faith has a long history. There are descriptions of Christian pilgrimages from southern Europe to the Holy Land from the fourth century, and such pilgrimages were encouraged by Church fathers such as St Jerome. Pilgrimages also began to be made to Rome and other sites associated with the Apostles, saints and Christian martyrs. In addition, pilgrimages occurred to places where it was believed the Virgin Mary had revealed herself. The Crusades to the Holy Land were also considered to be pilgrimages – of a military kind.

Pilgrimage in the Middle Ages frequently started with a vow being made before a parish priest. In this the would-be pilgrim would often negotiate areas for which he or she was seeking forgiveness, or requests for answered prayer. Sometimes pilgrims would be asked to pray for someone else, unable to travel, as they journeyed. At times their expenses were met by a supporter who hoped for spiritual benefits in return.

The sites to be visited varied from those in the Holy Land (access to which fluctuated given the changing politics of the region from the eleventh century onwards) to sites in Europe such as Rome itself or Santiago de Compostela (the shrine of St James in Spain), as well as places in England. English sites were many and varied. That of St Thomas of Canterbury dated from his murder in 1170. He was rapidly canonized and the process was completed in 1173. In 1220, Becket's remains were relocated from his first tomb to a shrine in the recently completed Trinity Chapel. This became one of the most visited pilgrim sites in England. Pilgrimages to the tomb of St Richard of Chichester dated from his canonization in 1262. Here in the Lady Chapel – in which pilgrims prayed after visiting his shrine – can still be found marks carved by pilgrims into the stone: crosses, three circles representing the trinity, and squares representing the four Evangelists (Matthew, Mark, Luke and John). These are not simply graffiti; they were public proof that pilgrims had completed their journey. Similar marks have been discovered carved into churches on the route to Chichester.[17]

Walsingham (Norfolk) became one of northern Europe's greatest places of pilgrimage in the eleventh century, following a vision of the Virgin Mary to the noblewoman Richeldis de Faverches in 1061. According to the Walsingham tradition, the Virgin instructed her to build a replica of the house of the Holy Family in Nazareth, in honour of the Annunciation. The Holy House was panelled with wood and held a wooden statue of an enthroned Virgin Mary with the child Jesus seated on her lap. Founded in the time of Edward the Confessor, the chapel of Our Lady of Walsingham was granted to the Augustinian Canons when an Augustinian priory was established on the site in 1153 and enclosed within the priory.

Some of the many other places attracting pilgrims included Glastonbury (Somerset), claiming to be the burial place of Saints Patrick, David and Dunstan, as well as King Arthur; Hailes Abbey (Gloucestershire), claiming a phial containing the blood of Christ; and Durham, with the body of St Cuthbert and the head of St Oswald.

The importance of pilgrimage can be seen in the famous life of Margery Kempe. Born Margery Brunham in King's Lynn (then Bishop's Lynn), Norfolk, in about 1373, she was married at the age of 20 to a local Norfolk man named John Kempe. With John she had 14 children. Following the birth of her first child, Margery fell ill and may have suffered from post-natal depression. She later said she suffered at this time from 'madness' which culminated in a life-changing vision of Jesus Christ at her bedside. According to Margery, he asked her: 'Daughter, why have you forsaken Me, and I never forsook you?' Following this she decided to open first a brewery and later a grain mill. Both enterprises failed. Though she had tried to live a more holy life after her vision, she was tempted by sexual desire and jealousy of neighbours for some years. In the end she gave up her business enterprises and dedicated herself completely to the spiritual calling which she felt her vision required. In order to do so she began to live a chaste marriage with her husband and began to make pilgrimages around Europe. On these journeys she visited Rome, Jerusalem and Santiago de Compostela. She wrote of her experiences – or rather dictated them to scribes – in *The Book of Margery Kempe*. In her book she recounted her experiences on these spiritual journeys; the final section included a number of prayers. During this time Margery recounts how she had a number of conversations with Christ. As well as describing her journeys and spiritual experiences, she also recorded the conflicts she had with Church authorities – many of whom did not quite know what to make of this woman. Was she mad? A heretic? Or saintly? Opinions were clearly divided. She was tried on different occasions for allegedly reading scripture, for teaching and preaching on scripture and faith, and for wearing white clothes which was considered inappropriate as she was no longer a virgin. In each case she succeeded in clearing herself of charges laid against her. Between 1413 and 1420 she also visited important sites and Church leaders in England. These included visits to Philip Repyngdon, Bishop of Lincoln; Henry Chichele, Archbishop of Canterbury; and the anchorite (hermit) Julian of Norwich. The last section of her book deals with a journey she made in the 1430s to Norway and to the Holy Roman Empire. Margery died in about 1438.

The controversial nature of Margery Kempe's spiritual experience is a reminder that medieval Christians expressed their faith in many and complex ways. Some, like Kempe, were marked out by their personal understanding of their relationship with God. For others the complexity was more problematic. This was because many medieval Christians in England combined a very real and energetic commitment to Christian beliefs, as defined and articulated by the Catholic Church, with additional activities which were often throwbacks to pre-Christian practices (but now shorn of pagan religious ideology). This raises the question of how far these practices undermined Catholic orthodoxy.

Superstitious practices are recorded from a number of sources. Some of these show the persistence of folk superstitions over centuries, adapting themselves to the religious ideas of their day. Charms are known from late Anglo-Saxon sources and clearly were rooted in beliefs in magic and in attempts to gain control over apparently uncontrollable aspects of life (such as sickness, loss and death) through possession of certain items, or by performing certain patterns of behaviour. What is interesting is that these folk superstitions took on the form of official religious beliefs but used them in inappropriate and unorthodox ways. In 2006 a slightly battered thirteenth-century gold annular brooch was found at Godshill on the Isle of Wight and reported under the 'Portable Antiquities Scheme'. The ring was inscribed with crosses and the letters '+A+G+L+A'. These letters represent a Latinized version of a Hebrew phrase 'Atha Gebri Leilan Adonai', meaning 'Thou art mighty forever O Lord'. In itself this is completely orthodox, as it represents an Old Testament Biblical concept which is completely in line with Christian beliefs. What is revealing, though, is that evidence from other sources suggests that this phrase was invoked as a charm against fever.[18] The owner of the ring was almost certainly completely orthodox in his or her Christian faith but was expressing it in a way which was bordering on magical. In other words he or she was diluting Christian beliefs rather than acting in a deviant way.

More obvious examples of blatant superstitions are found in the chickens entombed in the hollow walls of medieval buildings, vividly reconstructed in the Museum of London from finds dating to the Middle Ages in the city. These practices had no veneer of Christian belief and are comparable with records of people passing their children through holes in trees to cure illness. But even here there is no evidence whatsoever that such people invested such actions with any ideology, or belief system, at odds with their membership of the Church. Rather they bolted these attempts at gaining good luck on to Christian beliefs. Their priests would have been understandably concerned but we would be wrong to see these actions as challenges to Christianity. As with so much of England in the Middle Ages the evidence is complicated and the medieval reality is likely to have been more nuanced than the simplistic interpretations which are sometimes imposed on it.

This is not to assume, however, that such practices were appropriate. Within orthodox Catholicism there was a constant teaching mission designed to keep behaviour within acceptable boundaries. But the Catholicism of the Middle Ages had itself accrued a vast amount of semi-superstitious and non-Biblical practices, beliefs and claims. And as the Middle Ages progressed there were those within the Church in England who became more critical and vocal in their condemnation of what they felt was a falling away from New Testament faith. The question is: to what extent were these people hoping to reform the Catholic Church and to what extent were they rejecting it in order to replace it with a new concept of 'Church' altogether? In most cases it was almost certainly the former but this did not apply to all critics of the Church, and of all the critics of the Catholic Church none were more vocal than those who became known by their opponents as *Lollards*.

Radical attacks of the Lollards

The term 'Lollards' covers a wide range of critics of the way the Church was run in the late fourteenth and early fifteenth centuries. Those who are often described under this umbrella term held mixed beliefs that were not part of a unified system. Some hoped to reform the Church. Some thought the institution of the Church was irrelevant to a person's salvation. Some condemned all religious images. Some called for new and purer images to be produced to help people come closer to God. Most rejected the formal attempts at holiness such as institutional fasting, and it is interesting to note that the early fifteenth-century Lollard, Margery Baxter, was apprehended in Norwich because she was caught cooking bacon on a Friday (the traditional fast-and-fish day). But one thing all Lollards had in common was their attack on the worldly power and wealth of the Church.

A central figure in this challenge to the Church was John Wyclif. Wyclif had a number of key beliefs, the first of which was of predestination. This idea – that those who would be saved had already been determined since eternity – was not new. The New Testament writings of the Apostle Paul had emphasized the complementary ideas that salvation came from a personal faith in the Lord Jesus combined with living out this faith through good works. He also wrote that from eternity God had foreknowledge of those who would respond in faith and be saved. This idea had later featured in the writings of St Augustine of Hippo in the early fifth century, who had developed it considerably. What was radical about Wyclif's interpretation of this belief was his conclusion that no one on Earth could know whether or not they were members of the elect and therefore both the Church hierarchy and its membership contained both those who would be saved and those who would not. A person's position as priest, for example, did not automatically make him a member of the elect. This could be a spiritually levelling idea since it undermined the complex hierarchy of authority which was a fundamental feature of the Catholic Church in the Middle Ages. Thus it was a seismic shift in belief which threatened to bring down many of the carefully constructed power structures of the medieval Church. No longer was it necessary for salvation to rely on a priest with the power to hear confession, absolve sins, give penance and excommunicate those who disobeyed. In fact, it might not be necessary to have a priest at all. The most radical Lollards suggested that the 'priesthood of all believers' (a New Testament teaching which was downplayed by the medieval Church) meant that any good Christian man – and maybe even woman – could preach and administer the sacraments. The pope became an irrelevance, as did pilgrimages and images. Instead, all Christians should seek understanding of the nature of God and their faith through their own personal study of the Bible.

This was radical enough, but Wyclif went further. He rejected the Catholic doctrine of *transubstantiation*, which held that the bread and wine of the Mass became, at the moment of consecration, the body and blood of Christ. Later Lollards went further and claimed – as most modern Protestants do – that the Eucharist was a commemoration and symbolic. Under this belief the power of the priest to administer a miraculous experience was totally rejected. Along with the belief in making the Bible available in English and the acceptability of married clergy, the later Lollards were undermining the whole Catholic priestly system – although most still accepted a role for a transformed priesthood. And the attack continued. Lollards believed that social crimes such as adultery and fornication should be tried in royal – not Church – courts. Criminal clerics should face the same courts as anyone else, since the king had authority over the Church. In addition, priests should not hold secular jobs. The estates of bishops and the leading monasteries should be confiscated.

Many of these ideas were based on existing trends, since Papal taxation was no longer allowed in England, there was royal control over appeals to Rome and there were widespread criticisms of the worldliness of the clergy. Some of it echoed the ideas which appeared in the revolutionary preaching of John Ball during the 1381 Peasants' Revolt. Even the call for an English Bible was not as extreme as it came to appear, since the translation of the Bible from Latin into contemporary languages was not forbidden.

However, the Lollards faced a number of serious problems. Firstly, they failed to inspire sufficient support amongst the gentry and nobility. This support was needed to protect the Lollards from Church reprisals. Secondly, Lollard beliefs became associated with social and political revolution. This was fatal and meant that the elite failed to take up the cause for reform. The accusation was partly 'spin' developed by the enemies of the Lollards to discredit them, but it was also partly based on the way in which Lollard beliefs were taken up by more radical groups, or coincided with those beliefs held by more radical elements. The fact that similar dissatisfaction with the Church fed into both Wyclif's circle of Oxford intellectuals and the radical hedge-priests of the Peasants' Revolt was not the result of conspiracy, or a common organization – but it could easily appear so, or be made to appear so.

The final crisis for the Lollards came with the Oldcastle Revolt of 1414. Under Henry IV, Sir John Oldcastle saw military service in Wales but, in 1413, his association with the ideas of Wyclif led to his condemnation for heresy. Arrested and imprisoned, Oldcastle managed to escape from the Tower of London and, as well as being involved in the failed eponymous uprising in 1414, he was involved in Lollard conspiracies until 1417 when he was finally captured and executed by hanging over a slow fire. Until this time the passing of the statute *De heretico comburendo* ('The Necessity of Burning Heretics') in 1401 had achieved little by way of crushing Lollardy. But after the Oldcastle Revolt, Lollard beliefs and insurrectionary threats were firmly linked – at least in the minds of the elite – and gentry support melted away as the death penalty began to be applied to those lower-class Lollards who persisted in their beliefs. When eventually the Catholic Church in England faced a radical attack on its structures, wealth and authority in the 1530s it was not the result of a bottom-up movement like the Lollards. Instead, it resulted from a top-down, state-led, cultural revolution.

The Catholic Church in crisis?

This exploration of the impact of the Lollards brings us to a key issue. There is ongoing debate as to the state of the Catholic Church in England in the late fifteenth and early sixteenth centuries. Critics at the time and since were quick to point out its shortcomings, and some historians have suggested that these were part of developments which would culminate in the Reformation – in other words, that it was genuine dissatisfaction with real problems which led to massive restructuring of the medieval Church in the 1530s.

That there were problems in a number of monasteries in the later Middle Ages cannot be denied. Clearly, in these the original high standards of spiritual activity and strict discipline had slipped. At the Fourth Lateran Council of 1215, the pope insisted that all religious orders should tighten up their internal government and arrange regular visitations to correct any examples of falling standards. It is clear this was a response to problems which were ongoing. Following the bishop's inspection of Keynsham Abbey (Somerset) in 1348 it was ordered, amongst other disciplinary matters, that: 'Secular persons not to be present at meals. The porter of the outer gate ordered to let no one in or out after the hour of compline [dusk] . . . Canons keeping sporting dogs inside the monastery to be punished by being deprived of meat for a month and of fish for a fortnight.' In 1352, despite these criticisms, it was found that women were being allowed to enter the monastery, vows of silence were being ignored, the giving of food to the poor had been neglected and gambling was taking place. These were not isolated incidents. A century later, in 1455, the bishop was again concerned at the indiscipline in the abbey and ordered that the abbot should not allow 'any of his canons to sell wine at public fairs or markets'.[19] The fact that representatives of the Benedictine monasteries opposed efforts to reform the lifestyle of the order in 1421 indicates that they had got used to meat eating, receiving money payments, living in individual rooms and travelling outside their monasteries.

But is it taking these criticisms out of proportion to assume that monastic life was in crisis? After all, in any community it is possible to identify areas of indiscipline and room for improvement without condemning the entire institution. Was monasticism really in terminal decline by 1500? The answer seems to be that, while monasticism could have survived in England (as it did in Catholic countries in Europe), its future was indeed under threat. By 1500 there were about 26,500 clerics in parishes and about 10,000 monks, plus 2,100 nuns. They made up about 2 per cent of the total population. This is high but the number was declining, while the wealth of the religious houses was out of all proportion to their declining numbers within a national community where a significant proportion of people no longer felt attracted to the liturgy and discipline of the monastic life. However, this would suggest that monasticism by 1500 faced a slow decline, not a sudden collapse.

A similar dilemma exists concerning how we should interpret attacks on the clergy. In December 1349, the Bishop of Bath and Wells was attacked at Yeovil (Somerset) by certain 'sons of perdition' who, armed with 'bows, arrows, iron bars and other kinds of arms attacked the church', injured many of his attendants and kept the bishop a prisoner there until dark. The bishop having moved to the nearby rectory, the siege was reinforced and lasted until the next day, when loyal supporters rescued him. Other accounts exist of village priests, accused of sexual misconduct, being castrated by angry parishioners. Is this evidence of a collapse in support for the traditional Catholic Church? Or does it simply indicate, in the former case, anger against the ruling class at a time of crisis and, in the latter case, high expectations of what a priest *should* be like and anger when trust in a vital and loved institution was betrayed? It is not unreasonable to interpret the evidence in this way, though this does not deny the strong pressures for reform of the Church by 1500.

There is plenty of evidence that religious devotion was vibrant and very real at the end of the Middle Ages. And it frequently expressed itself in ways which were quite consistent with Catholic systems of belief and practice. Rood screens – which divided the chancel from the nave – can be read as cutting off the laity from the Mass, or as heightening the drama. Many Books of Hours were written so that literate laity could pray as part of their personal devotions during the Mass. This same devotion to the Mass helps explain the large number of pilgrims coming to visit the Holy Blood at Hailes Abbey (Gloucestershire) and the relic of the True Cross at Bromholm Priory (Norfolk). Similarly large numbers visited the shrine of Our Lady of Doncaster as late as the 1520s. Likewise, the shrine at Walsingham continued to draw pilgrims, and in 1534 income from offerings stood at £260. Overall, pilgrimage as an activity declined in the early sixteenth century but it was still significant. In fact, many local shrines grew in popularity as more famous national ones faced declining visitor numbers. Devotion to the Mass meant that Corpus Christi plays survived Henry VIII's dissolution of the monasteries and were not banned until the state-run Reformation of Edward VI. It is significant that it was the banner of the Five Wounds of Christ which became the rallying flag of the Pilgrimage of Grace in 1536–7. Other expressions of this traditional Catholic devotion can be found in the popularity of the image of Mary cradling the body of Jesus, known as 'Our Lady of Pity'. If the medieval English Church faced great challenges in 1500, none need have been fatal to the continued development of a Catholic spirituality which had continued unbroken since the late sixth century. That this was not to be the case was the result of developments which could not have been foreseen as the sixteenth century opened.

Chapter 5

POPULATION, DIET AND HEALTH

One major problem in the Middle Ages was sewage disposal. Much of the waste of London ended up in the Thames, but not everyone was conveniently situated close to this open sewer. Others dumped their sewage into slower-moving waterways. For example, in 1355 it was found that the Fleet Prison ditch, which was designed to be 10 feet (3 metres) wide, was so choked with the sewage of eleven latrines and twelve sewers that water no longer flowed along it. Faced with the need to remove household toilet waste, some turned to piping it into the unused cellars of unwary neighbours. Two men were fined for this in 1347. More often householders dug cesspools in their yards and constructed latrines over them. One such enterprising Londoner was Roger the Raker. Unfortunately, over the years this pit filled to capacity and rotted the floorboards. When Roger eventually plunged through these floorboards and drowned in his own accumulated excrement, it raised questions not only about the quality of London carpentry but also about the way in which health and well-being in the Middle Ages were affected by the sanitation of the time.[1] But before this is explored it is necessary to address the complex issue of the rise and fall of the medieval population.

Population statistics: an overview of change

The total number of Norman immigrants and their followers probably made up only about 5 per cent of the English population of about 2.5 million in the late 1060s. With the Norman core of William's supporters came others who had connections with him in Normandy and for whom the conquest of England offered opportunities both financial and social. These included Flemings, Bretons and Frenchmen and later a small population of Jewish and Italian bankers and merchants. But there was no major change to the ethnic make-up of England, and there was genetic continuity for almost the entire Middle Ages.

Evidence to support population estimates for the Middle Ages is limited and means that there are wide variations in possible figures. Three major pieces of evidence used are Domesday Book (1086), the Poll Tax returns for 1377 and the registration of baptisms, marriages and burials which began in 1538. These provide a basis for 'guesstimates' of population levels at key points in the Middle Ages.[2]

These 'guesstimates', as we have seen, hover around 2.5 million for 1086. By 1300 the population probably stood at 5.5 million and may have been as many as 6.5 million. By 1377, however, the population of England had fallen to about 2.5 million (following disastrous harvests, livestock diseases and the Black Death) and it would not exceed this figure until after1520 (with a likely low point in1450 of somewhere in the region of 2 million). The figure for 1377 can be gauged from the number of tax payers listed under the Poll Tax figures for that year, and the reasonable nature of the first Poll Tax suggests that tax evasion was probably relatively low. The pattern of declining population continued into the fifteenth century and it is actually possible that the population in 1525 was even a little lower (at about 2.3 million) than it had been in 1377. By 1541 a likely figure is 2.7 million and by 1551 about 3 million. The steady increase in population levels as the sixteenth century progressed was probably due to a mixture of reasons: higher rates of marriage for the size of the population, younger age of marriage for women, and possibly a slight reduction in occurrences of epidemics. What is so striking about this pattern is the realization that in 1300 the English population was comparable with 1750 but it took 450 years to reach this level again following the great fall in numbers in the 150 years after 1300. The fact that the mid-eighteenth-century population only then entered a rapid trajectory of growth as a result of the Agricultural and Industrial Revolutions suggests that, without these twin developments, population had hit a 'glass ceiling' at about the 1300/1750 level. Prior to the upward leap in population after 1750, it seems that the available agricultural techniques – coupled with the limited movement of foodstuffs on pre-industrial transport systems – were unable to support the kind of population levels that have been sustained since 1750.

The distribution of the medieval population was in striking contrast with the modern English population. In 1086 the greatest concentration of population lay in eastern England (Norfolk, Suffolk, Kent and Lincolnshire). By 1377 this had evened out a little as a result of a rising population in the Midlands, but the north and west still remained more thinly populated. This distribution of population in 1377 is, unsurprisingly, similar to the distribution of wealth seen in the tax returns of the Lay Subsidy in 1334.

Life expectancy in the Middle Ages followed a similar roller-coaster pattern and there was certainly no inevitable upward trajectory. On the eve of the Norman Conquest life expectancy was in the region of 35 years for a man and 25 years for a woman. By the 1390s life expectancy amongst Essex peasants has been calculated to have been 54 years (an average of male and female expectancy), and monks at Westminster Abbey at this time had a life expectancy of about 50 years. But by the 1490s this had declined to 48 years for the same Essex peasants and 40 years for the Westminster monks. The repeated cycles of infectious diseases after 1348 had taken their toll.

Diet and health: fat friars and hungry peasants?

Life expectancy is clearly affected by many factors, among them diet and nutrition. Gluttony was one of the Seven Deadly Sins, and episcopal visitations condemned monks for gluttony and for eating food intended for the poor. This criticism of monks increased from the late fourteenth century and was a product of 'a critical middle class willing to denounce the failings of both secular and religious authorities'.[3] But were these accusations of gluttony justified? It seems they may have been. Accounts from Westminster Abbey suggest that monks – even when fasting – consumed above the modern nutritional recommended daily allowance (RDA). Late fifteenth-century monks at St Swithun's Priory, Winchester, consumed per day: 1.5 lb (0.68 kg) of meat, five eggs, vegetable soup, bread and ale. Research on skeletons of 376 men over the age of 45 from three London monasteries – Merton Priory, Bermondsey Abbey and St Mary Graces – found that monks (compared with secular evidence) were almost five times as likely to develop obesity-related joint disease. These included a specific form of degenerative arthritis characterized by excessive bone growth along the sides of the vertebrae of the spine and other bones, known as diffuse idiopathic skeletal hyperostosis (or DISH), and other types of osteoarthritis.[4] DISH occurs today in about 2–4 per cent of modern populations but is as high as 10 per cent in the medieval monastic cemeteries of London. Over 11 per cent of those buried at Eynsham Abbey (Oxfordshire) suffered from DISH and similar evidence comes from other monastic cemeteries. Large-scale studies of DISH on medieval skeletons reveal that 87 per cent of sufferers were men, and that it was more likely to be found among the better-fed and less physically active monks of the Benedictine and Cluniac orders than among the vegetarian Carthusians and physically active friars.[5]

On the other hand, among the majority rural population diet varied with the success of the harvest. Poor weather in the early fourteenth century, for example, led to starvation. Indeed it was not until 1437–40 that the last great period of famine in the English Middle Ages occurred, due to the impact of the weather. At Chester in 1437 there are records of peasants making bread from peas and even from fern roots, so scare were supplies of wheat and the price so high. Paradoxically, the previous 60 years had seen improvements in access to food due to falling prices in basic foodstuffs from 1375. This variability means that it is difficult to generalize about the dietary experiences of ordinary people in the later Middle Ages. However, we can glimpse something of their nutritional reality.

Osteo-archaeologists (bone specialists) can identify evidence for problems in diet and nutrition in the form of *Harris lines*, or 'growth arrest lines' on skeletons. These lines appear in bones due to temporary retardation of bone growth. They appear as dense lines parallel to the growth plates in the long bones such as the leg (i.e. they appear as horizontal lines across the bone). They are caused by starvation or malnutrition, and some types of sickness. By identifying these lines it is possible to see how often an individual underwent severe stresses of this sort and how severe this stress was. It is also possible to get some idea as to how old the person was when the line was formed, by looking at where it appears on the bone. Regular occurrences of Harris lines may be an indication of seasonal stresses, which may imply that food was short at certain times of the year or at certain periods in the life of an individual. Studies comparing medieval and modern populations in Switzerland have found that: 'A high incidence of Harris lines was found in the medieval population, perhaps reflecting difficult living and hygienic conditions, but also the poor care and neglect of the child population'.[6] However, in England the evidence suggests that, while there *were* periods of real shortage, this problem was not generally widespread or persistent. Based on a study of over 16,000 Late Medieval skeletons this gives a picture of a reasonably well-fed population with occasional crises.[7]

There is evidence to suggest that, despite the problems in trade experienced by a number of industries in the early fifteenth century, many in the population were in fact able to use an improvement in wages to increase their consumption of ale and meat. No longer were they spending the greater proportion of their available cash on basic foodstuffs. In this respect standards of living seem to have been rising for a while after 1400, until recovering population and rising inflation depressed it again by the later fifteenth and early sixteenth centuries. Analysis of the food consumption of harvest workers at Sedgeford (Norfolk) in 1424 shows that the daily food intake was 1lb (0.45 kg) of meat and at least 6 pints (3.4 litres) of ale for every 2lb (0.9 kg) of bread consumed. The increase in meat consumption is in marked contrast to evidence for food intake a century earlier. Wheat-flour bread was replacing barley bread, and fresh beef was replacing bacon. In this improved consumption standards of living were coming into line with those which had previously been enjoyed only by better-off townspeople, clergy and gentry.[8]

Evidence about health, as well as nutrition, comes from a small selection of written sources but mostly from archaeological evidence. Bones reveal signs of infection in cases of tuberculosis, leprosy and syphilis. However, not all diseases show themselves in this way and those which impact on the soft tissues only cannot be detected. At times, though, the information from bones is quite specific. At Edix Hill, Barrington (Cambridgeshire), for example, in a cemetery used from the fifth to the seventh century, two skeletons show signs of leprosy in the bony growth found on the skull and extremities of the limbs.

Other evidence from skeletons can be even more revealing. Work at the cemetery of the deserted medieval village (DMV) of Wharram Percy (Yorkshire) has provided a detailed insight into both the health and diet of this farming community from the eleventh to the thirteenth centuries. Of the 687 skeletons examined, 15 per cent were babies. Their bones suggest that they were breastfed for up to 18 months. Modern research on the effects of breastfeeding show that this will have doubled these children's chances of survival in their first year. Even more revealing is the evidence for the long-term relationship between nutrition and overall health. By the age of ten the average height of children at Wharram Percy was 120cm (47.2 inches); less than the modern average figure of 137cm (53.9 inches) for a ten-year-old. Furthermore, the medieval children did not reach the height of a modern ten-year-old until the age of 14. In this they were similar to nineteenth-century factory children. However, despite a longer growing period the medieval inhabitants still grew relatively tall. The average height achieved at Wharram Percy was 169cm (66.5 inches) for men; national data for the Late Medieval period gives an average of 171cm (67.3 inches), compared with 175cm (68.8 inches) today. At Wharram Percy the average height for women was 158cm (62.2 inches); the Late Medieval average was 159cm (62.5 inches), compared with162cm (63.7 inches) today.

For those surviving into adulthood the chances of a relatively long life were good, as about 40 per cent of adults lived to 50 years or more. Regarding adult health, women suffered a high incidence of osteoporosis (loss of bone density in old age), while the men suffered it in the same proportion as modern men. An interesting statistic relating to women is that it seems that the minimum interval between births was probably 2.5 years. So, ignoring other factors, women would probably only have had eight children at most in their lifetime.

Skeletons from nearby York, from the same period, are also very revealing concerning social and health trends. At York there was a gender-ratio of ten women to nine men in the later Middle Ages; in the countryside the ratio was three men to every two women. It is possible that women were more geographically mobile, leaving villages for markets, workshops and service in grand houses. Skeletons also suggest that urban women did less physically demanding work than rural women. In contrast, rural women had osteoarthritis concentrated in their legs and back, suggesting gender-specific jobs such as grinding corn. Overall, the evidence for anaemia and infection was frequently found in skeletons from York, suggesting that crowded conditions and contaminated water produced 'a greater pathogen load in the urban environment'. Similar evidence from the cemetery at St Mary Spital, London, revealed high levels of rickets (averaging at about 24 per cent of the skeletons excavated) and suggests that these medieval Londoners also experienced poorer health than their rural neighbours, lacking sunlight and a balanced diet. Life could be more dangerous in an urban setting in others ways too: evidence for violent injury, for example, was higher in York than at Wharram Percy.[9]

Unlike the overweight monks discussed earlier, diet for the rural population was carbohydrate based. Rye bread and porridge were consumed, along with large quantities of ale. There was fairly easy access to dairy products but not in the quantities consumed by the DISH-exhibiting monks. On the other hand, cabbages, leeks and onions frequently occur in medieval descriptions of peasant food. Meat featured more in the diets of the better-off. Honey was the usual sweetener. Generally, dental caries (the term for tooth decay or cavities) remained relatively low until the seventeenth century, when it increased due to more dietary intake of refined carbohydrates, especially sugar. The relative rarity of sugar meant that in 1334 it cost 7 pence a pound (0.45 kg), which was more than a day's wages for a skilled archer in the Hundred Years' War. Even its increasing availability over the next century did not prevent it from remaining an expensive luxury. However, teeth still suffered – but from grits in cheap bread and poor oral hygiene, which will have encouraged infection and abscesses.

So, there does seem to be some validity in the stereotypes of portly monks and thin peasants. Rural populations were more prone to fluctuations in their nutritional consumption, as revealed by such things as Harris lines, than were the well-fed members of monastic houses. On the other hand, the evidence does not support the idea of a *starving* peasantry. However, it is clear that until the middle of the fifteenth century such a fate was never far away and that, in times of climatic deterioration or animal disease, it could suddenly become an all-too-present reality.

Sanitation and concepts of cleanliness

Health, of course, is also affected by levels of cleanliness. The importance of soap was recognized in the Middle Ages, and fifteenth-century 'white soap' was made from a mixture of fern ash and unslaked lime which was allowed to stand for two days. After this it was mixed with oil and tallow (usually beef or mutton fat) and heated before finally being mixed with bean flour and moulded into cakes.

In Britain references to soap begin to appear from about the year 1000. The chronicler John of Wallingford (died 1214), recording traditions from the early eleventh century, referred disparagingly to the fact that Danish immigrants bathed every Saturday. He accused them of carrying out this strange practice, alongside combing their hair daily and frequently changing their woollen clothes, in order to seduce English women! In 1192 the chronicler Richard of Devizes referred to the number of soap makers in Bristol. In the late thirteenth century soap making was reported in Coventry, while other early soap-making centres were in York and Hull. In the fifteenth century a London *sopehouse* was located in Bishopsgate and others were found on Cheapside. The Cheapside site left evidence in Soper's Lane, now Queen Street.[10] The *Proceedings, Minutes and Enrolments* of the Bristol Company of Soapmakers survive from the years 1562–1642 and record the names of over 180 people engaged in the trade in the city. A type of black soft soap was called 'Bristol soap' and a harder type, known as 'Bristol grey soap', was supplied to London by 1523 at the price of one penny per pound.[11]

However, personal cleanliness has only limited impact without clean water and sewage disposal, and before the later nineteenth century these two factors were the greater influences on public health. Also, medieval people had a different concept of the link between cleanliness and health. For them, the actual smell itself was the threat – the smell spread disease. Most had no idea that hand washing, bathing or cleaning food would combat illness. Archaeological studies reveal the outcome of such limited understanding of the link between dirt and disease: conditions such as amoebic dysentery, tapeworms, boreworms and whipworms were widespread.

In addition, society in the Middle Ages lacked coordinated systems of delivering clean water and (as we have seen) removing sewage. In this sense medieval towns and cities were inevitably dirty and unhealthy. This is not to suggest that men and women were complacent about these matters. A large amount of evidence suggests that, while the absence of a germ theory meant that there was no real understanding of what caused disease, there was a clear association between filth and bad health. At the very least, dirty water tastes foul, and rubbish and sewage stink. For these reasons alone authorities in towns made frequent efforts to clean up the environment. By 1285 the Great Conduit had been built to supply London with clean water (its intact fountain house has been excavated under the modern road of Cheapside). But this could not overcome the terrible conditions facing Londoners. We saw at the start of this chapter that complaints exist in the medieval records of cesspits leaking into the cellars of nearby properties, and of citizens even piping their sewage into their neighbours' cellars. The fact that such complaints exist show that the authorities were not taking the state of London for granted. The appropriately named *Assize of Nuisances* was established in London to settle disputes between neighbours over sewage and other actions which polluted the city. Even Edward III (1327–77) was moved to complain to the authorities about the foul state of the capital, which he suspected would lead to disaster:

When passing along the water of Thames, we have beheld dung
and lay stools and other filth accumulated in diverse places
within the city, and have also perceived the fumes and other
abominable stenches arising therefrom, from the corruption of
which great peril to persons dwelling within the said city will, it
is feared, ensue.[12]

Furthermore, industry and housing was not separated, so
pollution impacted on the lives of citizens. This would have
been particularly the case with industries such as butchers and
fishmongers which produced health-threatening waste by-
products. As one modern historian, Professor Hutchinson,
has put it:

It's difficult for us today to understand the medieval city as a
multitude of simultaneous activities. People living, people
bringing up families, being educated, worshipping and, most
important of all, making and trading. But all cheek by jowl.
They don't separate industry and living.[13]

The shifting – after protests from the prior of St John of
Jerusalem – of the butchers' quarter out of the city to Stratford,
or Knightsbridge, would have helped overcome at least this
menace to health. But the fact that the butchers' waste was then
dumped in the Thames will have threatened the health of those
who used it as their water supply. The waste of tanners and
dyers was added to this foul cocktail. And this is the key point
in explaining much of medieval ill health: sewage/waste and
drinking water were often in dangerously close proximity. This
was either because the same river was used as a water source
and a disposal system, or because groundwater supplies in
springs and wells were easily contaminated by nearby latrines
and cesspits.

The London city authorities attempted to meet the challenges by employing street cleaners and *night-soil* (sewage)
collectors, and citizens were fined for polluting communal
water supplies. One peddler was killed in a brawl when

passers-by objected to an eel skin he had thrown into the street, which could have led to a communal fine. But the task was beyond the available resources and technology. Philip Ziegler, who has made a detailed study of the Black Death, sums up the state of fourteenth-century London:

> By our standards, London would have been a very unpleasant, dirty, smelly place to live. The streets were always narrow; now they were cramped. The houses grew together. The streets would have a gutter on each side, and between these a muddy track that divided the houses. It was a pretty squalid scene.[14]

The killer diseases of the Middle Ages

The contrast between our modern affection for surviving medieval towns and the reality of medieval sanitation and cleanliness is well expressed in the words of David Dimbleby, in the 2007 BBC series *How We Built Britain*. Regarding the much-visited East Anglian town of Lavenham (Suffolk) he commented:

> To our modern eyes, Lavenham is a perfect picture-postcard town. Thousands of visitors go each year to photograph the houses with their beam and plaster walls; a style of building that still seems to appeal to us above all others. But there was nothing twee about the town in the fourteenth century. The stench from the roadway would have been overpowering, as waste from the dye vats mixed with offal from the butchers, dung from horses, and human excrement.[15]

The general state of sanitation in the Middle Ages (polluted drinking water in towns, problems in urban waste disposal, close proximity of rat and human populations, and absence of any germ theory) meant that, at any time, epidemics could break out and spread. This helps explain the high rate of infant mortality and the death rate of women in childbirth (due to infections introduced during labour); it also helps explain the generally low life expectancy – similar to those in less economically developed countries of the twenty-first century. This situation meant that life in the Middle Ages was lived in a context where killer diseases were endemic and accidents and minor infections could easily escalate into life-threatening conditions.

However, the fact that the population more than doubled between 1066 and 1300 reminds us that, in the competition between endemic disease and a high birth rate, the human population was capable of growing against these medical odds. This would have been assisted by the fact that the vast majority of people living in the countryside would have been less prone to illness which thrived in cramped and unsanitary urban conditions. Had this continued to be the overall medical experience of the Middle Ages then the population would have continued to grow despite the appalling death rate and would have been comparable with the booming populations in many modern developing countries. The reality, however, was far more complex and more terrible. The collapse of population after the 1350s, and its failure to recover to the level of 1300 over the next 150 years, reminds us that the medieval community did not only face an ongoing battle with endemic illness but also faced the intrusion of new and deadlier diseases which it had neither the medical knowledge nor the social organization to resist.

Of all the intrusive new killer diseases of the Middle Ages none compares with the Black Death, which swept the British Isles after 1348. First arriving in the port of Melcombe Regis (opposite Weymouth, Dorset) shortly before 24 June (the Feast of St John the Baptist), the disease had been moving westward across Europe for several years. This disease is usually identified as bubonic plague (*Yersinia pestis*), although other possibilities have been suggested, including anthrax, haemorrhagic fever and even Ebola. However, current evidence from plague victims in southern France supports the traditional identification. Contemporary chroniclers were understandably confused, as it seemed to come in a number of forms. The first exhibited characteristic swellings of the lymph glands in the groin and armpits (the infamous *buboes*). The second was a pneumonic form which infected the lungs and spread through coughing and sneezing. The third was a form which gave rise to septicaemia. Since all had different symptoms they appeared to be different diseases. The bubonic form may have thrived in summer and given way to the pneumonic form over the winter.

The spread of the disease seems linked to movements of infected rats. Black rats (*Rattus rattus*) live in close relationship with people. Thatched roofs and cob-and-timber-walled houses were easily infiltrated by rats; waste in urban streets would have supported large rat populations. Excavations in Southampton suggest that the rat population increased noticeably from the thirteenth to the fourteenth century. As rats fell victim to bubonic plague their rat fleas transferred to human hosts and the disease jumped the species barrier. It is interesting that in the European legend of the Pied Piper, the Piper (plague) first kills the rats before he carries off (kills) the children. And this reminds us of another feature of variants of bubonic plague – its (at times) disproportionate impact on the young and healthy.

The exact circumstances by which this disease reached western Europe is disputed, but the general consensus is that its medieval origins lay among the rodent population of central Asia. Environmental factors caused a movement of infected rodents out of this area, which then infected other rodents (e.g. rats). As these rodents died the disease passed to humans. The developing trade routes between the Middle East and China meant that a disease which was soon ravaging the Far East eventually spread to the Mediterranean and western Europe. The immediate link to the Mediterranean may have been via a Mongol army besieging the Crimean port of Caffa, which was occupied by the Genoese. Near-contemporary chroniclers suggest this connection. From there the disease spread to Italy. Environmental factors such as mild, wet weather may have encouraged the survival of the disease in host populations.

By the summer of 1348 the disease was in Dorset, by August it had reached Bristol, by September it was raging in London and the eastern ports of Ireland, and by 1350 it had reached northern Scotland. Nowhere escaped. The precise death toll is disputed but was very high: suggestions range from 35–50 per cent of the English population, and individual statistics bear this out. The manors of Glastonbury Abbey lost 50 per cent of their tenants, 40 per cent of the English parish clergy died, as did 27 per cent of the nobility (helped to avoid plague by less cramped conditions and fewer rats in close proximity). In January 1349, Ralph of Shrewsbury, Bishop of Bath and Wells, wrote a circular letter to his diocese in which he described how the disease 'has left many parish churches and other livings in our diocese without a priest or a parson to care for the parishioners.'[16] On the wall of the church at Ashwell (Hertfordshire) are scratched these enigmatic words: 'There was a plague, 1000, three times 100, five times 10 [1350], a pitiable, fierce violent . . .; a wretched populace survives to witness and in the end a mighty wind, Maurus, thunders in this year in the world, 1361.'[17]

The outbreak of 1348–50 was not all that was heard of bubonic plague. That of 1361 was remembered as 'the mortality of the children', as it seemed to target the young (probably those born since 1348 and without the immunity gained from surviving the first outbreak). Later outbreaks occurred in 1369 and in 1375. It would continue to return in cycles until its last great outbreak in 1665.

It is easy to assess the impact of the Black Death solely in its economic and class terms: the impact on wages, or the end of villeinage. This is very important but we must never lose sight of the emotional impact. It must have felt as if the world was coming to an end. Even to a community used to high mortality rates the seismic effect of what happened in the middle of the fourteenth century must have been impossible to comprehend. Because we cannot measure this, we are forced to recognize that we cannot fully grasp it – but this does not mean we should ignore it. People's spiritual, emotional, mental, economic and social worlds were changed as a result of the cataclysm that had befallen them. As the poet John Gower noted in the 1390s:

> The world is changed and overthrown,
> That it is well-nigh upside down,
> Compared with days of long ago.[18]

The bubonic plague was not, of course, the only killer disease of the Middle Ages. In fact, a study of death rates at Christchurch, in Canterbury (Kent) between 1395 and 1505 concluded that one year in every four was a 'crisis' year. From about 1450 these 'crisis years' happened less frequently but the crises themselves were more acute and killed more people than the earlier – more frequent – outbreaks of disease.[19] Other evidence from Canterbury suggests that its killer diseases included 'sweating sickness' (possibly influenza), plague, tuberculosis and fever. Records from fifteenth-century Westminster point to summer and autumn as the seasons most closely associated with epidemics.

An occurrence of the epidemic known as the 'sweating sickness' in 1485 killed two mayors of London and six aldermen within one week. Thomas Hille, who was mayor at the time of the outbreak, died on 23 September and was succeeded by William Stokker, appointed the following day. Within four days Stokker himself was dead, and on the 29 of September John Warde was elected mayor for the remainder of the official year. There was no mayoralty banquet, which is hardly surprising in the disastrous circumstances.[20] Other outbreaks of this disease are recorded in 1508, 1517 and 1528. Tentative evidence suggests that mortality rates in the fifteenth century were highest in the population group aged 25–34 and this may have suppressed fertility and population recovery in the 150 years after the outbreak of the Black Death.

Tuberculosis (TB) may also have been a significant killer disease in the fifteenth century. Its alternative name of 'consumption' sums up the effects of untreated tuberculosis – the victim is (almost) literally consumed by loss of weight and breathlessness. The disease has also gone under the name of the 'White Plague'. Tuberculosis bacteria most commonly affect the lungs (termed pulmonary TB), with about 75 per cent of those affected experiencing this. However, it can also affect the central nervous system, the lymph system, the circulatory system, bones and joints. It is a common and deadly disease. The bacteria is easily spread by coughing, sneezing, kissing and spitting, and a reservoir of the disease no doubt existed then – as potentially now – amongst cattle, in the form of bovine tuberculosis. This form may also be spread by badgers, amongst which the disease is also endemic. The dependence of the spread of the disease on environmental factors and inadequacies in knowledge of treatment has led a recent chronicler of the history of the disease to comment that 'Tuberculosis has been called the perfect expression of our imperfect civilization.'[21] Evidence from excavated skeletons is supporting the belief that the disease was present in the medieval population. Molecular biologist Ronald A. Dixon of the University of Bradford, has commented that 'The historical record suggests a much larger number [of cases] than the cemeteries indicate.' This is because only about 3–5 per cent of its victims develop lesions on their skeletons. However, in an effort to test the archaeological evidence, he and his colleague Charlotte Roberts have isolated fragments of DNA from eight skeletons taken from a medieval graveyard in northern England. One of these skeletons had lesions which suggested tuberculosis and from this individual they identified a section of DNA unique to *Mycobacterium tuberculosis*, the pathogen responsible for TB. There is now the likelihood that future studies of genetic material will confirm more examples of TB in medieval skeletons than were previously revealed by conventional bone analysis.[22]

Leprosy too was a killer in medieval England. Spread by skin contact, coughing and sneezing, it can take as long as five years before symptoms appear. In later medieval England leprosy may have declined because those who suffered from tuberculosis developed a cross-immunity. And to this list of killer diseases should be added dysentery, typhus and malnutrition.

Occasionally, evidence emerges in contemporary accounts which may point to other diseases that are difficult to identify without more detailed descriptions. One of these occurs in *Knighton's Chronicle, 1337–1396*:

> In the summer, that is, in the year of grace 1340, there occurred a repugnant and widespread sickness almost everywhere in England, and especially in Leicestershire, during which men emitted a sound like dogs barking, and suffered almost unbearable pain while it lasted. And a great many people were infected.

While it is impossible to be certain, the 'barking' voice may indicate an outbreak of diphtheria, or a streptococcal throat infection. The same chronicler also records under the summer of 1355 a disease with the following characteristics:

> ... people went out of their minds, and behaved like madmen in field and township. Some thus deranged fled into woods and dense places, as though they were wild beasts shunning the presence of men, whilst others ran from the fields into the townships, and from the townships into the fields, now here, now there, without regard for themselves, and it was extremely difficult to catch them. And some wounded themselves with knives or tore with their teeth those who tried to capture them. And many were taken and led into church, and left there bound until they received some relief from God, and in some churches you might see ten or a dozen of them, or more, or fewer, and it was a great sorrow to behold their suffering.

Knighton concludes that the sickness was possibly due to evil spirits, but the symptoms suggest the crisis may have been an outbreak of ergotism. This occurs when damp, cool weather leads to cereals (particularly rye) being contaminated with a hallucinogenic fungus.[23]

There has long been an assumption that syphilis entered the European population following the discovery of the Americas. However, definite medieval examples have been discovered in York, Ipswich, Hull and Carmarthen in Wales. One expert in the field believes that 'venereal syphilis is a late medieval, newly evolved form, probably derived from endemic syphilis in Southwest Asia', and that its late appearance in England was not due to transfer of the disease from the Americas but rather that the disease 'was late in adapting to populations living in colder northern European climates and societies, and had to become more aggressive and venereal in transmission.'[24] The symptoms of syphilis (which can take up to 20 years to show themselves) would have resembled leprosy, and it was probably treated as if it were this disease.

Hospitals, medicine and surgery

Medieval medical care was a complex mixture of Christian theology, Greek and Roman medical concepts, astrology and traditional practices. In such a profoundly Christian environment spiritual causes of disease were frequently sought and an association often suggested between disease and sin. Christian compassion also led to active care for the sick and the establishment of early hospitals from the fourteenth century onwards, staffed by those in religious orders. In the same way infirmaries were an important feature of monasteries. These focused as much on spiritual health as on physical recovery, and even though medical remedies would have been limited in their effects the care, improved diet and increased cleanliness would in many cases have assisted recovery.

St Mary Spital was one of the great hospitals of medieval London, alongside St Bartholomew's. Founded in 1197 as a refuge for women in childbirth, it was greatly enlarged in the thirteenth century. A two-storey infirmary was built and this was extended in the fourteenth century when new stone buildings were constructed for the lay sisters. Later still, tenements were built for wealthier residents. By the fifteenth century doctors were working in the hospital. The cemetery increased in size at the same time, suggesting that St Mary's was operating more as a hospital than as a shelter for travellers. By the time of its dissolution in 1538 it had 180 beds and was one of the largest hospitals in England. Excavations on the site of the infirmary suggest a more likely figure of 90 beds but these might have been shared. A large north–south channel seems to have been dug as part of a water-supply system. While this was silting up by the fourteenth century it may still have assisted drainage.[25]

But the key question was, how was illness to be treated? There was no clear-cut answer. Increased interaction with the Middle East from the twelfth century led to a resurgence of Greek ideas, which had survived in the Islamic world. On one hand this encouraged a more critical – observational – approach towards diagnosis and treatment. On the other, the veneration given these ancient texts made their assertions unassailable even when wrong. A classic example lies in the Greek 'Theory of Humours', which asserted that human bodies were composed of blood, yellow and black bile and phlegm, and that illness was frequently caused by an imbalance between these humours. This flawed understanding led to frequent recourse to *phlebotomy* (blood letting), which would dominate medical practice for centuries. The colour of patients' urine often dictated diagnosis. Astrology too dominated many treatments. Finally, in a pre-scientific environment, actual medicine was a mixture of tried-and-tested herbal remedies and others ranging from the bizarre to the dangerous. In this way helpful remedies such as feverfew to cure a headache, henbane smoke and raspberry-leaf tea to soothe pain, and poultices on inflamed wounds stood alongside fried mouse to cure whooping cough, quartz crystals to stop bleeding and badger droppings to stop toothache. Treacle appears as a much-sought-after remedy for reducing fever in the Paston Letters, and other sources refer to mustard for use in poultices. At Merton Abbey, London, archaeologists have discovered a dump of mustard seeds which were presumably shipped in along the river Wandle and used in the abbey's infirmary.

Medical professionals were divided between physicians (who had completed years of study of the Greek texts) and lower-status surgeons who set bones and operated. Medicines and some medical advice would also have been dispensed by *apothecaries*. Only the wealthiest could afford such professionals and most would, instead, have relied on traditional folk remedies and local herbalists. By the fifteenth century increased understanding of anatomy assisted in wound treatment; literary evidence suggests the existence of cataract operations and archaeology reveals *trepanation* (drilling a hole in the scull). However, the absence of anaesthetics and antiseptics will have meant that much surgery was defeated by shock and infection. In this – as in many areas of sanitation, health and medicine – what we might call 'the long Middle Ages' lasted, for most ordinary people, into the nineteenth century. At the largest excavated medieval cemetery outside London (at Barton-upon-Humber, Lincolnshire) this reality was apparent in the fact that the skeletons revealed no significant differences in health over 900 years, from c.950 to c.1850.[26] In this sense the Middle Ages lasted a very long time indeed.

Chapter 6

WOMEN AND THE FAMILY

When, in 1469, Margery Paston, the daughter of a wealthy Norfolk family, became secretly engaged to her family's estate bailiff Richard Calle, she found herself in the middle of a bitter dispute which pitted her against her own mother and brother because she had challenged the conventions of her gender and class. The family hoped to marry her into a noble family, whereas Richard came from a family of shopkeepers. All the anger and genuine sense of betrayal is revealed in the letter that her mother wrote to her son, Margery's brother.

> On Friday the bishop sent for her and he spoke to her clearly and reminded her of her position in society and who were her family and friends. And that she would have more friends if she followed their advice. And if she did not, what rebuke and shame and loss she would suffer. And she said again what she had promised [to Richard Calle] and she said boldly that if these words did not make it final then she would make it quite clear before she left! These shameless words shocked me and her grandmother . . . I ordered my servants that she should be

banned from my house . . . I beg you that you do not take this
too badly. For I know well that it goes to your heart and it is the
same to me and to others. But remember, as I do, that all we
have lost is a worthless person. For if she had been good, this
would never have happened. Even if he [Calle] were to die at
this very hour, I would not take her back.[1]

Despite all this, Margery succeeded in marrying Richard and
her family were forced to accept this. Furthermore, the family
found that they needed Richard's bookkeeping and organizational skills and were losing money without him. So, he was
reinstated to his post – but was never truly accepted by
Margery's relatives. Her story reveals the severe constraints
facing medieval women. This was due to a range of factors, not
least of which was the medieval understanding of what was the
fundamental character of 'Woman'. This was an understanding
which was affected by the Norman Conquest but went much
deeper than this event and its social repercussions.

The position of women in society suffered a setback in
1066. While female land ownership occurred to a significant
extent in Anglo-Saxon society, the Norman preoccupation
with linking land to military obligations reduced the role of
women as landowners. Moreover, developments within
Canon (Church) law also reduced the status of women.
Whether this would have happened if the Conquest had not
occurred is a matter of debate.

What is clear is that women had a complex image in the
Middle Ages. Eve was a woman; the Virgin Mary was a
woman. On the one hand it was a woman who was blamed for
the Fall and the origin of the sinful nature of humanity (along
with Adam of course). On the other it was a woman whom
God had honoured by making the mother of Christ. And in
medieval Catholic theology Mary was a woman exalted far
beyond the relatively limited information provided by the
New Testament. Yet it was this very Church which greatly
emphasized the particular responsibility of Woman in the fall

and whose male-dominated celibate clergy could sometimes be highly misogynistic in the way they described and related to women.

The medieval legal definition of women, outlined in 1180, was that 'every married woman is a sort of infant'. As a result even adult married women had few rights since, in most circumstances, the existence of a male (whether father or husband) meant that he was in control. Consequently, when a woman married, her property automatically belonged to her husband for as long as he lived. Furthermore, Canon Law permitted a man to beat his wife if he considered her lazy or disobedient. This was not a licence for unrestrained violence since manorial courts contain plenty of evidence that if violence was thought excessive neighbours might intervene, but this fact does not reduce the significance of this power over women. Within marriage a woman's infidelity was more likely to be severely judged than that of a man. And the simple facts of biology meant that a woman – via pregnancy – was easily identified as having engaged in sex outside of marriage. In such a society the very fact of being female could at times be considered a reproach, and words such as 'womanish', 'effeminate' and 'feminine' were used against men as terms of abuse. Edward II and his favourites were attacked for their 'effeminacy' and this was one of the contributory factors leading to his overthrow and murder at Berkley Castle (Gloucestershire) in 1327.

Women were also frequently regarded as being less rational and intelligent than men and more easily tempted into sexual sin. This latter point owes a great deal to Church writers and probably reflects the projecting of blame on to women for the sexual desire which these men felt, having been forced to adopt celibacy. In such circumstances it was invariably the woman who was blamed for tempting the man, rather than the man being blamed for sexual desire. Despite these so-called characteristics of women there were clearly women who prospered in this male-dominated world and did not conform to the stereotype. The countess Hawisa, wife of the Earl of Essex in 1180, was described by a monastic chronicler as 'almost a man to whom nothing masculine is lacking save virility'. In exceptional cases such characteristics might even be reluctantly admired, but they were not to be emulated by women as a general rule. It comes as no surprise to discover that women could not normally hold responsible roles within government or in law courts and they could not attend university.

That women should be quiet and docile was a frequent – male – preoccupation in literature. The *Ancrene Riwle* suggested that the Virgin Mary was the model in this, since she said so little that her words are only recorded four times in the New Testament. It is interesting how often women are fined in manor court records having 'scolded and quarrelled' with another woman. The manor court rolls for Yeadon (Yorkshire) for 1449 record Joanna, wife of Richard Couper, fined for doing this to Margaret the wife of Thomas Piper 'in contravention of a penalty imposed for this' (suggesting it was not a one-off offence). Sibell, wife of John Watson, was similarly fined for doing this to the same Margaret, but this picture of village bickering is further complicated because Joanna was also fined because she 'equally has scolded and quarrelled with Sibell' as well! The court protested that these quarrelling women had disturbed the 'good order' of the manor.[2]

Sex and marriage

There was much debate as to what caused the development of gender. A common assumption was that a child was formed by a man's seed mixing with matter from the mother. If this occurred on the woman's left side it produced a girl; if on her right side it led to the birth of a boy. It was also thought that any difference in the size of a woman's breasts indicated the gender of the child to be born. Other writers suggested that girls were produced by defective semen. This, it was suggested, made women long for sexual union with – more perfect – males. Whilst not all thinkers agreed with this (Aquinas for example), the dominant opinion was that reproduction was the result of an active male force acting on passive female material.

In addition, there was an assumption that women's reproductive organs were an inverted version of a man's. This was part of the idea that women were, in some sense, defective males. Furthermore, the popularity of the ancient Greek theory that human bodies were dominated by four 'humours' led to the idea that, whereas men were dominated by hot and dry humours, women were dominated by cold and moist humours. The need to remove excess quantities of the latter was understood to be the reason for menstrual bleeding.

Finally, regarding conception, many medieval scholars believed that conception only occurred when both partners were sexually aroused. This idea caused acute problems for women made pregnant by rape, since it was assumed that they were willing partners in an act which they found pleasurable. Male theorizing overrode these abused women's experiences of reality. As with most matters concerned with medieval women and their nature, it was men who articulated it and who stamped it with their masculine authority. Linked to this idea was the view that it was the semen of the man, not actual penetration, that caused sexual pleasure in a woman. And the expectation was that all legitimate sexual activity should occur within marriage.

Although it would accrue a wide range of rituals, the Church's definition of marriage was remarkably simple. It rested on consent and on the simple exchange of words indicating agreement to be married. Though not a new definition, this was formally ratified by the Fourth Lateran Council in 1215; at the same time marriage was, for the first time, defined as a *sacrament*. If the promise indicated a future intent this became marriage if the couple later began a sexual relationship. Sex alone, though, did not make a relationship a marriage, since Church law pointed to the valid – though always chaste in Catholic theology – marriage of Joseph to the Virgin Mary. However, the reality was that abduction and rape (or seduction) was used to force some women into marriages and clearly played upon a family's desire to regularize what had been done without consent. If the woman became pregnant, then consent to the sexual act was assumed to have occurred anyway.

Evidence for the period around 1400 suggests that marriage usually took place when couples were in their mid-twenties (men a little older than women), which allowed a man time to secure an income. This evidence is from the church court at York, and it seems that rural couples married a little earlier, with a slightly bigger age difference between husband and wife. Overall, it appears that common assumptions about an early age for marriage actually conflict with the evidence for this economically prudent approach dictating later marriage. Later marriage also meant a smaller family size, which assisted in keeping together the small estate gathered through parents' lifetimes.

Parental consent was usually sought but was not essential. Most marriages took place in church, but this was not stipulated in law and often it was sufficient to state marriage vows in front of witnesses. The minimum age for marriage under Church and Common Law was 12 for girls and 14 for boys. Nobles operated under a different set of rules, and much younger betrothals were common amongst the elites. Sexual maturity for medieval girls was probably achieved at about 14 years. The minimum age for marriage contrasted with coming of age regarding property rights and inheritance, which, though fixed at 15 for girls, was 21 for aristocratic men (the position for those men lower down the social scale not being so clear).

Strict rules established the family boundaries within which marriage could be contracted in order to avoid technical and actual incest. Restrictions based on blood ties, or *consanguinity*, were added to by restrictions concerning sexual proximity, or *affinity* (such as marrying the sister of a woman with whom one had had sexual relations, or someone for whom one acted as a godparent [*spiritual affinity*]). A growing trend, seen by the fifteenth century, was for common rituals – such as a pre-contract or engagement (which might be made before witnesses such as a priest) – to mark out the significance of marriage, then a public formal contract made within the home of the parents of one of the parties, followed by exchange of vows at the church door (*solemnization*). This was sometimes followed by a marriage meal and later by the blessing of the marriage bed and sometimes viewing the married couple getting into bed! Sex, though, frequently occurred between the pre-contract and the solemnization. This was not regarded as fornication since the declared intention to marry counted as a key stage in the process of getting married. By 1500, however, this practice was increasingly being frowned on by Church authorities and the emphasis was shifting towards marriage solemnization itself as the only legitimate start for sexual relations. From the 1520s a women made pregnant by her husband before solemnization was regarded as soiled by sin and in need of penitence and purification.

Divorce was not an option for medieval people unless they could prove that the marriage should not have occurred in the first place. In such cases it was necessary to prove that the original 'marriage' had involved people whose family ties were such that they broke Church rules on consanguinity, affinity or spiritual affinity. This was often not a straightforward matter, as even Henry VIII found when trying to divorce Katherine of Aragon (claiming she had been a sexual partner with his brother and therefore his brother's wife, not just 'his brother's intended'). Such matters might be complicated by politics, as in the above case where the pope was unwilling to anger Katherine's relative the Holy Roman Emperor. It was also complicated by the hypocrisy of powerful people, as when Henry married Anne Boleyn, with whose sister he had definitely had the same level of sexual relationship which he claimed made it unlawful for Katherine to have married him. Other complications existed where claims could be made that a pre-contract between two individuals meant they were not technically free to later marry someone else. This occurred following the death of Edward IV in 1483, when Robert

Stillington, the Bishop of Bath and Wells, disclosed to the dead king's brother, the Duke of Gloucester (later Richard III) and the royal council the existence of a pre-contract between Edward IV and a woman named Eleanor Butler. This pre-contract (if real) made Edward's later marriage to Elizabeth Woodville invalid and his children, by her, illegitimate. As a result of this 'evidence' Parliament declared Richard to be England's legal king, since the two sons of Edward were in effect bastards. But for ordinary people such manipulation of the law was out of the question and marriage was for life. Impotence was also a ground for separation but it had to be proven, and examples exist of authorities testing the husband's ability to get an erection by exposing him to other women. Similarly, proving a woman to have been unchaste at marriage could also cause a marriage to be annulled but was difficult to prove and open to abuse.

Many Church writers described marriage as an acceptable state for those not able to achieve the higher calling of chastity. For these writers marriage was a concession to human weakness and clearly a second-class form of life. However, not all writers expressed such a negative view. Thomas of Cobham, in 1215, suggested a wife had the power to persuade her husband to act morally, and Robert Mannyng reminded his readers that God had ordained marriage in the Garden of Eden.

As the earlier evidence from the 1520s reminds us, sex outside marriage – *fornication* –was considered very sinful. However, much evidence exists regarding its frequency. Lords of the manor could even make a profit from it, with fines imposed on village women for fornication and for bearing illegitimate children. At Wakefield Manor in 1316, seven female villeins were fined for '*lechery*'. In the manor court rolls for Walsham-le-Willows (Suffolk) in 1340, Agnes Fitte was fined 2 shillings and 8 pence because she 'gave birth outside wedlock'. This was the fine known as *childwyte*. A similar attempt to enforce sexual morality in a manor court can be found at Downham (Cambridgeshire) in 1311, when 'Twelve jurors present that Alice, the daughter of Amicia committed adultery and is therefore in mercy'.[3] The phrase *in mercy* found in legal documents is a common abbreviation of *amercement* and means that she was fined. That the jurors accused Alice may be as much explained by the fact that they would be fined it they did not do so as by their own sense of moral disapproval. In 1316 the community at Osset, near Wakefield, was fined 40 pence because they concealed the existence of the sisters Eva, Alice and Annabel who had apparently all been '*deflowered*' and were accused of being *lecherwytes*, that is, sexually promiscuous.[4]

The Catholic Church taught that within marriage the main purpose of sex was to reproduce, although the liturgical calendar was full of feast days and fast days (plus Sunday) on which marital intercourse was forbidden. In addition, couples were also not supposed to have sex during the woman's menstrual period.

Marriage for aristocratic women was frequently a business deal. Love between the partners was not seen as important. Instead, marriages were made to create territorial alliances or to increase the wealth of the families involved. The evidence of Magna Carta reminds us that the king had the right to sell off widowed noble women to the highest bidder, and female wards were particularly prone to being manipulated as financial assets. Lower-class unfree women could similarly be forced to marry by their lord. Agnes Seynpel in Cambridgeshire, in 1289, had to pay a fine of 12 shillings to be allowed a few months to find a husband of her own choosing.

Women could inherit if there was no male heir, and as long as she remained single a woman could hold property like a man. But this right was lost on marriage. Remaining single was a virtual impossibility for a woman who inherited substantial property. About 93 per cent of all daughters of the most powerful landowning families between 1330 and 1479 were married by the time they were 35 years old. And such women remained as wards of their overlord, who had final say on whom they could marry. However, Magna Carta insisted that no widow should be forced to remarry. The Common Law decreed that any items which a woman owned on marriage became the outright property of her husband. This was even more severe than a husband's guardianship of his wife's landed property. As a result, some fathers without sons disinherited their daughters in order to keep their lands within their family.

Given both the importance of marriage (as a context for sexual activity and the organization of inheritance) and the church's exaltation of virginity, it comes as no surprise to discover two very different views of sex in medieval written sources. This duality has been explored by the historian Ruth Mazo Karras.[5] The first is a very negative view which is often found in theological and medical books and which described sex as sinful and a threat to the soul. The other view is earthier and found in evidence such as chroniclers, manor records and the courtly love literature, and describes sexually active priests, aristocratic mistresses and lower-class sex between peasants. It still reflects medieval ideas about sex but suggests that many people did not share the horror of it found in the writings of many celibate clergy. So, the medieval attitude towards sex was complicated and the practice was often very different from the theory. Karras has also shown how many medieval people saw love and friendship differently from the modern ideal, which sees sexual intimacy as principally concerned with relationships. Medieval people, however, appear to have more commonly considered sex as an act of lesser importance, something somebody did to somebody else, and not part of a mutual relationship. This was strongly linked to both the passive view of women's role within sex and the subservient view of women in general, which reduced the emphasis on them as friends and partners with men. Karras even subtitled her book 'Doing Unto Others' to emphasize this point. It shows an interesting contrast between the medieval and the modern outlook on sexual relationships. But it has to be borne in mind that the twenty-first century sex industry and pornography reveal that this attitude towards women as sexual objects cannot be solely regarded as a medieval characteristic.

The complex medieval attitude towards sex is seen in the view of virginity. As we have seen, for medieval Church writers and opinion formers virginity was highly prized. Although for the first thousand years of Church history it was possible to be a priest and be married, this became increasingly frowned upon. For those who chose the 'religious life' in a monastery, chastity was one of the essential characteristics of their calling and discipline. From the 1070s onwards in England the campaign against married parish priests intensified. All of this created a mindset in which marriage and sexual activity was regarded as being for those who were not able to meet the higher calling of celibacy.

Modern historians, such as Sarah Salih, who have studied the way in which virginity was regarded in the Middle Ages, have revealed that for medieval writers there was more to virginity than sexual inexperience, and that virginity could almost be considered as a gendered identity; a role which was performed rather than biologically determined. By exploring versions of virginity as they appear in medieval saints' lives, in the regulated chastity of nuns, and as shown in the book of Margery Kempe, she has demonstrated that it was an active role, much debated, considered clearly vulnerable but also *recoverable*.[6] This last point is particularly interesting because it reminds us that in the mindset of the Middle Ages repenting of sexual activity – particularly if accompanied by vows of chastity from that point – was tantamount to becoming a virgin again. And this explains the outlook of those married people who made the decision to enter the 'religious life' after years of marriage and those who sought – often successfully – to encourage prostitutes to repent and 'retire' into specialist nunneries. The complex idea of virginity – both holy and yet requiring great effort to maintain . . . elusive yet appealing . . . seductively presented in some literature and yet removed from earthly desire – embodies much of the complex attitude towards sex in the Middle Ages.[7] The value placed on virginity is seen in the fact that in the design of religious houses access to a female dormitory was as difficult as that to a sacristy (where sacred vessels were stored) in a male religious house.[8]

Women's role in society

Sexuality could define women in economic terms too. Ploughing, hedging and ditching were seen as typically male occupations, whereas planting, winnowing, weeding and looking after the chickens and cows was seen as female. Where women did comparable jobs to men they seem to have been paid the same rate, but women traditionally did less well-paid jobs. However, women were clearly experienced workers and organizers, and in many surviving wills husbands name their wives as their executors.

Single women had greater freedom if they were below the rank of major landowner, and this was particularly so in the developing towns. In some towns – such as Exeter, Lincoln, London, Torksey and Worcester – even married women could trade freely as if they were single. This was particularly so if a wife's trade was different from the trade of her husband. Such women could also take on apprentices and this is specified in ordinances from London. Girl apprentices were not at all unusual in trades such as the silk industry, but Agnes Hecche's apprenticeship to her armour-making father, in early-fifteenth-century York, is unusual to say the least. Widows were particularly prominent in town trade and in some towns in the later Middle Ages they constituted up to 20 per cent of those classed as heads of households. Mostly they traded in food, drink and clothing. About 50 per cent of the women workers in late-fourteenth-century Exeter were engaged in such trades. In many towns it was the textile trades in which female labour was dominant, though they were usually as employees, not as owners of the business. Others were employed in laundries. Nevertheless, their economic activities in towns did not extend to government, from which they were totally excluded. In

London in 1422 it was decided that women would not even be allowed to oversee the trading in oysters at Queenhithe. In short, as in the countryside, women might find greater economic opportunities after the Black Death but this was not allowed to develop into political power. And, despite the evidence for some women prospering within marriage and continuing to do so on being widowed, it should also be remembered that many widows lived in terrible poverty.

Despite this, widowhood could sometimes give women an opportunity to escape the marriage market, which especially dominated aristocratic life. This was achieved by entering a religious house as a nun. This same opportunity was sometimes taken up by older married women. Since nuns were the best-educated women in the country this did allow some women the right to exercise considerable power. A woman – often a widow, or an unmarried woman – who was not attracted by the regulations of convent life might become an *anchoress*, following a hermit lifestyle of prayer and contemplation. However, for most medieval women the context for most of their activities lay within the family.

Family life
Throughout the Middle Ages the prime time for child bearing was the early to mid-twenties. A woman close to the time of giving birth was ideally *confined* in a warm, dark room and attended by a midwife and female helpers. Males were excluded. Newborn babies were baptized within two or three days, for fear they die unbaptized and be thus excluded from salvation. In an emergency a lay person could baptize a dying baby rather than risk waiting for a priest. Children – certainly of elite parents for whom we have more information – were often given three godparents, two of the same gender and one of the opposite.

Contrary to many assumptions it seems that extended families of three generations were relatively rare across much of the Middle Ages. Fourteenth-century poll tax records indicate few families contained members beyond parents and their children. The resulting picture is largely of nuclear families. However, there are some complexities which the available evidence does not allow us to disentangle. The poll tax groupings of couples with the same surnames in the same small settlement probably indicates separate households of married brothers, but it may represent a system known as *frérèche*, in which two or more married couples lived under the same roof. The married 'units' in such a situation were usually organized around brothers. Suggestions have been made that this can be demonstrated in a number of cases using court roll evidence from Halesowen (Worcestershire) prior to the 1350s.[9] Similar conclusions have been drawn for Leicestershire in 1379 from poll tax returns, but not for Essex, which appears more consistently 'nuclear'.[10] What these studies may indicate is that there was no consistent family form across England, with East Anglia characterized by nuclear families while other structures (extended and *frérèche*) were found in the Midlands and West Midlands up until the 1380s. This same pattern of nuclear families appears in towns in the Middle Ages.

The development of such an apparently 'modern' family structure may have been encouraged by living in regions which were less conservative and were characterized by the active buying and selling of land, division of peasant land units, greater geographical mobility and a more varied and active economy – in which smaller family units could be economically viable without having to inherit land. In areas associated with arable agriculture, villeinage and the demands of lords, the need of assistance from close family members (accompanied by the landlord's desire to avoid splitting peasant land units) may have encouraged extended family patterns. If this is the case it may explain why the nuclear pattern seems to increase from the later fourteenth century, as villeinage declined. By the sixteenth century it was the dominant family structure across much of England (and north-western Europe). This trend was accompanied by the placing of adolescent children as servants in nearby households: a practice more pronounced in towns than in the countryside, though it was also found there. This was known as *life-cycle service*, since it was not a permanent career choice but one lasting until the individuals married and set up their own households. It gave access to training in craft skills and increased as the wages of day labourers mounted in the late fourteenth century – live-in servants offering a cheaper alternative to hired hands.

When it comes to relationships within such families, it is tempting to assume that the high rate of infant mortality meant that people in the Middle Ages had looser emotional attachments to their children than modern parents. Indeed, in the 1960s the French historian Philippe Ariès argued that 'childhood' was invented after the Middle Ages and that medieval children were considered as little adults.[11] Ariès pointed out that most medieval young people were apprenticed like adults, or worked in agriculture like adults. In short, they entered into adult society at a very early age. As evidence he cited art. In medieval art there are few recognizable children, or babies. The physical build of those painted, their clothing, expressions, and mannerisms all reflect adult norms. In the medieval world a young person of seven years old was already considered an adult. In medieval church writings this was the age of reason – the age when it was considered that a child could begin to commit sin. As a result, Ariès argued, 'there was no place for childhood in the medieval world.'[12]

This view has not gone unchallenged. Following more recent examinations of the evidence, historical sociologists have countered Ariès' view by claiming that, in fact, it convincingly demonstrates the extent to which the relationship between parents and children was a fundamental element in medieval European society.[13] The contemporary 'accounts' of the so-called martyr William of Norwich seem to challenge the idea that what little childhood there was ended early. Despite being 12 years old at the time of his death, it is clear that (although he was already a tanner's apprentice and living away from home) he was clearly considered a child. It was his apparent youth and innocence which made him such a useful figure to anti-Semites seeking to blame Jews for ritually murdering him. In the *Life and Miracles of St William of Norwich*, written by Thomas of Monmouth between about 1150 and 1173, the handling of the death of William only makes sense against a background of adult fears concerning the vulnerability and innocence of children.[14]

With regard to relationships between parents and children, the medieval ideal was for men to hold authority over their wives and children. In the poem *Piers Plowman*, William Langland puts these instructions into the mouth of 'Reason':

> He warned Walter that his wife was much to be blamed for wearing a headdress worth five guineas, while his ragged old hood would hardly fetch threepence. And he bade Mr Bett cut himself some birch-rods, and beat his daughter Betty till she was willing to work.[15]

Women by the end of the Middle Ages

There is evidence that during the fifteenth century there occurred a hardening of male attitudes towards women and what we would now call gender roles, and that some economic and social freedoms, which had been increasing before this, were reduced. For example, it seemed that men and women were increasingly segregated in church.[16] This shows itself in churches where the provision of pews were primarily for the use of women; men presumably standing as before. By 1500 there had also been an increase in the number of separate maidens' and young men's guilds, which may reflect the same trend in segregation of men and women.[17] In the same way, clues suggest that women no longer played female parts in the Mystery Plays from the 1450s onwards. That men (in drag) came to play these parts is clear from accounts such as those from Coventry in 1499 detailing payments 'to pylatts wyffe

[Pilate's wife] for *his* wages'. The fact that the plays with most female parts are associated with female crafts suggests that, at an earlier time, these parts were once played by women. In addition, many of the female characters which emerge by 1500 appear based on negative stereotypes of women.[18] This downplaying of female roles, in addition to the propagation of anti-female humour, is striking.

This trend was accompanied by attempts to restrict women's working opportunities in order to protect the jobs of men in the economically troubled years of the fifteenth century. In 1453 regulations in Coventry barred women from working at the broad-looms of the city. A similar ordinance was passed in Bristol in 1461. Other laws against women weavers occur from Hull in 1490 and Norwich in 1511. Similar fear of the 'ungoverned woman' shows itself in stricter town ordinances concerning prostitution in Nottingham in 1463, Leicester in 1467 and York in 1482. The same trend made it increasingly difficult for women to keep alehouses (a common occupation for centuries prior to the late fifteenth century). Such women were now accused of being sexually lax, of receiving stolen goods and of corrupting young men. This move to drive women out of the marketplace is seen across northern Europe at this time and is by no means confined to England. The new emphasis was on women as economically dependent home-makers and men as financially independent breadwinners. These economic changes were accompanied by increased regulation of sexual behaviour, as attitudes towards sex changed during the later Middle Ages. In short, there was far more regulation in the later Middle Ages than in the earlier period.

This increased attempt to control women, both socially and economically, coincided with an increased interest in the role of alleged female sexuality in witchcraft. For most of the medieval period there was virtually no punishment of men and women for witchcraft. The 'Great Witch Hunt' is a feature of the end of the Middle Ages and the start of what historians call the Early Modern period (in the sixteenth and seventeenth centuries). At this time anxieties about economic problems and schisms in the Church coincided with an increased fear of women's sexuality. This latter issue became one of the strangest factors in the development of the concept of witchcraft, which occurred only at the very end of the Middle Ages, and led to a widespread belief that witchcraft came from uncontrolled sexual desire on the part of women. As such it was part of a trend which blamed marginal members of the community, and those least able to defend themselves, for problems in society. The story of the Great Witch Hunt lies outside the scope of this book but its roots lay in the increasingly tough later-medieval attitudes towards women, particularly unmarried ones or widows. In this way, the focus on supposed female sexual promiscuity and the fact that most of those accused of witchcraft were female, poor and old came to be combined in a process of deadly scapegoating.

In many other ways, however, the late-fifteenth- and early-sixteenth-century expectations of women remain consistent with those of earlier centuries. The Sarum Missal taught that at marriage a wife should be 'bonair [courteous] and buxom [obliging] in bed and at board.' Other conduct books taught the virtues of meekness, modesty, fertility and subservience to her husband. That not all women accepted these characteristics is clear from evidence across the Middle Ages, but there is an increase in their prevalence from 1500. In 1531 the Venetian ambassador noted that a crowd of up to 8,000 women had attempted to lynch Anne Boleyn at a Thameside residence. His report suggested that the women were not severely punished because they were female, and this clearly made the attack feel less of a threat to those in authority (though probably not to Anne). The action of these women is a curious mixture of 'medieval feminine characteristics'. On the one hand the women were conservative and traditional. They were pro-Catholic and antagonistic to Anne's disruption of the relationship between Henry VIII and Katherine of Aragon. Their light treatment by the authorities shows that they were still regarded, condescendingly, as the weaker sex. On the other hand they were aggressive and subversive and made the most of their social position to attempt actions which would have seen a man hanged. In fact, the ambassador claims that some of the 'women' were in fact men in female clothing!

The fact is that many women resisted the trend to control them more closely. As literacy increased it was reflected in a growing number of women who could read. Even the religiously conservative Thomas More ensured his daughters received a full humanist education. Such attitudes were most likely to be found amongst a small group of the elite families and this had, to some extent, been true throughout the Middle Ages. Diane Watt has recently argued that women in the period 1100 to 1500 contributed (as patrons, readers, audiences and subjects) both to the production of texts and their meanings, whether these were written by men or by women.[19] But women's involvement in radical trends and challenges to social norms was not restricted to female aristocrats and families of courtiers; it is also evident in those women who appear amongst the early Protestant martyrs under Henry VIII. When Anne Askew was burnt for heresy in 1546, she was not unique in her female membership of the emerging Protestant community. Clearly, she did not consider it her role to sit submissively under an authority she believed wrong – in this case the Catholic hierarchy.[20] Her assertiveness reminds us that not all women accepted a role of passivity.

Chapter 7

LAW AND ORDER

Justice in late Anglo-Saxon England centred on the shire court, which met twice yearly and was overseen by the ealdorman and bishop. Direct responsibility for law and order fell to the sheriff, who supervised the work of local – *hundred* – courts. These met every four weeks. In addition to these, manor courts had delegated powers to deal with lesser offences. All those over the age of 12 were required to attend these courts. It was on this foundation that later medieval legal developments were built.

As the medieval period progressed the dispensing of justice became increasingly more formalized, with clearly defined responsibilities for dealing with different levels of crime. The royal courts and royal judges appointed by the Crown had jurisdiction over all *felonies*. This arrangement was known as the *Common Law* because it applied across the whole country. Even the so-called palatinates of Chester and Durham (where bishops ruled with powers normally associated with princes) and, after 1351, Lancaster were still subject to the Common Law. An early explanation of what was understood to be covered by these laws was written in the 1230s by Henry of Bratton (known as Bracton) in a work entitled *On the Laws and Customs of England*. The laws passed by Parliament and known as *Statute Law* continually added to this body of laws and differentiated between levels of crime. The term *felony* was used in Common Law to describe very serious crimes, whereas misdemeanours, or in the Middle Ages *trespasses*, were considered to be less serious actions. In the Middle Ages crimes considered as felonies included murder, rape, robbery (taking the property of another by means of force or fear), theft of goods worth more than 5 pence and arson. These crimes were punished by hanging. A number of trespasses were also dealt with by royal judges and these covered crimes such as assault and the fourteenth-century laws relating to contracts, wages and prices. In the absence of a police force, law enforcement from the twelfth century relied on *juries of presentment*, which set up groups of jurors sworn to accuse anyone suspected of committing a crime in their local area. This replaced a system which relied on private prosecutions and by 1400 it was the source of almost all prosecutions.

A key feature of the administration of local justice was a system known as *Frankpledge*. With its roots in Late Anglo-Saxon times it made all freemen (except for clergy and knights) join a *tithing* of ten men, who were responsible for the behaviour of each other. In the event of one of them being accused of a crime, the other members of the tithing had the task of bringing the accused to face justice, or compensating the injured party. In practice the checking that everyone was a member of a tithing – called the *View of Frankpledge* – was the task of the manorial *Court Leet*. Any man not in a tithing was fined and the money went to the lord of the manor. In this way the system acted as a bridging structure between the control of petty local offences and more serious crimes. By making it a responsibility of the manorial court the task was offloaded from central government onto local lords, but the local lords could themselves profit from the administration of the system.

At Weston (Hertfordshire) in 1340 the manorial court record listed the responsibilities involved in the Frankpledge system: to account for all members; to ensure all aged 12 years and over were members of a tithing; whether a *hue and cry* (hunt for a criminal) had occurred since the last meeting of the court; whether blood had been shed and, if so, by whom; whether any trespassing offences had been committed (e.g. a dung heap placed on the street, ploughing on a neighbours land, etc); naming those accused of theft; naming of receivers of stolen goods and counterfeiters of coins; names of any woman who has been raped; whether treasure has been unearthed; whether any use of false weights and measures had occurred. And the list goes on.[1]

Below the tier of the royal courts (administering the common law) and the intermediate layer of the system of Frankpledge were the manorial courts, which enforced the customary rules and obligations of local manors, punishing offenders with fines. In these courts actions were brought not only by the lord of the manor, since tenants could also bring complaints against other tenants, as when in 1331 Thomas de Totehille successfully brought a complaint against a neighbour for letting his dogs kill six of Thomas's pigs. Or when John Packard was fined because he had not paid a fine of 13 shillings and 4 pence, owed on account of his wife Alice striking Margery, wife of William Wodebite, which 'drew blood'. Or when, at Downham (Cambridgeshire) in 1311, William Bunting was forced to compensate Peter Gill 2 shillings for 'beating and ill treating him'.[2]

The final form of law in England was *Canon Law*. This was the law of the Church: it applied across the whole of Western Europe and was administered in Church courts. It mostly dealt with behaviour amongst the clergy but also affected the laity since these courts had authority over the payment of tithes, sexual misconduct, validity of marriages, wills, heresy and witchcraft. There could be real tensions between this system and that of the royal courts, since clergy who had committed serious offences were tried in Church courts rather than in royal courts and were thus subject to much less rigorous punishment. Claiming 'benefit of clergy' meant a person claimed to be eligible for trial under a Church court, and this system was subject to much abuse. The proof of whether a person really was a member of the clergy was the ability to recite a Biblical passage in Latin. So, in addition to the whole issue of whether the clergy should escape the more rigorous justice of the royal courts for the same crimes as a lay person was the fact that anyone who could read (or memorize) a Biblical passage could claim they were a member of the clergy, whether they were or not. (For more information on 'benefit of clergy' and the definition of who was a cleric, see Chapter 4.) It was this issue of clergy exemption from royal justice for serious crimes which lay at the heart of the dispute between Henry II and Thomas Becket, Archbishop of Canterbury, in the twelfth century. After 1489 'benefit of clergy' could be claimed by a lay person only on one occasion, but the fact that this could apply to crimes as serious as murder meant that it remained very controversial. Punishments in Church courts included public whippings (in the earlier centuries of the Middle Ages) and, more usually, public penance such as standing in the marketplace in undergarments holding a lighted candle. In Church courts men and women had equal status, although, as with courts operating under the Common Law, the unfree could not bring cases to these courts.

Access to these courts was denied to villeins, and women's actions in law were limited to the prosecution of the murder of her husband (but only if he died in her arms), action which led to the loss of an unborn child and rape. Magna Carta (1215), in Article 54, asserts: 'No one shall be arrested or imprisoned on the appeal of a woman for the death of any person except her husband'. Also, the evidence suggests that it was very unlikely that charges of rape would result in successful prosecution of the perpetrator. This was particularly so if pregnancy ensued since it was assumed that conception could only occur if sexual pleasure was mutual. The subservient status of women could, conversely, operate in a woman's favour if she was charged as complicit in crimes committed by her husband, since it was judged that if she acted on her husband's instructions it was he who carried the blame, since she was bound to obey him.

The two highest courts in England by 1250 were the court of *common pleas* (normally sitting in Westminster although in the fourteenth century occasionally in York) and the court of *king's bench* (meant to travel with the king, though by the second half of the fourteenth century also usually sitting in Westminster). The court of common pleas dealt with disputes over property and that of king's bench dealt with felonies and with appeals from lesser courts. To open a case in common pleas a person first had to pay for a *writ* to be issued (which identified the complaint, named the defendant and compelled them to answer the complaint before the court) and then pay for an attorney to plead the case before the royal judges. This could be an expensive business.

In addition to this system, royal judges were also sent out into the regions on tours known as *eyres*. These tours were meant to happen every seven years. After 1294 this was abandoned and replaced by local *assize judges* and *commissions of oyer and terminer*. The assize judges moved through circuits of adjacent counties and dealt with offences which had occurred there since their last sitting. This was meant to happen at least three times a year. Commissions of oyer and terminer, on the other hand, were sent out to deal swiftly with local disorders and local abuses of power. A similar system was the *commission of Trailbaston*, sent out to deal with the organized criminal activities of armed gangs. While these illustrate the problems of local lawlessness they themselves were often accused of corruption and of being arbitrary in their actions. They failed to stop the Folvilles and the Coterels (organized crime gangs, see pp. 156–7), for example. During the late thirteenth century *keepers of the peace* were also appointed with some policing duties and, by 1400, these had evolved into local

Justices of the Peace (a title first used in 1361), who sat in judgement at least four times a year (in *Quarter Sessions*) and dealt with less serious offences. They came to be a vital local arm of government: fixing wages and prices, building and controlling the use of roads and bridges, and supervising those local services thought by the Crown and Parliament to be necessary for the welfare of the country. The Quarter Sessions were not replaced by Crown Courts until 1972 and reveal the long-lived nature of many medieval institutions. By a law of 1389 the early Justices of the Peace received a subsistence allowance of 4 shillings a day. This appears to have soon lapsed, since most JPs were drawn from the local elites and, as wealthy landowners, could manage without this assistance.

Punishment and criminal burials

Despite the changing nature of the medieval justice system, one surprising aspect is how little it relied on prisons. Prison as a major form of punishment is largely a modern invention, dating from the later eighteenth and early nineteenth century. It was not until 1576 that JPs were required to build *houses of correction* in which rogues and vagabonds could be detained. These were apprehended by village constables, who were unpaid members of their local parish and were conscripted for service annually. Prior to this, punishment relied far more heavily on execution, other forms of physical violence, outlawry and fining. Medieval prisons were primarily holding places for those awaiting trial, rather than the place of punishment itself. In London in 1475 arrangements for bringing prisoners to trial changed. Instead of so-called *gaol delivery* taking place once a year (as was usually the case under the old system), it was now to be held at least five times a year. This must have been a relief to the prisoners awaiting trial.

However, medieval prisons certainly existed. One of the more famous was Clink Prison, set up in the twelfth century under the authority of the bishop of Winchester in Southwark, on the south side of London Bridge. In the area today known

as Bankside the bishop built separate prisons for men and
women. The fact that a prison was sited here was a product
both of the bishop's authority and the criminality of the area.
This is because Southwark was complex, both socially and
legally. The borough contained inns and public gardens and
was fashionable as the residence of great men. By the end of the
thirteenth century a number of town houses of powerful
Churchmen and nobles were sited south of the Thames here –
from this position the river provided them with easy access to
Westminster. Sir John Fastolf, who gained fame in the French
wars, was among the well-known inhabitants of Southwark.
He owned a considerable establishment there during the fourteenth century. Even more impressive was the bishop of
Winchester's house, just west of the bridgehead. Traditionally,
this was an area where lay and ecclesiastical franchises had
grown up and claimed independence from royal justice. As
such, they offered privileged positions to these landowners but
also afforded shelter to fugitive criminals and debtors. This led
to increased criminality in the area. In a number of cases, land
leased from the Church in Southwark became used for *stews*
(brothels), since they were out of the stricter control of royal
authority or that of the City of London to the north of the
Thames. This applied to land owned by the bishop of
Winchester and the prioress and nuns of St Leonard's Priory,
Stratford at Bow. Hence the bitter jibe of Duke Humphrey to
his uncle Cardinal Beaufort – bishop of Winchester 1404–47 –
in Shakespeare's *Henry VI, part I*: 'Thou that givest whores
indulgences to sin' (1.3.35).

One of the reasons why prison appeared low on the
sentencing options was the prevalence of capital punishment.
And this reveals itself in the oft-neglected area of medieval
execution cemeteries. Even as men and women in mid- to late
Anglo-Saxon England were subscribing to burial in cemeteries
around churches, another form of burial rite is noticeable in the
archaeological record. These *deviant burials* occur away from
community cemeteries. This became particularly significant

since, from about 850, the community cemeteries were in ground that was regarded as being hallowed by its proximity to a Christian place of worship. In this way both the living and the dead formed one Christian community – those on earth and those in heaven (with their mortal remains buried near a church and awaiting the Last Judgement). In view of this the rejection of certain burials (and their placing elsewhere) is all the more striking and must have been regarded as so by the contemporaries of those categorized as deviant.

Both small and large execution cemeteries are known from the middle to later Anglo-Saxon period and into the twelfth century. A number of very characteristic deviant burials, in which bodies show signs of violence or strange orientations very different from the norm, occur around Mound 5 at Sutton Hoo (Suffolk) and were probably placed there when this (once-elite) burial ground had become taboo due to its use in pagan times. Another very striking example was discovered beheaded and buried at the world-famous site of Stonehenge in Wiltshire. This was radiocarbon dated in 2001 to between 600 and 690, although this date has since been revised and this particular execution burial may have occurred as late as 890.[3] Similarly, archaeologists excavating a large Bronze Age round barrow at South Acre (Norfolk) found it was reused in the Anglo-Saxon period, with over 100 secondary burials. Many of these were in shallow graves. Some graves contained multiple burials and none showed signs of being ceremonially placed in their graves. There were no children and most were young adults. Eight appeared to have been decapitated, seven were buried facing into the earth, while others appeared to have been bound. This was almost certainly a *cwealmstow* – an execution place.[4] Many of these places were sited at boundaries of hundreds and shires and became locations of both execution and burial of excommunicated criminals. It is likely that many of the references to 'heathen burials' found on charter boundaries refer to these execution cemeteries, rather than to burial grounds dating from before the conversion to Christianity.[5]

Evidence from both archaeology and charters suggests that by the tenth century this separation of criminals and social outcasts from cemeteries used by the rest of the community had become widespread in England. There are some clues which suggest that drowning was sometimes used both as a method of execution and of disposal of the body, and may be linked to the belief that water acted as a barrier to ghosts.

During the eleventh century the practice of burying criminals at boundaries began to be replaced by the claiming of bodies of criminals for burial by certain monastic orders. The order most commonly associated with this was that of the Knights Hospitaller. Sometimes these burials took place in parish churchyards, or in churchyards of the order, such as the Pardon Churchyard in Clerkenwell, London. There are examples of Hospitallers claiming the bodies of executed criminals in places as varied as Ilchester (Somerset), Aylesbury (Buckinghamshire) and York.[6]

Throughout the Middle Ages the death penalty was used for a wide range of offences including property crimes where items stolen were worth more than 12 pence. This applied to all over the age of ten, which is when children were regarded as having reached the age of criminal responsibility. The most usual method of execution was hanging, although a woman found guilty of murdering her husband could be burnt at the stake. This was because this was regarded as *petty treason*.

Crime levels and 'moral panics'

The study of medieval law and order raises an important question: how criminal were the Middle Ages? The answer is that levels of criminality varied across the period but were surprisingly high. Murder rates for East Anglia in the fourteenth century were comparable with those of modern-day New York. In England generally the homicide rate was far higher than that of urban USA today.[7] Evidence from traditional rural peasant communities – such as Russia before Collectivization in the late 1920s – reveals that a great deal of

violence occurred both in domestic disputes (particularly
involving male violence against women and children) and in
disputes between neighbours. No doubt those involved would
have recognized the scenario, from 1312, in which Robert of
Starston (Norfolk) threatened Thomas his brother with a
knife; the dispute was over land. In retaliation, Thomas killed
Robert with a cart shaft. As Bruce Campbell has noted, such
acts of violence between tenants were related to the scarcity of
land in Norfolk at the time and 'are generally passed over with
less comment [in medieval records] than those between tenants
and landlords', for the simple reason that they did not threaten
the social order. A peasant killing another was a crime but not a
challenge to the position of the local elites.[8] Overall, then, it is
justifiable to say: 'There was clearly a casual and easy resort to
violence, not just the minor fist fights and assaults with sticks,
pitch-forks and knives recorded in manorial court rolls but
also murder . . .'[9]

However, certain specific events seemed to have triggered an
upsurge in the rate of crime, such as the return of Edward III's
army from the siege of Calais in 1347 and the return of soldiers
from more general campaigning in France in 1361. Such was the
scale of the problem that local Justices of the Peace were
empowered to force these returning soldiers to take up jobs in an
effort to prevent them from turning to crime. No doubt crime
rates rose at other times too, due to similar war-related circumstances, but we lack the detailed records necessary to chart the
effects. As an aside, the conduct of these returning soldiers in
England makes one realize the appalling impact of English
'military adventures' on French communities during the
Hundred Years' War. This can often be overlooked in favour of
the heroic clash of arms involved in a Crécy, or an Agincourt. In
between times many of the common soldiers would have been
looting and raping and murdering defenceless French civilians.
War provoked increased crime in other ways too. Increased
taxation and forced sales of provisions for the army struck at
commercial activities and could cause middle-men and -women

to pass on the demand for cash as they, in turn, put pressure on their debtors further down the social scale. This tendency is very noticeable following the Scottish victory over the English in 1314 and the resumption of war with France after 1337. The result of this pressure shows itself in poor peasants selling tiny pieces of land in a desperate effort to pay their debts. In 1315–21 many people begged and stole to survive and 'crimes against property mushroomed'.[10] For much longer periods the unsettled conditions on the northern border with Scotland allowed criminal activities – often under cover of acts of war – to go unpunished.[11]

Crime rates might rise in the specific circumstances outlined above but, as in modern societies, would more usually have been related to downturns in the economy and other social and economic causes. The structure of the medieval economy aggravated this tendency as some historians have observed: 'A market economy and a subsistence level of production – this could be a most unfortunate combination, and those who lived with it lived dangerously'.[12] For many such people drifting into petty crime to avoid destitution would have been a temptation at times of economic recession. Evidence from court sources suggests that the period around 1300 saw an upsurge in petty crime which accompanied just such a period of economic distress. For example, a close relationship has been shown between women stealing food and clothing and years of poor harvests.[13] And if the items stolen were worth more than 12 pence these criminals were hanged. The unsettled years of the later fourteenth century were similarly accompanied by increased crime, as well as by societal anxieties which are not unique to the Middle Ages. In 1376 the House of Commons petitioned for stricter penalties against vagrants. This was one of a number of such petitions associated with falling grain prices and landlords laying off large numbers of agricultural labourers. The interesting point is that it was the increase in the numbers of mobile workers which alarmed the propertied classes, and indeed it may well have been the case that among such groups of wandering and begging workers there was an increased inclination towards crime. There are echoes here of the later Elizabethan laws against vagrancy during another economic downturn in the later sixteenth century.

The problem did not go away and further laws against vagrants were passed in 1414 and 1446. The later Vagrancy Act of 1495 stated that beggars should be arrested, put in the stocks for three days and afterwards returned to their original place of residence. The idea was taken up by local authorities in a number of cases. In 1500 city authorities in Gloucester ordered the registration of all beggars and, in 1504, expelled most from the city. In 1515 the authorities in York issued official badges to beggars who – due to illness or injury – were considered legitimate, in order to differentiate them from those considered work-shy and a social nuisance. These latter, termed throughout the sixteenth century as *sturdy beggars*, were the subject of a long-lived social panic but may indeed have been associated with rising crime statistics. In 1531 a national law took up practices already experimented with in places such as York; by this act all beggars were to be classed as either worthy of licence or liable to punishment. Justices of the Peace were ordered to put the new law into effect. More and more towns adopted the badge scheme. In 1533 an ordinance in London banned begging, put beggars to work (paid for by charitable gifts to a central fund) and sent their children into household service. As with so much of such legislation, in which experiments in social policy in different towns were later taken up by national government, this radical scheme became effective nationwide by a law of 1536. This decision was accelerated by the problems caused by closing down monastic almshouses and hospitals which had previously assisted many poor people. The new law may have been thought necessary because of the closing of Catholic institutions, but its implementation was slowed down by Catholic practices. Alms giving was too strong a tradition within medieval Christianity to ban it. In 1552 the government again attempted legislation to enforce the law of 1536, but this time without attempting to ban voluntary alms giving.

The extent of the 'moral panic' over beggars is seen in the attempt, in 1547, by the Vagrancy Act to temporarily enslave beggars as a way of forcing them to work. This law was impossible to enforce, however, and was repealed, but it reveals the depth of the concern gripping the minds of lawmakers in the mid-sixteenth century. That there was a major social problem lying behind this anxiety cannot be denied. In 1549 and 1550 both Norwich and York introduced compulsory taxes to support the *deserving poor*. And earlier, in 1546, a textile factory employing about 2,000 unemployed people was established in Oxford. While this illustrates a concern with separating out the 'deserving' from the 'undeserving' (without tackling the underlying causes of the increase in unemployment), at least these responses attempted to provide some relief to the unemployed as opposed to criminalizing them.

Given the heightened activities against groups of lower-class beggars, it is a revealing contrast to examine the impotence of the law when facing organized crime. Some of the most striking examples of crime of the fourteenth century were caused by organized gangs of criminals, often linked to members of the lower aristocracy. Such gangs of well-connected thugs could terrorize a region. This was certainly the case in the early fourteenth century with the Folville and the Coterel gangs.[14]

Medieval criminality flourished especially in times of political turbulence. During the reign of Edward II and the early years of the reign of Edward III a number of well-connected gangs terrorized large areas of England with virtual impunity. The status of their leaders as members of the local aristocracy gave them power and connections which allowed them to escape royal justice and to further their careers of criminal brutality. In their levels of criminality and in their apparent immunity to government action they resembled the organized crime gangs that have at times plagued modern states. None were more notorious that the Folvilles and the Coterels. The Folvilles were a group of younger brothers from a Leicestershire gentry family.

For about a decade they terrorized their local community from their base at Ashby Folville, which they called 'The Castle of the Four Winds'. They committed murder, rape, assault, robbery and kidnapping. In 1326 the Folville brothers murdered a senior member of the government tax-gathering service. In 1332 they kidnapped and ransomed a royal judge, Sir Richard Willoughby. Through their intimidation of local juries and assisted by the corruption of judges and sheriffs they escaped punishment. In alliance with another criminal gang – the Coterel brothers – their reign of crime extended into Nottinghamshire and Derbyshire. In the absence of an effective policing system such violent and determined medieval criminals were more common than might otherwise be imagined.

The tendency of such gangs to target certain vulnerable groups, such as travellers on the open road, led to the Statute of Winchester in 1285 ordering that a verge should be cleared of brushwood for 200 feet on either side of the highway, in order to avoid providing cover for thieves preying on travellers. The road between London and Winchester was so regularly menaced by gangs of robbers at the time of Winchester's St Giles' Fair each September that the city authorities at Winchester organized patrols along the road to deter these criminals.

These organized criminal gangs often escaped the application of the full rigour of the law because of their powerful connections and a significant level of corruption amongst the law enforcement agencies in the regions. This stands in marked contrast with the amount of energy such agencies put into punishing beggars. More common than such well-connected criminal gangs were cases where peasant families cooperated in less serious crimes such as sheep stealing.[15] The crimes of theft, burglary and receiving stolen goods appear frequently in manorial records as indicators of these local webs of criminality. In this way, at Wakefield (Yorkshire) in 1316, Adam Vapurnient of Wiveley and Agnes Spire were accused of 'burgling the house of Robert Alayn of Bretton and stealing woollen and linen clothes, meat and other goods to the value of

5 marks. Margaret of the Wodhall of Wiveley to be attached [arrested] for receiving them and the stolen goods.' There was clearly a rash of such crimes in Wakefield since the record relating to the opening of the manor court had earlier referred to 'frequent burglaries and the great number of thieves' in the area. The same court then went on to list some 8 acts of violence and 16 thefts under investigation. Within the latter were the cases of Eva and William, who had received stolen goods; John Maufesour for burglary; Thomas the forester for stealing a dish and a carpet from the same house; Mauger the Turner for assisting thieves; Henry Shepherd and his brother John who were hanged for stealing horses and cattle; Marjory for burglary and stealing money, a tunic, a surcoat and a silver buckle; Richard of the Ker who caught a nameless thief burgling his own house but, as well as retrieving a stolen shirt, also recovered (but kept for himself) a shirt the thief had taken from the house of Robert the Leper; and at the same time Maud the daughter of Richard of the Ker had stolen food from this same Robert the Leper's house. Finally, there was Elias the Saucer who stole 40 herrings which were worth 4 pence. In addition, the above-mentioned Richard of the Ker was apparently keeping 'Margaret daughter of Thomas in incest', though what this meant is unclear.[16] All of this speaks of a high level of criminality in one community.

The continued economic problems of the mid-fifteenth century saw increased anxiety on the part of lawmakers and law enforcers concerning the criminality of the lower classes. Some of this has already been touched on with regard to begging, but the concern ran deeper and wider than anxieties over vagrancy. Local courts were increasingly concerned with matters relating to unrest at alehouses, problems of gambling, and accusations of prostitution and other forms of sexual immorality. Disorder seemed to be on the increase, and the court records from 1450 onwards reflect this 'reality', or this 'anxiety'; it is difficult to tell which word best describes what was occurring. What was definitely going on was a growing willingness of courts to take on matters of morality which before 1400 would have been considered the responsibility of Church courts. Prosecution of adultery and fornication and punishing of prostitutes increasingly became matters of concern to local courts. Priests occur in increasing numbers among those accused of sexual offences, including charges of rape. When this is viewed alongside a number of examples of parishioners castrating their local priest it seems clear that the moral mood was changing within a significant section of the population. In this there was a flowing together of two currents: anxieties over increasing disorder on one hand, and on the other a trend towards personal spirituality that was more focused on expectations of holy living.

How far these currents flowed across society is difficult to judge, but they were clearly highly influential as the fifteenth century gave way to the sixteenth, and would influence how many areas of society would develop in the later Middle Ages and beyond. In 1492 this new mood was summed up in new civic laws passed in Coventry. The intention was to radically reform the moral structure and character of the town and threatened the disciplining of urban officials found guilty of adultery and the punishment of barmaids if they were considered to be acting as prostitutes. The reference to women was telling. The new mood contained a high level of anxiety over illicit sexual activity, which was increasingly being regarded as a crime, with lone women accused of encouraging prostitution and petty criminality. The Coventry ordinances attempted to put an end to economically (and hence socially) independent single women by insisting that any single women younger than 50 should go into service with a household until they were married.

The abuses and limitations of the law

As with all systems, the system of law in the Middle Ages was open to abuse. Royal justices were at times accused of corruption. Indeed, Sir Thomas Willoughby, who was kidnapped by the Folville gang, was himself accused of selling laws 'as if they had been oxen or cattle'. As we saw earlier, under Canon Law those lay people who were able to quote a memorized Latin verse of the Bible could escape the punishments of the royal courts by claiming the right to be tried by Church courts instead. In addition, the cost of litigation meant that wealthy landowners could financially cripple rivals by bringing land disputes to court even if the case was dubious. Numerous examples exist of such cases and also of aggressive litigants accompanying these actions with violence and intimidation as part of a campaign against a rival. By the fifteenth century such disputes had become so widespread that many landowners thought it prudent to send a son to the Inns of Court, in London, where lawyers were trained. Having a lawyer in the family was a useful weapon in a local landowner's arsenal of defence (and attack). The increasing scale of legal property disputes can be seen in the fact that while some 900 writs were issued in the early fourteenth century, about 2,500 were issued in the early sixteenth century.

The Paston family of East Anglia (famous for their surviving letters) were locked in just such a bitter dispute with a rival – Lord Moleyns – over the ownership of the manor of Gresham (Norfolk). Each side used violence at different times to take control of the manor. John's wife, Margaret, wrote to him in 1449:

> Get some crossbows and wyndlacs [hooks to wind back the bow] to wind them with and quarrels [crossbow bolts]. For this house has so few of them that none of our men can shoot out, although we have never had so much need.
>
> Partryche [one of Lord Moleyn's men] and his friends are frightened that you will get in [to the house they had taken from the Pastons]. They have made bars to bar the doors, and they have made wykets [holes to fire through] on every corner of the house to shoot out through, both with bows and hand-guns.
>
> I ask that you will make sure that you buy me 1 lb of almonds and sugar and that you will buy some frese [cloth] to make a gown for your child.

Crossbows, arrows, some almonds and sugar, plus some cloth for a spot of home-tailoring . . . Just an everyday shopping list for Margaret Paston! While this may have been a rather extreme example, it illustrates how violent such disputes over land could become. And it could occur on a much smaller scale too. In 1451 the Pastons were in dispute with neighbours again. This time it was over a wall which neighbours claimed encroached on their land. John Paston's mother, Agnes, wrote to him: 'Someone came from church and pushed down all that was built there and trod on the wall and broke some – but I cannot discover who it was.' Later, in November 1451, she wrote to him again of a report that she had received: 'Men from Paston [village] would not go on procession further than the churchyard on St Mark's day. For the route of the procession was blocked, and that men hoped that in a short time the wall would be broken down again.'[17]

Despite the problems of the Pastons, the legal system in the Middle Ages was fairly effective at protecting property rights and titles but much less effective in tackling crimes of violence against the person. It was almost totally ineffective, for example, in punishing rape. Such ineffectiveness was aggravated when the accused were well connected and able to intimidate jurors and/or bribe judges. As with much crime prior to the twentieth century with its modern forensic aids, detection was almost impossible and most successful prosecutions relied on a criminal being caught in the act, or being accused by someone who had (or claimed to have) knowledge of the crime. Court records reveal the kinds of cases in which justice was most easily applied: 'Wakelin the son of Ranulf killed Matilda Day with a knife. The village, and twelve jurors, testify that he was caught in the act with a bloodstained knife, and so it cannot be denied. He is to be hanged.'[18] However, at times careful investigation might lead to successful prosecution if witnesses could be tracked down and persuaded to speak. In this way, in 1248, the gang of people responsible for robbing two foreign merchants at Alton (Hampshire) were eventually tracked down and several hanged. A similar process tracked down those responsible for attacking and robbing Geoffrey Chaucer at New Cross, in 1390. But, of course, both these crimes affected members of the elite, who were well placed to put pressure on the authorities to pursue those responsible. In the event of such a crime being discovered it was the duty of any citizen who became aware of it to raise the *hue and cry*, and it was then the duty of all who heard to join in and attempt to catch the offender. For raising the hue and cry unjustly against another, a person could be fined, as was Agnes Brigge, who was fined 3 pence at Brandon (Suffolk) in 1385 for wrongly raising the hue and cry against John Folsham.[19]

When a crime was brought to court the medieval system faced the difficult question of how to prove guilt, or establish innocence. Early answers to this quandary relied on processes which were designed to test innocence by reference to God, or the neighbours of an accused. With regard to God, the use of *ordeal* involved a defendant undergoing a severe physical test. For example, the defendant was required to pick up a hot object and the state of the wound was then checked after three days; healing being taken to indicate innocence. An alternative was *trial by combat*, in which defendant and accuser faced each other in battle and victory was thought to go to the one of which God approved. Trial by ordeal was abolished in 1215 and trial by battle declined quickly, but was not formally abolished until 1819! On the other hand reliance on neighbours involved an accused person finding enough people of sufficient standing who would be willing to swear on oath concerning the good behaviour and character of the accused. The flaws of this procedure are immediately apparent. Firstly, a person's previous actions are not necessarily a guarantee of their innocence in a current accusation. Secondly, it raised the obvious problem of a defendant's innocence being established solely on the basis of their skills at social networking.

The system of oath swearers developed into the more effective system of *trial by jury* during the thirteenth century.

In this system elements of the previous system were combined with an attempt to create a more neutral and effective approach, as local juries were supposedly selected from reliable people who then swore to reach a verdict based on local knowledge of events and reputations. Such a system could be very effective. Henry of Bretteby killed his son when the two were out ploughing. But the jury of local men knew the two well and were sure it was an accident because, as the verdict records: 'They know for a truth that Henry would rather have killed himself than his only son'.[20] This use of juries increasingly developed into a system which examined the limited evidence in order to reach a verdict. It was this system of evidence and of trial by jury which Magna Carta refers to:

> Article 38: In future no official shall place a man on trial upon his own unsupported statement, without producing credible witnesses to the truth of it.
>
> Article 39: No free man shall be seized or imprisoned, or stripped of his rights or possessions, or outlawed or exiled, or deprived of his standing in any other way, nor will we proceed with force against him, or send others to do so, except by the lawful judgement of his equals or by the law of the land.[21]

However, in deciding guilt, or innocence, the very severity of the law was itself a problem. It was common for juries to declare an item was worth less than a shilling (12 pence) in order to avoid a crime incurring the death penalty. More complex was the matter of pardons. By the mid-fourteenth century it was common for violent criminals to be given a royal pardon in return for military service in the French wars. Charters of pardon could also be bought as a way of raising money for the Crown. This was corruption of justice originating at the highest level. And it helps explain the behaviour, referred to earlier, of some members of the English army in France and on their return to England.

Attitudes towards law: the legend of Robin Hood

The legend of Robin Hood has so coloured our image both of
'him' and of medieval outlaws that it is difficult now to think of
criminality in the Middle Ages without this romantic – and
mythologized – image springing to mind. When, in 2007, a
British Chancellor of the Exchequer presented his budget to
Parliament, the *Independent* newspaper could rest assured that
its readers would fully understand the allusion in its comment:
'Old-style socialists liken themselves to Robin Hood by
seeking to tax the rich to help the poor. But when it comes to
British business, the Chancellor has become a latter-day Sheriff
of Nottingham.'[22] Regardless of whether its readers agreed, or
disagreed, with the political judgement, all will have understood the basis of the characterization Robin Hood = good,
Sherriff of Nottingham = bad. Indeed, so positive is the
modern image of Robin Hood that when a modern Wiltshire-
based Christian charity sought to engage individuals and
companies in Britain with its work among some of the poorest
communities of Eastern Europe, its mission statement declared
it was '. . . committed to relieving poverty through direct
action'. And its name? 'Robin Hood Ministries'.[23] Once again,
we understand the reference and the values of sharing out
wealth to those in need which are inherent in the name. What is
more intriguing is that a fifteenth-century audience would
have understood the reference just as well. We know this
because the first poem celebrating the deeds of Robin Hood
appeared in 1450 (*Robin Hood and the Monk*) and a large
number of records from the same date reveal that dressing up
as Robin Hood was one of the most popular options among
rural communities collecting money for their local church at
celebrations called *May Games*. But who and what was Robin
Hood? And what does the growth of his legend tell us about
popular attitudes towards law and order and definitions of
crime in the Middle Ages?

Firstly, what are the historic origins of the Robin Hood
legend? Perhaps the most detailed analysis of the large amount

of evidence relating to this elusive outlaw has been carried out by Professor James Holt.[24] In short, what emerges from the analysis of a vast amount of complex evidence is that probably the first (securely datable) reference to such a criminal – in this case named *Robert Hod* – is from the York Assizes of 25 June 1225. In this year the king's judges ordered the seizing of the goods of 'Robert Hod, fugitive'. A year after this original record there occurs another reference to this action but this time the outlaw is given the more colloquial name of 'Hobbehod'. Whether this man was the original Robin Hood is impossible to say. The record gives no more information about his crimes, nor his modus operandi, nor the location of his activities. But what is clear is that within about 50 years the same name was appearing as the adopted name of a significant number of criminals. And in these cases they are adopting the *whole name* as a surname, which suggests they considered it an appropriate 'tag' for themselves and their activities. They include:

1262. *William Robehod*, in Berkshire. Crime: membership of an outlaw gang and robbery.

1272. *John Rabunhod*, in Hampshire. Crime: murder.

1272. *Alexander Robehod*, in Essex. Crime: theft.

1286. *Gilbert Robehod*, in Suffolk. Crime: unspecified.

1294. *Robert Robehod*, in Hampshire. Crime: sheep stealing.

These are by no means isolated examples[25] – the name appears again and again in similar circumstances. Clearly, Robin Hood had become a national legend before the end of the thirteenth century. And the criminal nicknames apparently refer to more than just Robin himself. In 1313, in Kent, the search was on for a fugitive accused of murder, named 'John of Shorne, called Little John', a character closely associated with Robin Hood in the later legends. It is likely that the emerging legend owed its origins to the actions of a number of these Robin Hoods: '. . . there was not just one "original" Robin Hood, real or fictional, but many. Each one acknowledged the legend by adopting the surname or by accepting it from others. Each one contributed to it and thereby became difficult to distinguish from the legend itself. Each one was real, committing real crimes, engaged in real adventures . . .'[26]

During the fourteenth century tales associated with Robin Hood became firmly embedded in popular culture. In William Langland's poem *Piers Plowman* (dating from about 1377) the character 'Sloth' confesses:

> I do not know my paternoster perfectly as the priest sings it.
> But I know rhymes of Robin Hood [written as Robyn hood]
> and Randolf, earl of Chester.[27]

We would like to know more about what specific activities had become associated with the legendary outlaw by this period. However, while there is little specific information regarding the 'shape' of the legend in the fourteenth century, this is remedied in the fifteenth century when the content of the legends becomes more apparent from the surviving sources. In 1420 Andrew de Wyntoun wrote a rhyming chronicle in which under the years 1283–5 he claimed:

> Then Little John and Robin Hood
> As forest outlaws were well renowned,
> In Inglewood and Barnsdale
> All this time they plied their trade[28]

In the 1440s another Scots writer referred to 'the famous murderer, Robert Hood, as well as Little John' coming to prominence in 1266.[28] Another of the earliest examples of evidence is a piece of graffiti-poetry written on the edge of a 1432 document listing those elected to Parliament from Wiltshire. It pretended to list the surnames of those elected but instead carried the contrived message:

> Robyn,
> hode,
> Inne,

Grenewode,
Stode,
Godeman,
was,
hee.[29]

The question then arises: what are the common features of
these early legends? Certain themes run through a number of
them: the virtue of life in the Greenwood; quarrels amongst the
outlaw band; Robin's devotion to the Virgin Mary; Robin
rewarded by a post in royal service; disguise used to defeat
enemies; villains are the Sheriff of Nottingham, bishops, a
greedy abbot and a treacherous monk; Robin is a yeoman; he is
based in south Yorkshire and Nottinghamshire. What is
missing is rather striking: no battles with quarter-staffs, no
Maid Marian, no mention of Richard the Lionheart (only
'Edward our comely king' is referred to), little mention of
oppressive taxes, no reference to Robin as a dispossessed
nobleman – and there is little about robbing the rich and giving
to the poor! The earliest discernible Robin Hood is a complex
character. He attacks rich monks, the royal Forest Law and the
local sheriff. But he is not a revolutionary. He reveres the king
and there is little evidence of a campaign for social justice.
There is no romance. As a ribald disturber of the peace, he is
the spokesman of the middling sort of yeomen against those
who irritated them and thwarted their ambitions, and he is the
enemy of corrupt and powerful men.

So what does his popularity tell us about medieval attitudes
towards crime? The first thing is that the earlier supporters of
Robin Hood's fame were not deluded into thinking crime was
likely to right wrongs. It was not that which appealed to them.
The evidence suggests that it was a rough-and-ready attraction
towards outlaws who lived by their wits, and to crime which
seemed acceptable because it targeted popular figures of
resentment – such as local government officials and wealthy
Churchmen. Mixed in with this was a romantic notion of life

'in the Greenwood'. In the same way mythologized views of more modern criminals – such as Jesse James, Bonnie and Clyde in the USA, the Great Train Robbers in the UK – offer similar and surprisingly sympathetic views of criminals on the run. These gloss over the violence of their crimes while seeking to reduce the criminality of their actions by defining their victims as depersonalized institutions (such as banks). If the popularity of Robin Hood tells us anything about medieval attitudes towards crime it is probably that, in an environment of fairly widespread petty criminality, people were prepared to tolerate it in others when they themselves were not affected by it and when victims did not evoke sympathy. This sounds very like the reality expressed in the court record of Richard of the Ker apprehending a thief who was stealing from him, but being quite prepared to help himself to the shirt of Robert the Leper. In the absence of more detailed crime statistics, this is probably as far as the analysis will take us. But it does seem to offer an insight into a fairly common medieval outlook.

Chapter 8

LANGUAGE, CULTURE AND ENTERTAINMENT

Before the Norman Conquest the native speech of the Anglo-Saxons was high status enough for legal and government documents to use it alongside the universal language of Western Christendom – Latin. The technical name for this Anglo-Saxon language is *Old English*. It is found in sources as varied as charters, government writs and translations of the Bible. The particular dialect that had become dominant by the eleventh century was that of central southern England – the Old English of Wessex.

For two centuries after 1066 the English language went into social decline. Norman-French and Latin (the educated language of the Church) replaced Old English for the elite and the upwardly mobile. William I gave up his early attempts to learn English and England would not have a ruler whose first language was English until Henry IV in 1399. This linguistic social divide is fossilized in the modern English language. We eat *beef*, *mutton* and *pork* (derived from Norman-French *boef*, *moton, porc*); but those who care for them in the fields and barns labour with *cows, sheep* and *pigs/swine* (derived from Old English *cu, sceap* and Middle English *pigge*/Old English *swin*). The language of the worker and the language of the one who enjoyed the product of their labour was not the same. It is a post-1066 linguistic and social separation.

However, English remained the language of the majority of the population even if the more upwardly mobile and economically active needed to learn Norman-French as well. Norman-French itself began to develop into a rather provincial form of French and this increased as English rulers lost land in France in the early thirteenth century. This left the French language of England increasingly isolated, although it took another 150 years and the growing patriotism which accompanied the upsurge of wars against France in the fourteenth century for English to finally regain social acceptability in England. When Chaucer wrote *Troilus and Criseyde* in about 1380 and later went on to write the *Canterbury Tales* it was English that he used. And about this time a number of French books began to be translated into English.

But even during the period 1066–1380, English did not vanish as a literary language. It continued to be used in some areas of government: royal charters, for example. Even during the late eleventh to mid-twelfth centuries Old English texts (especially saints' lives and grammar books) continued to be copied and adapted. From the later twelfth and thirteenth centuries there survive many examples of written material in English: song lyrics, saints' lives, devotional manuals, histories and poems. Early-fourteenth-century romances, such as *Havelok the Dane*, illustrate the influence of English among educated members of the urban merchant class. During this period the English that was emerging was different from the Wessex-based Old English of late Anglo-Saxon government and literature. What was emerging was *Middle English*.

Middle English is the name given to the forms of the English language spoken between the Norman invasion and the late fifteenth century. After this period *Chancery Standard*, a form of London-based English, began to become widespread. This later process was aided by the introduction of the printing press into England by William Caxton in the 1470s. The language of England spoken after this time, up to 1650, is known as *Early Modern English*. In the north other changes occurred, as the Northumbrian dialect of Middle English spoken in south-east Scotland developed into a dialect known as *Scots*.

By the time Middle English emerged as a high-status language in the literature of the late fourteenth century it had gained a great deal of vocabulary from French. This was not surprising. Ranulph Higden, in his Latin work of history, the *Polychronicon* of 1330, commented that educated children were 'compelled to abandon their own language and to construe their lessons and their tasks in French' and the ambitious learnt French 'in order to be more highly thought of.' It is therefore no surprise that many of the French words which entered regular English usage are from relatively high on the social scale: *abbey, beauty, fashion, government, music, nation, parliament, prince.* Others had a more immediate impact: *colour, parish, prayer, saint.* By 1350, though, French was losing the battle with Middle English.

The Middle English of the fourteenth and fifteenth centuries was an amalgamation of the dialects and vocabularies of the literary cultures of the West Midlands, London and East Anglia. It was not the language of southern and western England, whose dialects were already sounding parochial and rural and would later feature in the way 'rustics' talk in Shakespearean plays. If English was on the way up, it was not the direct descendant of the kings of Wessex. But it was this new kind of English which appeared in the works of Geoffrey Chaucer, William Langland, Thomas Occleve, Thomas Malory and William Caxton. English had once again become the respectable language of literature and culture. This coincided with increasing literacy. The early fifteenth century witnessed the first attempt by ordinary laypeople to write their own history, in the so-called *London Chronicles*. The earliest of these chronicles represents the first generation of historical writing to be undertaken in English since the writing of the Anglo-Saxon Chronicle stopped in the mid-twelfth century.[1]

The exception to this progress in the use of English was the Bible. Bibles in English had existed in Anglo-Saxon times and, as early as the late seventh century, the Northumbrian monk Bede started to translate the Bible into Old English. In a similar way, the West Saxon scholar Aldhelm (640–709) translated the Book of Psalms and large parts of other books of the Bible into Old English. Then in the eleventh century, Elfric translated most of the Old Testament into Old English. In short, the English Bible was not an invention of Wyclif in the late fourteenth century, as is often assumed. There was, in fact, no prohibition on non-Latin Bibles, and Bibles in French as well as selections of the Bible in English were used by some aristocrats before the fourteenth century. But the problem was twofold. Firstly, the earliest complete translation of the Bible in the late fourteenth century was associated with the Lollards and so the whole enterprise became suspect. Secondly, even as late as 1400 English had not yet achieved the status which made it acceptable amongst the most educated of the elite. As a result, in 1409 strict controls were placed on translating the Bible into English. Possession of English Bibles had become associated with heresy and the link would not be broken until the English *Great Bible* of 1539 was ordered to be placed in every parish church.

Personal names
The decline of English after 1066 revealed itself in many ways. Anglo-Saxon personal names were very varied, from complex two-element names such as Ethelred, Wulfstan, Ethelthryth and Elfgifu to simpler forms such as Cutha, Hwituc, Duduc and Tuma, which had themselves been created as pet forms of more complex names. Into this situation the Norman

Conquest brought a raft of new names (often Germanic but influenced by French): William, Henry, Geoffrey, Robert, Odo, Matilda, Rosamund. Accompanying this was a trend to name from the Bible (which was a fashion being seen across western Europe): Andrew, Matthew, Stephen. The growing cult of the Virgin increased the giving of the name Mary from the mid-twelfth century. A similar process, but focused on John the Baptist, encouraged the use of the names John and Joan from the 1160s.

Anglo-Saxon and Danish names continued to be given into the twelfth century but then went into a steep decline in favour of the new personal names which had a higher social cachet since they were the names favoured by the new elite. In Lincolnshire, around Louth, by the 1220s only 6 per cent of tenants listed in a survey of 624 people had pre-Conquest names of any kind, but 14 per cent were called William, 9.5 per cent were called Robert and 6.5 per cent were named John. These three 'new' names alone made up 30 per cent of the total name stock! The trend continued to accelerate. By 1300 male names were dominated by John, Peter, Thomas and William; female names by Elizabeth, Mary and Anne.[2] Analysis of the Poll Tax returns for Sheffield in 1379 shows that of the 715 men assessed for tax, 33 per cent were named John and 19 per cent William; a total of 52 per cent of males carrying just these two names. The only Anglo-Saxon name used was Edward and it was not found among the top eight names, which were, in descending order: John, William, Thomas, Richard, Robert, Adam, Henry and Roger.[3] It is little wonder that manorial court records from the thirteenth century have clerks wearily noting 'another William . . .' as they record those paying fines and taking part in the proceedings.

One spin-off from this implosion of names from the great variety which had existed before 1066 was the rise of the hereditary surname. This was a development accelerated by an increase in government taxation bureaucracy and a rise in population, which meant it was becoming difficult to differentiate people by given (Christian) name alone. The Anglo-Norman aristocracy first experimented with surnames, or bynames. The fashion rippled out to better-off Londoners by about 1150 and across society during the thirteenth century. By the Lay Subsidy Roll taxation return of 1327 surnaming was well established, though not absolute. These early surnames, though, were highly flexible and not yet necessarily hereditary. Such names might vary across a person's lifetime and change from one generation to another, but the hereditary principle was growing – assisted by the permanence encouraged by official record keeping. Consequently, by 1400 almost everyone had a hereditary surname.

Of all surnames the largest number were 'local surnames', named from local places. Of these, some indicated foreign origins – such as Fleming and Bremner (from Barbant) – but most were named from English towns, villages and farmsteads such as Wiltshire, Ashley and *Bristow* (from Bristol). Others were more local still and referred to intimate details of the local landscape. Examples include: *Uppehulle* (up hill), *atte Forde*, *atte Crosse*, *West*, *atte Tonesend* (town's end) and *atte Bakhouse* (Bakehouse), all found in one Somerset village (Keynsham) in the Lay Subsidy tax returns for 1327 (the last one being as much an occupational as a locational name). Many of these, as these examples show, were originally preceded by a preposition such as *de*, *at*, *by*, *in*. Examples include Richard *de Hadestoke*, a London alderman in 1240 and named from Hadstock (Essex), or William *Attebroc*, recorded in 1199. These prepositions began to be dropped after 1400 though some, such as *atte Wode* and *by Field*, survived into modern surnames such as Atwood and Byfield.

Another large group of names indicated a person's relationship to another. Many were *patronymics* of the type which would eventually give us Jackson, Hodgson, Richardson. Others referred to different relationships, such as the examples *Hannebrothir* and *Ibbotdoghter* recorded in 1324 in the Manor of Wakefield, or *Spenserdoghter* and *Jacksonwyf* recorded in the 1379 Poll Tax for Lancashire. Few of these survived to become modern surnames, the exceptions being those few containing the relationship word *magh* (brother-in-law), such as Hitchmough and Hickmott.

Many surnames were occupational names: such as Webster, Weaver, Fletcher, Smith. Some survive in modern surnames long after their specialist medieval craft terms have been forgotten: Billeter (bell founder), Chaucer (shoe maker) and Harbisher (maker of knight's mail hauberks). A small number of these might have been given in jest, such as in the cases of Roger *le Mounk*, recorded in Norwich in 1318, who was actually a baker, or the Londoner, William called *le Clerk*, who was in reality a butcher in 1336.

Others surnames were nicknames. William *catface* is found in at least one manorial record! It has not survived as a modern surname and neither did the names of William *Two yer old*, from the estate of Ronton Priory in Staffordshire in 1311, or Margaret *Tenwynter*, in Suffolk in 1476 (what these meant as adult surnames is unknown). But Vidler (wolf-face) has, and so has Gulliver (glutton). There are many such modern surnames which derive from the observations of medieval neighbours and workmates. Some probably reveal characteristics well known to neighbours, such as Henry *Nevereafered* (never afraid), recorded in 1334 at Keynsham (Somerset). Then there was William *Standupryght*, recorded at Ricknall (County Durham) in 1355, whose bad behaviour was causing his neighbours to leave the manor. So, was his surname ironic, or a reference to a man who aggressively defended his own interests? Or was he named this for another reason entirely? The name is intriguing but we cannot now say why it was conferred.

A relatively small number of modern surnames have their origins in pre-1066 personal names. These names (about 560 in total) make up about 4.6 per cent of modern British surnames and derive from names which had already become hereditary by the time they appear in fourteenth-century taxation returns[4] – when other, emerging, surnames were still in a state of flux. Clearly, after 1066 some families (for reasons that are now unrecoverable) persisted in giving Anglo-Saxon, or Anglo-Scandinavian, personal names until these names became so associated with their family that they developed into hereditary medieval surnames. Names such as Whittock (recorded in the Lay Subsidy Roll for Somerset in 1327, in the form *Wyttok* but ultimately derived from the Old English, *Hwituc*) are a thread connecting the 'medieval invention' of surnames with the Anglo-Saxon past. They were like fossils embedded in the shifting matrix of changing medieval naming fashions, which had otherwise abandoned the forms and conventions of pre-1066 name giving.

Education

Many people in the Middle Ages were illiterate, but amongst elite families and the upwardly mobile there was greater emphasis on education. However, in the earlier Middle Ages many within the elite (despite the very early attempts of Alfred of Wessex in the ninth century to force the governing classes to learn to read and write) would have relied on the clerks in their households to provide the necessary literacy. Where there was education among such families it would have been based on home tutoring. From the later fourteenth century, grammar schools provided instruction in Latin grammar for the upwardly mobile in towns. Parish priests at times offered assistance to those lower down the social scale. This was sometimes provided by priests in chantries. At Rothwell (Yorkshire, West Riding) a priest ran a small school in 1408 and nunneries often provided elementary education for both girls and boys. Some elementary education may have been provided outside the oversight of the Church, but the evidence for this is slight. During the fifteenth century evidence increases for the provision of grammar schools in a number of towns. By the later fifteenth century most middle- and upper-class males were literate, as were many women in these classes. Even lower down the social scale there was a surprising degree of literacy, if measured by the ability to read, rather than to write.

To be educated beyond the grammar school involved attendance at one of the two universities of Oxford and Cambridge. Evidence for organization of colleges at these two towns dates from 1214, in the case of Oxford, and 1225, in the case of Cambridge. In this earlier period the education was controlled by the friars, although Benedictines were also active at Oxford. From the 1450s the Cistercians and Augustinians also became involved in running colleges.

Around 1380 there may have been as many as 2,000 students at Oxford and Cambridge (most were at Oxford). By 1450 it had risen to about 3,000. Many of these students would have been young men hoping to follow a career in the Church; others would have been existing clergy working to improve the level of their learning. Many of the former would have been in their mid-teens. Lodging privately gave way, over time, to living communally in halls. From the mid-fourteenth century these were replaced by the emerging colleges, which provided lecturers and lodging for students. The process began earlier at Cambridge than at Oxford. Early colleges at Cambridge included Peterhouse (1284), Clare (1326), Pembroke (1347), Gonville (1348, refounded 1351), Trinity Hall (1350) and Corpus Christi (1352); early Oxford colleges included New College (1379), All Souls (1438) and Magdalene (1448). A statute of 1406 ordered that any family could send its children for education. This overturned earlier customs which stopped villeins from doing this and their sons from being ordained into the Church. By 1500 about 66 per cent of students at New College were from upwardly mobile farming families.

At these universities the majority of students studied arts degrees. These were comprised of the *trivium* of grammar, rhetoric and dialectic (resolving disagreements through rational discussion) and the *quadrivium* of arithmetic, music, astronomy and geometry. Only about 33 per cent of fifteenth-century Oxford students completed the degree course to bachelor graduation after up to six years. Others stayed much shorter times and covered only part of the available course. For those wishing to study the Common Law (see Chapter 7), alternative establishments existed in the Inns of Court in London. From about 1250 collections of students receiving instruction from lawyers grew up there in the same process which lay behind the creation of the university halls and colleges. These colleges were Inner Temple, New Temple, Gray's Inn and Lincoln's Inn. Nearby, another tier of colleges grew up – the Inns of Chancery – at which many students started to study before progressing to the Inns of Court.

The written word

This restricted access to education in the era before the printing press exalted the status of the handwritten word. The most famous examples of the Latin script of the Middle Ages are those found in the handwritten documents produced in monastic scriptoria. These were often elaborately orna-mented, giving us the term *illuminated writing*. The whole process was time consuming: from scraping and stretching the finest calfskin to make the *vellum*, to ruling the guide lines, to writing and illustrating the text. The ink used varied from the fading oak apple gall to the messy lampblack. Any errors might be carefully incorporated into the design by a skilled scribe but would be a major problem for a less accomplished writer. As one scribe apologetically commented on a spoiled page: 'Bad vellum, new ink'.

In the 1250s most manuscripts contained theological, litur-gical and academic material. However, this changed over the next 250 years. By the fifteenth century the variety increased dramatically to include romances, chronicles, medical texts, rolls of coats-of-arms and aristocratic family trees (such as the *Rous Roll* and the *Beauchamp Pageant*), guild records from towns, texts of plays and musical scores. Some, such as the *Confessio Amantis* (*The Lover's Confession*), combined themes of Christian confession with Classical mythology and the exploration of courtly love. This particular work is a 33,000-line Middle English poem by John Gower. In it a lover complains first to Venus and later confesses to her priest, Genius. The *Confessio*, probably completed by about 1390, is an important addition to courtly love literature in English. This shift of emphasis in subject matter is explained by a number of different factors such as increasing literacy, rising living standards and intellectual expectations of urban groups, the appearance of paper during the fourteenth century (cheaper than vellum) and the development of printing after the middle of the fifteenth century. All of this greatly expanded the number of lay consumers of books. It is significant that when, in 1476, William Caxton established the first printing press in England (at Westminster), the first books he printed included Chaucer's *Canterbury Tales*, Gower's *Confessio Amantis* and Malory's *Le Morte d'Arthur*. This was a little light reading for the new class of lay readers. There is something surprisingly modern in Caxton's choice of genre – gossip, 'kiss and tell' and high drama among the rich and famous.

As noted above, the invention of printing had a great impact on medieval libraries, as handwritten texts were replaced by printed ones. The arrival of these early printed books, or *incunabula*, as they are termed, meant that many handwritten manuscripts were discarded long before the Reformation. This was accelerated by manuscripts passing out of the protective ownership of the great monastic libraries. For example, the library of Christ Church, Canterbury lost about half of its manuscripts to Oxford *before* the Reformation. This was because as individual monks went to study in Oxford they took manuscripts with them which they then treated as their own personal property. These were often then sold or pawned in Oxford. By the sixteenth century Oxford bookbinders often used leaves from old manuscripts to strengthen the covers of printed books, which clearly suggests that the market had been flooded with these handwritten manuscripts.[5]

Later, during the Reformation, many monastic libraries were devastated. The Act against Superstitious Books and Images (1550) ordered that service books which did not comply with the latest liturgy should be destroyed. This resulted in a huge loss of books. For example, only six books are known to survive from the 350 held by Meaux Abbey in Yorkshire. The only medieval libraries which survived intact were those belonging to the cathedrals of Durham, Exeter, Hereford, Salisbury and Worcester. In these cases monastic collections were protected because they were passed on to secular communities. Some monks attempted to preserve collections by taking books with them when monasteries were dissolved. At Monk Bretton (in Yorkshire), the last prior had possession of 142 former monastic books as late as 1558. John Bale, a collector of medieval manuscripts, wrote with sorrow in 1549 how collections of manuscripts were taken 'some to serue (serve) theyr iakes (privies as toilet paper), some to scoure theyr candelstyckes, and some to rubbe their bootes.'[6] The seventeenth-century writer John Aubrey wrote of how medieval manuscripts were treated in Malmesbury (Wiltshire). Here the destruction was that of the library of Malmesbury Abbey – a religious community whose roots went back to the eighth century or earlier. But this was no barrier to those who used its manuscripts as dustcovers for school books, stoppers for barrels of ale and scourers for cleaning the barrels of guns. When one considers this treatment of the accumulated libraries of the Middle Ages, the sheer shock and extent of this cultural vandalism is difficult to express. The work of scriptoria over the centuries went to toilet paper and cleaning kitchen utensils.

Of course this was not the fate of all such books. Matthew Parker, Archbishop of Canterbury (died 1575), was one of many collectors who protected great numbers of books. His collection included many priceless Anglo-Saxon manuscripts, including the oldest version of the *Anglo-Saxon Chronicle* and copies of translations of Latin texts made at the ninth-century court of Alfred of Wessex. Sir Robert Cotton (died 1631) attempted to create a national library, and his collection included manuscripts of such astonishing value as the *Lindisfarne Gospels*, two original copies of *Magna Carta*, *Beowulf* and versions of the

Anglo-Saxon Chronicle. Some account books and registers passed to the new owners of monastic land. Some were taken abroad, such as the *Psalter of Christina of Markyate* (made at St Albans Abbey in the 1130s), which now belongs to the church at Hildesheim in Germany. These are today some of the intellectual treasures of the English language. But they are only a tiny fraction of what had once existed but were destroyed.

Despite the fact that access to written forms of expression was limited to the literate minority, aspects of literate culture were sometimes seized on by non-literate members of society in order to express their own individuality. This is clearly seen in the use of wax seals, with which important written documents in the Middle Ages were frequently completed. Most were made and used in the thirteenth and early fourteenth centuries, with their use declining in the fifteenth and sixteenth centuries. In the later period, as literacy increased, the seal gave way to the signature. However, in the earlier period even many nobles could not write and the seal offered a combination of personal flourish and official statement. These often consisted of two parts – a central symbol representing the person and a text running round the edge. The word *seal* can be applied to both the wax impression and the *die*, or *matrix*, used to make it. The most famous of these are those associated with royalty and nobles. Royal seals, called *Seals of Majesty* (showing the seated ruler) first appear in the eleventh century. That of Edward the Confessor (1042–66) survives and shows the king enthroned, holding sceptre and sword. These were used on the writs (administrative commands) of later Anglo-Saxon England. William the Conqueror's seal, like that of Edward the Confessor, was a double-sided one and showed him on horseback on one side and enthroned on the other. Knights' seals also usually showed them armed and on horseback. Some showed them hunting. However, seals were not just associated with government and the powerful.

A number of lower-class people signalled their individual identities with the use of seals and these are interesting insights into both medieval individualism and humour. Some, such as the scissors of Geoffrey Le Barbur, found in Berkshire, showed their trade. Many were mass produced and contained no name or personal identification. Instead, they were chosen by the purchaser from a range of options. They might carry legends which were supposed to be humorous, such as: 'Bi the rood Wimen are wode' ('By the Cross, women are mad').[7] In these ways some rather quirky aspects of medieval individuality survive.

Dining and table etiquette

Lords ate in public as part of their social status and relationship with retainers and clients. Paying for great feasts – such as the Duke of Buckingham's Christmas Day dinner for 294 people in 1507 – was a clear statement of power and influence. Kings and archbishops dined in state every day, and access to them was blocked for all but the most powerful. Lesser lords might be more accessible, but etiquette was still strictly adhered to. Raised up on a dais in the Great Hall a lord and his family were literally above those who were socially beneath them. The table nearest the dais, on the lord's right, was called the *Rewarde*, from the fact that it received food from the dishes used on the lord's own table. The table opposite was called the *Second Messe* and the other tables were ranked as they fell further away from the high table. Even the *trenchers* (the bread used instead of plates) were ranked according to quality and freshness and provided in a strict hierarchy amongst the tables. In a similar way the different tables did not enjoy the same choice of dishes.

Children, it was thought, needed a lot of milk but no red meat and – more surprisingly – no fruit. Different food would also be provided for clerics in the lord's household. Church ordinances decreed that no meat should be eaten on Wednesdays, Fridays or Saturdays, or during Lent. These became 'fish days'. However, some communities would eat barnacle goose as it was considered to be more fish than fowl.

Each course served consisted of mixed meat, fish, poultry and sweet dishes. These were served to those on the lord's table but on other tables people helped themselves; on these tables cups might be held in common too. Between courses in a high-status household *soteltes* would be served. These consisted of items sculpted in hard sugar, such as swans or peacocks. At the end of a meal the lord and guests were served with sweet wine, wafers and spices. Finally, grace concluded the meal and a toast was drunk to close the proceedings.

Serving the food was a large team of servants: *sewer* (head waiter), *pantler* (head of the pantry), *butler* (drinks), *ewerer* (hand washing and linen), chief cook, carver and lord's cup-bearer. Out of sight were waiters who brought food no further than the entrance of the hall, scullions, spit boys, pot boys and bottle washers. The laying of table was also complex. The ewerer laid cloths on the tables along with wash basins; the pantler laid out the lord's trencher, rolls wrapped in a napkin, the salt cellar and knives and spoons. It should be noted that forks did not appear in elite households until the fifteenth century.

Eating the meal took place according to strict rules. Hands were washed, the lord's food and drink were tasted, and cooked meats were carved according to exacting standards and formalized rules. Individual behaviour was also the subject of elaborate books of etiquette. These became more common from the thirteenth century but are particularly noticeable by the fifteenth century. Examples include the *Book of the Order of Chivalry*, translated from the French and published by Caxton in 1494, and *The Book of Good Manners*, by Jacques Legrand, along with the *Book of Nurture*, by John Russell, also published in the late fifteenth century. Sometimes the very fact they had to instruct guests not to do certain things suggests that these practices were all too common! Fingernails should be clean; drinking from a shared cup should be avoided so that bits of food did not end up floating in the drink; teeth should not be picked with a knife at table; hot food should not be blown on to cool it; bread should not be crumbled into the common dish; bones should not be gnawed; scratching the head should be avoided, as should spitting and belching.[8] All of which raises the question of how genteel such feasts really were the further one got away from the high table. Among the thirteenth-century table manners one book tells diners to 'refrain from falling upon the dish like a swine while eating, snorting disgustingly and smacking the lips'.

The food eaten at a wealthy feast was from a wider choice than would be acceptable to a modern table: starlings, gulls, herons, cormorants, swans, cranes, peacocks, capons, chickens, dogfish, porpoises, seals, whale, haddock, cod, salmon, sardines, lamprey eels, crayfish and oysters. Turnips, parsnips, carrots, peas and fava beans were common vegetables and the use of onions and garlic was common. Some of these are familiar, while others (seagull for instance) would not be acceptable to modern tastes. Inventories prepared for the 6,000 guests invited to the installation ceremonies of the archbishop of York in 1467 indicate that the guests consumed 300 caskets of ale, 100 caskets of wine, 1 large bottle of wine sweetened with sugar, nutmeg and ginger, 104 oxen, 6 wild bulls, 1,000 sheep, 304 calves, 400 swans, 2,000 geese, 1,000 capons, 2,000 pigs, 104 peacocks, over 13,500 other birds, 500 stags, bucks and roes, 1,500 venison pies, 608 pike and bream, 12 porpoises and seals, 13,000 dishes of jelly, cold baked tarts, custards and spices, sugared delicacies and wafers.

Such foodstuffs would have been beyond the wildest dreams of the vast majority of the population. Poorer peasants survived on broths thickened with barley, or other grains and oatcakes cooked in the ashes of fires or on heated stones. It was common to leave a stockpot on the fire embers during the day into which greens or other foods were added, which was then thickened before eating. However, as wages rose after 1350 larger amounts of meat entered the lower-class diet.

Fashion
Fashion is an important way in which identity, values and status can be displayed within society. Amongst the aristocracy

this could reach astonishing proportions, as when Thomas de Berkeley spent over 10 per cent of his total income on clothes in 1345–6. While leather shoes have been found in waterlogged archaeological deposits, very little else has survived of the fabrics of the Middle Ages. As a result, we have to rely on illustrations and insights into fashion from carvings. And what does survive in these illustrations tells us what the elite minority were wearing – or were expected to wear. We know much less about fashion lower down the social scale. When we learn that shoes with their pointed toes stuffed with moss were fashionable in the 1380s and again in the 1480s we can be sure that we are touching on a matter which affected only a tiny proportion of the total population.

So closely was fashion associated with status that the *sumptuary laws* of the mid-fourteenth century attempted to prescribe exactly who could wear what! There is no reason to think that it ever succeeded, but it gives a top-down view of how things should be. Before the 1320s status was mostly signalled by the amount and quality of clothes worn. After this period there appears to have been an acceleration in fashionable concerns with style and tailoring. This was greatly assisted by the innovation of buttons from around 1350 onwards. These made it easier to wear closer-fitting garments and greater differentiation appears between male and female fashion from this point onwards. This change was assisted by an increased range of imported dyes and fabrics for the elite who could afford the latest trends. The same elaboration shows itself in the greater use of fur and embroidery and the increased complexity of women's headgear as the fifteenth century progressed.

Lower down the social scale there is evidence for a greater impact of fashion after the 1350s, albeit on a much-reduced scale compared with the fashion leaders of society. This revealed itself in increased incidence of linen undergarments, tailored tunics and dyed hoods, hose and cloaks. By 1400 shorter and closer-fitting styles had descended the social ladder from the aristocracy, who had enjoyed these as the height of elite fashion in the 1350s. Cheap mass-produced jewellery also appears in greater quantities in urban sites and reveals a developing mass-production industry designed to meet increased lower-class consumer demand.

The origins of drama

The roots of modern drama lie in the more dramatic areas of Church liturgy in the Middle Ages and in other expressions of Christian faith such as the *Mystery Plays*. These plays were popular from the thirteenth to the sixteenth century. Only four complete cycles of these plays survive from York, Chester, Wakefield (also called the Towneley Cycle) and from an unidentified East Midlands town (the *Ludus Coventriae*). We know that such plays were also performed at the English towns of Bath, Beverley, Bristol, Canterbury, Chester, Coventry, Ipswich, Leicester, Norwich, Northampton, Newcastle-upon-Tyne, Wakefield and Worcester. Mystery Plays are also recorded as taking place at Brome in Suffolk. They provided popular medieval theatre with strong Christian themes. Experts are divided as to the exact origins of these plays but there seem to have been two 'currents' flowing into them. The first was that of liturgical drama. These were dramatic re-enactments of Biblical events which were added to the celebration of the Mass on major feast days. These started as brief explanations, or *tropes*, and developed into dramatic dialogues. On Easter Day, for example, there is evidence that some services included dramatic re-enactments of Mary Magdalene discovering the empty tomb of Christ. At the very least these set a precedent for more free-standing Christian drama and influenced the content of later Mystery Plays. The second 'current' was probably that of processions and folk plays associated with Plough Monday, May Day, Midsummer Day and Christmas. They were characterized by being performed in English, in public places, by amateurs.

The first Mystery Plays were based around the celebration of Corpus Christi, a feast which was initiated in 1264 but which became particularly popular from the early fourteenth century. Falling on the Thursday after Trinity Sunday, this was an early summer event and focused on Christ's saving power revealed in the host (bread) of the Mass. The groups of plays which were performed around this date made up a cycle which told the story of God's saving purposes from the Creation, through the life of Christ, to the Last Judgement. The plays were coordinated and run by a religious guild within the town, but the different parts were contributed to by craft guilds. It was these which gave the plays their names, since these guilds all had a specialist *mestier* (trade) which has given rise to the word *mystery* in the name of these plays. Incidentally this latter word also came to mean something 'hidden' because the trade secrets of such guilds were closely guarded.

The earliest examples of these plays – those in the York cycle – date from the 1370s. While there are similarities between component parts of the cycles from different towns (such as some in the Wakefield and York cycles), others reflect the particular characteristics of areas and composers. Most in the York cycle are very urban, while rural issues such as sheep stealing appear in the Wakefield cycle. This theme is used to both humorous and dramatic effect and highlights the skills of the original composer of the play. In some towns the plays were performed in one place. In most they took place from wagons sited at different places in the town, and people moved from wagon to wagon as the cycle of plays unfolded. Special effects made the performances even more engaging. In Coventry 4 pence was paid to the man keeping the fire burning in hell's mouth.

The religious teaching that was communicated through the Mystery Plays was often embedded in earthy humour and slapstick comedy. Noah's domestic conflicts with his fiery wife are a key feature of the Wakefield, or Towneley, Cycle of plays. The fifteenth-century additions to an earlier structure included raucous and violent comedy. Mrs Noah nags her husband; he calls her a *ramskyt* ('ram shit') and hits her; she thumps him back; later they complain about each other directly to the audience; they fight again. This bickering and domestic disharmony was encouraged by apocryphal stories of Noah and even in their own day were as controversial as they were popular. The Wakefield plays also include shepherds who moan about taxes, robbers, their wives and the weather. Chaucer, in *The Miller's Tale*, complained that such plays did more entertaining than educating. But their popularity clearly lay in more than their comedy – it surely lay in the attempt to make the Biblical accounts accessible and immediate. The Flood and the birth of Christ become events which are set in a world the audience would instantly recognize. When the shepherds, in the Wakefield Cycle, give baby Jesus a pet bird, some cherries, a ball to play with . . . there is no mockery intended. Instead, we see the gifts of poor men to the Son of God who has come amongst them in deepest poverty Himself. The message is simple: to such as us He has come! And when, within the York Cycle's portrayal of the crucifixion, the soldiers appear as everyday workmen amorally carrying out their brutal task, the audience is once more drawn into the drama. But this time the dramatic device is to confront them with the common guilt of Mankind which took Christ to the cross. This is drama with a profound meaning. It is more than entertainment. Those Church leaders who condemned it had not seen through its outer layers to its inner radicalism, which was profoundly Christian.

In the sixteenth century extreme Protestant distrust of Catholic pageantry led first to the censoring of these plays (removing such Catholic themes as the Assumption and coronation of the Virgin Mary) and eventually to their abandonment altogether. This trend was probably further accelerated by the rising costs of the plays at a time when many towns faced both financial difficulties and competition from travelling players offering secular plays. The year 1576 is the last year for which there is any record of performances of the Wakefield Cycle.[9]

The English at play: alcohol

The commonest drink for much of the Middle Ages was *ale*. Usually it was made from barley, oats, or a combination of the two known as *dredge*; wheat was occasionally mixed in but was expensive. The process involved malting the grain to stimulate germination, then drying it to stop the process. It was then threshed. The malted grain was then rough-milled and hot water was added and kept hot for several hours, which allowed the starch to convert to sugar and enter the water. This made a liquid called *wort*, which was left to cool and yeast was added. After several days the mixture would be ready, although herbs were often added (and sometimes spices). The residue was used for a second *mashing* to produce *small ale*, or *small beer* (a much weaker alcoholic drink). Hops were not involved in the process until the early fifteenth century. Ale went off very quickly and there was a swift movement from brewing to selling.

Many households – and certainly large aristocratic ones – brewed their own ale. The finished products were measured in *tuns* and *Winchester gallons*. A tun was the equivalent of 216 gallons of ale, or 252 gallons of wine. A Winchester gallon was the same as a modern US gallon. This made a Winchester gallon the equivalent of 0.8 of an Imperial gallon, later established in 1824 (which itself is about 4.5 litres). As early as Magna Carta, 1215, there was a concern over the reliability of measures for ale (and wine and corn). The Assize of Bread and Ale of 1266 allowed local assize courts the power to regulate the prices of these two essential commodities. The Oxford assize of 1310, for example, decided that ale should cost 1¼ pence a gallon and strong ale 1½ pence per gallon. To give this some meaning, a labourer at the time earned about 1 penny a day and a skilled craftsperson about 6 pence. Ale was sold in quantities of a gallon, quart (2 pints/quarter gallon, or 1.13 litres), or a *pottle* (4 pints, or 2.27 litres). These were measured via jugs carrying seals to confirm their accuracy. In 1364 the alewife Alice de Caustone was found guilty of having 1½ inches of pitch at the bottom of her quart measuring jug – instead of holding 2 pints, the pot's capacity was reduced by 25 per cent. Another issue concerned the strength of ale and it was this which caused the appointment of London's first *ale-conners* in 1377.

As a safer drink than water, ale was seen as a staple foodstuff. Much of the production was the work of women, although men were also involved and it has been estimated that the Cistercian monks of Fountains Abbey (Yorkshire) may have produced as much as 2,200 gallons (10,000 litres) every two weeks; both for consumption within the abbey and for sale outside it. In towns a great deal of the ale was sold via fast-food outlets which also sold pies and other delicacies of questionable quality. At these outlets ale was often sold in the 4-pint quantities called *pottles*. Other sources, of course, were taverns and alehouses. Such alehouses ranged in size from those accommodated in a home to larger establishments such as the alehouse in Paternoster Row, London, which had 60 seats on two floors. Those in a private house were usually run by women termed *ale-wives*. The surname Brewster derives from this occupation and is the female version of Brewer. Inns were much larger establishments, offering rooms for travellers, often with large shared beds. Many were linked to monasteries. Some have become associated with famous events, such as The Tabard at Southwark, where Chaucer's pilgrims gathered before setting out for Canterbury. Taverns, on the other hand, were establishments somewhere between private houses (operating as alehouses) and inns, and were often associated with bawdy behaviour and crime.

Despite the lower alcoholic content of small ale the impact of consuming large quantities of the full brew was as great then as now. The ale-wife Elynour Rummyng, in John Skelton's poem of 1517 (*The Tunning of Elynour Rummyng*), recounts how she and her husband cavorted together following a drinking session:

> Than swetely together we ly
> As two pygges in a sty.[10]

Many communal activities involved consumption of large quantities of alcohol. These were often organized by the church, or the lord, such as Church Ales, Whitsun Ales and Bride Ales. Money raised at these events was often ploughed back into community projects.

In the Middle Ages a clear distinction was drawn between *ale* and *beer*. In the Anglo-Saxon period the word 'beer' had been applied to the drink which was later termed ale. However, after 1066 the word fell out of general use and when it reappeared, in the early fifteenth century, it was used to describe a significantly different beverage. The new term 'beer' was applied to an alcoholic drink made from hops. This drink had a long history of popularity on the continent, but its introduction into England was resisted as a foreign intrusion. As late as 1512 the town authorities in Shrewsbury banned the use of hops in brewing. An interesting illustration of the fondness for the more traditional ale is revealed in the fact that Henry VIII gave his courtiers beer – but reserved ale for himself.

However, there was no resisting the new drink. Beer was more economical to produce since more could be made from the same amount of malt. Furthermore it was safer. Beer mash required boiling and this killed off bacteria. Andrew Boorde's *The Fyrste Boke of the Introduction of Knowlegde* (1540) reflected on health problems caused by bad ale in the lines:

Ich am a Cornishman, ale I can brew
It will make one cacke, also to spew.[10]

This boiling of beer mash also added to the economy of scale in producing beer, since this gave it a much greater shelf life than that of ale. If ale was often a cottage industry, beer was big business. The shift from home production to larger commercial enterprises in the second half of the fifteenth century is seen in the fact that at Havering (Essex) between 1465 and 1505, the 21 ale brewers fell to 15, of which only one was a woman. This growth in fewer – larger – breweries was a process accelerated by the closure of monastic breweries in the 1530s.[10]

The English at play: board games

A number of board games were played in the Middle Ages in England and have been the subject of specialist study.[11] In the twelfth century the card called *nard* was brought to England by crusaders returning from the Middle East. This game was played on a flat board, divided in two with a pair of dice determining moves. It is likely it was played in a similar way to backgammon and it may have been one of the ancestors of this game, via the game known as *tables*. An alternative possible ancestor for backgammon is the Roman game *tabula*, or *alea*, which was probably played in England before the introduction of *nard*.

Another popular board game was *Nine Men's Morris*, in which players have nine pieces, or 'men', each. These are moved about the board's 24 intersections. Similar to draughts, the aim of the game is to leave the opposing players with no pieces, or no legal moves open to them. *Nine Men's Morris* boards have been found carved into the cloister seats at Canterbury, Gloucester, Norwich and Salisbury cathedrals and in Westminster Abbey. These boards used holes, not lines, to represent the nine spaces on the board. Another board is carved into the bottom of a church pillar in Chester.

Chess had reached Spain by the eleventh century and was probably being played in England soon after this date. There were a number of differences between the medieval and modern games but in southern Europe at least, by about 1475, the two games were virtually the same.

The English at play: sport

Football has its origins in the Middle Ages, both as an informal game and as a village-wide game, such as that recorded as occurring at Wistow (Yorkshire, East Riding) on the eve of Lent 1422. In many areas of the country there was a strong association of mass games of football with this time of the year.

The ball may have been carried, as well as kicked, and there appear to have been few rules. At Gloucester Cathedral an engraving from the early fourteenth century shows two boys playing football and may suggest that hands, as well as feet, were used. Another medieval image suggests the ball was made from stitched leather, although it is often assumed (on the basis of little evidence) that it was made from an inflated pig's bladder. The same image that shows this stitching also seems to show a man with a broken arm, and this link between football and violence appears in many records. In 1314 football was banned in London, with little effect. In 1333 at Newton Aycliffe (County Durham), the manor court summoned William Colson, John de Redworth and five others to explain why they had not provided the names of those continuing to stage football games despite a warning of a fine of 20 shillings for those who kept on doing so. After heckling by Alicia de Redworth, the wife of John, the names of 18 men were finally given.[12] English football in the Middle Ages was clearly associated with popular enthusiasm and with disorder – two characteristics which still resonate with modern experiences.

After war broke out again with France in 1337, archery at local targets (*butts*) was increasingly encouraged for men. So important was this that attempts were made to ban football, and it is interesting that the illustrations in the Luttrell Psalter in about 1340 show archery but no football.

The English at play: a nation of pet lovers?

Keeping small animals as pets was a common practice in the Middle Ages, as has been revealed by recent work by Kathleen Walker-Meikle.[13] The animals involved included dogs, red squirrels, rabbits, cats and tame birds such as larks and starlings. Some were very exotic indeed. Eleanor, the wife of Edward I, owned a pair of parrots. Social status of owners could be displayed through fancy accessories such as collars, embroidered cushions and bells. Pets frequently appear in portraits and other works of art and seem to have been particularly associated with women, though men could be attached to more functional animals such as hunting dogs. However, this was not a hard-and-fast rule. Robert, Bishop of Durham in the late thirteenth century, owned two pet monkeys and was noted for the attention he gave them, feeding them peeled almonds (according to the chronicler Richard of Durham). A fourteenth-century priest, John Bromyard, complained that many priests cared more for their pets than for the human beings in their care. This may have simply been said because the idea of men keeping pets was frowned on and provided an easy target for someone looking to criticize worldly clerics. Nevertheless, the choice of pets as a means of making this attack does suggest that a lot of priests were keeping them. Whether pets were kept in peasant homes is difficult to say from the scant evidence.

Chapter 9

LIVING ON THE EDGE:
ALIENS AND OUTCASTS

The changing status of the Jews, 1066–1290

In 1210, King John arrested all the wealthy Jews in England and demanded a ransom for their release. This was a common way of extorting money from a vulnerable community which relied on royal 'protection' for its survival. However, this royal protection came at a very high price. The Crown used the Jewish community as a source of large sums of cash. These might be taken in loans or, as in the case of John, through direct force. John had already used this method on more than one occasion, including forcing the Jewish community to make a massive contribution towards the ransom earlier paid to gain the release of Richard I.

The sum John demanded in 1210 was huge and came to 66,000 *marks*. The mark was a unit of account and worth two-thirds of a pound (or 13 shillings and 4 pence). The amount demanded therefore came to £44,000. In Bristol the Jewish community was imprisoned in the castle until the money demanded was produced. The chronicler, Roger of Wendover, recorded the story of one 'Jew of Bristol' who refused to pay his ransom. The sum demanded from this unfortunate Jewish resident was 10,000 marks, or £6,600. Faced with his refusal to give in to this royal blackmail, the king ordered the royal torturers to work. Their brief was to pull out one of the Jew's molar teeth every day, until he paid the 10,000 marks. Each day, for seven days, the Jewish merchant, named Abraham of Bristol in some accounts, had one of his teeth pulled from his mouth using pliars and without the benefit of any substance to subdue the pain. And still he held out against his tormentors. On the eighth day, the torturers began preparation to rip out the eighth tooth. As they set to their bloody task, Abraham of Bristol finally gave way. After a week of excruciating pain he could take no more. He agreed to pay the sum demanded. Utterly vulnerable – as was the entire Jewish community – he could turn to no one for assistance or protection. He was living 'on the edge' in an increasingly hostile society.

William of Malmesbury records that the English Jewish community first appeared in the reign of William the Conqueror when he transferred a community from Rouen to England. In return for rights of residence and royal protection, Jews paid huge taxes to the Crown. Within the economy they were merchants, pawnbrokers and financiers. Among the goods they traded were precious metals, furs and jewellery. Within the financial sector their role included moneylending at interest: an occupation prohibited to Christians by the Church.

Around 1093, Gilbert Crispin, the Abbot of Westminster, published a record of his debate with a Jew, entitled *Disputation of a Jew with a Christian about the Christian Faith*. In it he revealed a friendly and open attitude towards the Jewish scholar: 'he was well versed even in our law and liter-ature, and had a mind practised in the Scriptures and in disputes against us. He often used to come to me as a friend both for business and to see me, since in certain things I was very necessary to him, and as often as we came together we would soon get talking in a friendly spirit about the Scriptures and our faith.'

It was at this time that an attempt was made to introduce the legal principle (already seen on the Continent) that all Jews were the 'king's property'. During Henry I's reign (1100–1135) a royal charter was granted to Joseph, the Chief Rabbi of London, and his followers. Under this charter, Jews were permitted to move about the country without paying tolls, they could buy and sell goods and property, in legal cases they were to be tried by their peers and oaths were to be sworn on the Torah rather than on the Bible. Special weight was attributed to a Jew's oath, which was valid against that of twelve Christian Englishmen.

However, despite this promising start this vulnerable community often experienced periods of persecution. These attacks were often centred on accusations of coin clipping and ritual murder of Christian children: the *Blood Libel*. These periodic accusations led to violent attacks on Jewish communities which usually ended with the payment of a huge fine to the Crown. There were three particularly famous Blood Libel cases. The first in Europe was the accusation that Jews had murdered a boy named William in Norwich (1144), who was later described as 'St' William of Norwich. This accusation was followed by that of 'St' Harold of Gloucester (1167) and Little 'St' Hugh of Lincoln (1255). Each of these dead children became the object of a cult of veneration at the cathedrals in these towns.

The first 'Blood Libel' occurred at a time of particular vulnerability, due to heightened ethnic tension following the First Crusade and political instability in England during the Civil War between Stephen and the Empress Matilda. Stephen burned down the house of a Jew in Oxford (some accounts add with the owner in it) because he refused to pay a contribution to the king's expenses, but otherwise attacks on Jews in England were, according to the Jewish chroniclers, prevented by Stephen.

Despite this vulnerability the Jewish community prospered. Within five years of the accession of Henry II, in 1154, Jews are recorded as resident in Bristol, Bungay, Cambridge, Gloucester, Lincoln, London, Northampton, Norwich, Oxford, Thetford, Winchester and York. However, they could only bury in London. This was a restriction which lasted until 1177. The financial importance of the Jewish community is seen in the fact that Strongbow's conquest of Ireland (1170) was financed by the Jewish financier Josce of Gloucester. Generally Henry II put few obstacles in the way of Jewish financial activities. However, in 1186, when raising money to pay for the crusade against Saladin, Henry took a 'tithe' (amounting to £70,000) from his English Christian subjects but a 'quarter' (valued at £60,000) from the English Jewish community. This enormous imposition assessed the Jewish community as being in possession of 25 per cent of the total movable wealth of the kingdom. This may partly reflect the real wealth of the community but more likely reveals the way in which the Jewish community was vulnerable to crippling extortion.

Henry was probably encouraged to do this by the huge amount of money which had gone to the Crown following the death of the Jewish financier Aaron of Lincoln. This had occurred because regulations stipulated that estates based on usury passed to the Crown on the death of the estate owner. It was Aaron who had loaned money to help pay for the building of the cathedrals at Lincoln and Peterborough and his estate (including £15,000 of debts owed to him) and a large treasure all passed to the Crown on his death. This amounted to 75 per cent of the usual annual government revenue – a vast sum in the hands of one man. A special branch of the Treasury was set up to deal with this large account and was called 'Aaron's Exchequer'. The treasure was shipped to France to help pay for the war Henry was waging against the king of France, but was lost at sea in February 1187.

Following Henry II's death, there were serious attacks on Jewish people at Richard I's coronation in 1189, which was followed by attacks at Colchester, Lynn, Norwich, Stamford and Thetford. At Lincoln, Jews took refuge in the castle. At Dunstable only accepting baptism saved the community from being murdered. The most terrible attack occurred at York on the nights of 16 March (the day of the Jewish feast of *Shabbat ha-Gadol*, the Sabbath before Passover) and 17 March 1190. The Jews of York were alarmed by massacres elsewhere in England and by a murderous attack on the family of the late Benedict of York, killing his widow and children, setting their house on fire and carrying away Benedict's treasure. Benedict had earlier died in Northampton of wounds caused by attacks on Jews at the coronation of Richard I. Those who murdered his family and looted his house in York were led by Richard Malebisse, who had borrowed money from the Jews of York.

The leader of the Jewish community in York, Josce, asked the warden of York Castle to protect them and the Jewish community were allowed into Clifford's Tower. However, the tower was besieged by a mob, demanding that the Jews convert to Christianity and be baptized. Trapped in the castle, the Jews were advised by their religious leader, Rabbi Yomtob of Joigney, to kill themselves rather than convert. Josce began the mass suicide by killing his wife, Anna and their two children and he was then killed by Yomtob. The father of each family followed suit, killing his wife and children and then Yomtob stabbed the men before killing himself. A small number of Jews who did not kill themselves surrendered to the mob at daybreak on 17 March. After leaving the castle, on a promise that they would not be harmed, they were also killed. Malebisse and his murderous mob then went to York Minster where they seized the financial records of the Jewish community (deposited there for safe keeping) and burnt them.

The persecution did not end there. When Richard I was imprisoned on his way back to England from the crusade, the Jewish community was loaded with a disproportionate amount of the taxation to be raised. They were forced to contribute 5,000 marks toward the king's ransom – over three times as much as the contribution of the City of London. On Richard's return the *Ordinance of the Jewry* (1194) ordered a tighter regulation of Jewish financial transactions, which finally led to the establishment of the *Exchequer of the Jews*. This made all the transactions of English Jews liable to taxation by the king of England, who thus became a silent partner in all the transactions of Jewish moneylending. The king also demanded two *bezants* (gold coins of variable value) in the pound; that is, 10 per cent of all sums recovered by the Jews through royal courts.

The increasing persecution was encouraged on 15 July 1205, when the pope laid down the principle that Jews were doomed to perpetual servitude because they had crucified Jesus. Earlier, in 1198, Pope Innocent III had written to all Christian princes, including Richard I of England, calling upon them to stop the charging of interest on money loaned by Jews to Christians. The new English king, John, at first treated Jews with tolerance. He confirmed the charter of Rabbi Josce and his sons and made it apply to all the Jews of England. He ordered the authorities in London to prevent attacks on Jews. He reappointed a Jew named Jacob as 'archpriest' of all the English Jews (12 July 1199). However, this did not last. In 1210 John demanded the sum of £100,000 from the religious houses of England, and 66,000 marks from the Jews. It was then that Abraham of Bristol refused to pay his quota of 10,000 marks and had seven of his teeth extracted until he finally agreed to pay.

This persecution, terrible as it was, was not continuous. The reigns of Henry II (1154–89) and the period of the minority of Henry III (1216–27) were peaceful times for the English Jewish community. However, when Henry III came of age this policy of relative toleration was reversed. The trend was already moving that way. The Third Lateran Council of 1179 had declared that no Jew should employ a Christian and that, in any matter of dispute, a Christian's testimony would always be accepted against that of a Jew. In 1215 Pope Innocent III went further, at the Fourth Lateran Council, and passed a law forcing all Jews to wear a badge. In 1218 Stephen Langton, Archbishop of Canterbury, brought it into operation in England. This badge took the form of an oblong white patch of two by four finger-lengths. The Synod of Oxford, 1222, barred Jews from employing Christian women and from building any new synagogues, and ordered that they would have to pay tithes despite not being members of the Church. In 1239 and 1244 Pope Gregory IX condemned the Jewish Talmud as blasphemous and heretical and set the Church up as the deciding authority of what was acceptable within Judaism. Jewish books which were deemed unacceptable were seized and burned. This was an important step in the increasing radicalization of anti-Jewish action, since it claimed that Jews had abandoned the Old Testament faith (by the creation of the beliefs and commentaries in the Talmud) and so were no longer eligible for the limited toleration previously allowed them. It accompanied a twelfth-century shift away from the traditional Church view that the Jews had rejected Christ out of spiritual blindness, and replaced it with the interpretation (which was not itself new) that they had wilfully rejected Jesus despite recognizing him as the Messiah and had therefore become heretics against the faith of the Old Testament and allies of the devil. This campaign against the Jews was headed by the new Dominican order who, as the military campaigns of the crusades declined in the thirteenth century, took up a kind of crusade against those defined as 'heretics' living within Christian societies. In 1221 the Dominican friars were given land inside the Oxford Jewry as part of a campaign to convert the Jews. The Franciscan friars played a similar role. This accompanied new assertions of papal power which were also supported by these preaching orders of friars.

Taking their cue from the papal actions, local communities made their own contributions to ethnic cleansing. Petitions were sent to the king to remove his Jews and they were expelled from Newcastle (1234), Wycombe (1235), Southampton (1236), Berkhamsted (1242) and Newbury (1244). Henry, in an attempt to raise money, sold the Jewish community to his brother Richard of Cornwall, in 1255, for 5,000 marks, and lost all rights over it for a year. In the following August a number of leading Jews, who had gathered at Lincoln to celebrate a marriage, were seized on a charge of having murdered a boy named Hugh. Ninety-one were sent to London. Of these, 18 were executed for refusal to plead and the rest were kept in prison till the expiry of Richard of Cornwall's control over their property. Clearly, the whole Jewish community was becoming increasingly vulnerable. In January 1275 Jews were expelled from the lands of Queen Dowager Eleanor. To this general atmosphere of increasing racial hatred Henry III seems to have made a personal and active anti-Jewish contribution. His sanctioning of an accusation of ritual murder against the Jewish community (regarding Little 'St' Hugh of Lincoln) was the first time an official 'green light' had been given to these racially motivated accusations. Similarly, it was his son – Edward I – who, in 1276, was to revive an accusation of ritual murder against London's Jewish community; a charge which had been ignored by the authorities when it was first made in 1272.

As political order broke down between Henry III and the supporters of Simon de Montfort, actions against the Jews escalated. Between 1263 and 1265 the Jewries at Cambridge, Canterbury, Lincoln, London, Northampton, Winchester and Worcester were all looted. In addition, Simon de Montfort (who had already expelled the Jews from Leicester) annulled all debts to the Jews. By this time the king and others were shifting most of their transactions to Italian bankers who were extending their influence in England.

Under Edward I the persecution of the Jews intensified. His 'Statute of the Jews' (1275) made it illegal for Jews to lend money at interest; something Italian bankers were allowed to do, having been exempted from the general condemnation of usury, and were increasingly doing to their great profit. This impoverished the whole Jewish community and this economic marginalization was a prelude to total expulsion. In 1278 the entire English

Jewish community was imprisoned and 293 Jews were executed at London, allegedly for coin clipping. The Synod of Exeter in 1287 added to previous discriminatory practices by banning Jews and Christians from eating together, banning Jewish doctors from treating Christian patients and forbidding Jews from leaving their houses during the Easter festival. Christians who mixed with Jews would be excommunicated.

On 18 July 1290 Edward issued *writs* to the sheriffs of all the English counties ordering them to enforce a decree that all Jews should leave England before All Saints' Day of that year (1 November). They were allowed to carry their portable property but their houses passed to the king, except in the case of a few favoured people who were allowed to sell theirs before they left. Somewhere in the region of 4,000 Jews were expelled. It is difficult to be precise on numbers, but in the 1280s about 1,100 paid a poll tax placed on all Jewish males over the age of 12 years. After 1290 there would not be a Jewish community in England again until the 1640s, when some Spanish and Portuguese Jewish merchants (living as Christians but secretly practising Judaism) lived in London. It was not until 1656 that they could live openly as members of the Jewish faith.

There is very little archaeological evidence for England's medieval Jewish community, although there is a lot of evidence in tax records. Living in some 26 towns and enjoying the same material culture as their Christian neighbours, these Jewish communities are hard to spot in the archaeological record. Medieval Jewish cemeteries have been excavated at London, Winchester and York. The London example (at Cripplegate) had all the graves emptied and desecrated after 1290. London's city walls have been found to contain six fragments of reused tombstones with Hebrew texts. Similarly, fragments of Jewish gravestones were found in the foundations of the Guildhall in Cambridge. Part of another one was reused in a medieval cellar wall in Northampton. Buildings which were probably constructed by Jewish merchants survive in 'Jew's House', Lincoln, 'Wensum Lodge', Norwich, and part of a building under the County Hotel in Canterbury. In London the Jewish community lived in the area known as 'the Jewry'. This was not a ghetto and Jews and Christians lived alongside each other here, close to the main trading and financial centre of the city. This area is commemorated in the street name Old Jewry and the name of a church, St Lawrence Jewry.

Given the rarity of archaeological evidence, the discovery of London's first Medieval *mikveh* (plural *mikva'ot*) – Jewish ritual bath – in 1986 during excavations in Gresham Street was particularly significant. A subterranean structure, it was lined with ashlar blocks and pottery dated it to the twelfth century. At first it was suggested it might be a strong room, but no other evidence for such a structure exists from medieval London. Interestingly, it was not in a synagogue but at the rear of a private house. However, this is similar to a type of small mikveh identified in Germany. In 2001 a second was found at Milk Street. Pottery dated this one to the mid-thirteenth century. Jewish ritual law dictates that the first 40 *seah* (c.750 litres, or 164.9 Imperial gallons) in a ritual bath must be spring water or rainwater, collected in cisterns and channelled to the mikveh. This must have been used in these two cases since neither was deep enough to reach groundwater.[1]

The Milk Street mikveh was owned by Jewish financiers, the Crespins, until 1290 and there were other Jewish occupiers of houses around the Gresham Street site. It is not possible to tell whether these two mikva'ot were built for private, or communal, use but they are fascinating and poignant reminders of a vanished community – a community which played such an important role within England between 1066 and 1290, including providing the financial capital to pay for palaces, cathedrals and the monastic building projects of the Cistercians in Yorkshire.

Prostitution: managing sin

Although fornication was condemned as a sin, prostitution was impossible to eradicate. This left the question of how such sin should be managed. Officially sanctioned brothels (or *stews*) existed in places such as Sandwich in Kent, Southwark (across the Thames from the City of London) and Cock Lane at Smithfield, in London. In Southwark, prostitutes were often called 'Winchester geese' since the brothels were sited on land owned by the bishop of Winchester, who collected rents from them. Local ordinances insisted that the *stewholders* were men and that women must stay with a client all night in order to avoid the charge of 'night-walking'. Technically women were not allowed to lodge at the brothel. However, despite these regulations, there existed illegal stews which were often run by women. In 1384, a London ordinance stated that any prostitute plying her trade away from Cock Lane would be held in the pillory at Aldwych.

The location of red-light areas was signalled in a number of towns by names such as Grope Lane (or even coarser and more explicit variants) found in Bristol, London, Oxford, Southampton and York. Often in locations close to markets and shops, they were tolerated – though officially disapproved of – centres of the medieval sex trade in these cities. However, during the fifteenth century urban authorities took an increasingly tough stance regarding prostitution. Behaviour which had been largely ignored before 1400 became the subject of official sanctions. The 1492 ordinances at Coventry attempted to control the activities of barmaids and ale-wives considered to be prostitutes. The 1500 Gloucester ordinances stated that prostitutes and their clients would be put on public display in the marketplace. This was part of a new moral mood which stemmed from increasing anxiety about social order and a wish to create a more morally stable and purified society, backed up by local courts. No longer was the regulation of sexual morality considered the prerogative of the Church courts.

Homosexuality

Homosexuality was considered a sin by the Church in the Middle Ages. This was on the basis of both Old and New

Testament condemnations of it as a perversion of sexuality as ordained by God. The phrase 'Sodomy', as an alternative term, takes its name from an account in *Genesis*, chapter 19, of the men of the city of Sodom who attempted to have homosexual sex with the angel-guests of Lot and who were punished for their sin. Following this, the cities of Sodom and Gomorrah were destroyed.

However, in single-sex religious communities it is likely that homosexuality occurred, even if excused as no more than brotherly, or sisterly, affection. Indeed, the very creation of such single-sex communities, linked with the suppressing of sexual desire, must have produced situations which were at times highly sexually charged. For men this would have been sharpened by the very negative image of women which was encouraged by many celibate (and probably sexually frustrated) male writers in the Middle Ages. Clearly, if close brotherly/sisterly affection passed beyond this, into sexual acts, it would be impossible to square with the Church's Biblical teaching. But there is clear evidence that it did – covertly – occur. However, in her review of sexual expression in the Middle Ages, Ruth Karras points out that the accusation of homosexual behaviour was often simply a charge against those considered to be 'outsiders'. For example, some English writers used it against the Normans and some Christian writers levelled the same accusation against Muslims. This means it is impossible to assess the frequency of its occurrence.

Although some writers have suggested that the Church tolerated it (and have interpreted ambiguous accounts and documents in the light of this interpretation), Karras rejects this suggestion and this does seem more in line with the available evidence and the official view of the medieval Church. She does identify a word used in some medieval literature – *adelphophilia* – which the historian John Boswell has suggested refers to homosexual marriage, but she rejects this interpretation and suggests that it, in fact, referred to a kind of intimate brotherhood.[2] Once again, this seems a far more likely situation, given official medieval condemnation of homosexual acts.

Lepers: judged by God or halfway to heaven?

Leprosy, or Hansen's Disease, seems to have reached Britain in the Late Roman period. Without modern treatment, there can be progressive and permanent damage to the nerves, skin, eyes and limbs. Its disfiguring effects have always made leprosy a much feared disease. It is impossible now to be sure of whether the recorded occurrences of the disease were always leprosy, since other skin diseases, such as severe *favus* and similar fungal diseases, severe *psoriasis* and some other diseases not caused by microorganisms may have been classified as 'leprosy'. The fear of contracting the disease meant that lepers were supposed to carry a clapper and a bell to warn others of their approach. The first recorded English use of the word 'leper', in the form *lepruse*, is from the thirteenth-century handbook for female hermits, the *Ancrene Riwle* (or *Ancrene Wisse*). Inspired by Jesus's compassion towards those suffering from the dreaded skin diseases of the first century, the Middle Ages saw many charitable donations by rulers, nobles and Church leaders to establish dedicated leper hospitals, or *leprosaria*. By 1230 there were about 250 leper hospitals in England.

Lepers were regarded as walking dead and before they entered such leper hospitals went through a form of burial ritual. Church writings refer to specific garments and utensils which were given to lepers for their sole use and which were blessed before being passed to them. This was not unlike what was done at the ordination of clerics, and highlights the strangely ambiguous role of lepers in medieval society. In some accounts it was suggested that lepers were experiencing a kind of purgatory in this life and, therefore, there was something holy as well as terrible about their suffering. Some accounts also refer to them as 'Nazirites', a Biblical term describing a person set apart and consecrated to the Lord. These are referred to in the Old Testament Law, in the *Book of Numbers* chapter 6, verses 1–21.

Separated from the rest of the population, both in life and death, these leper hospitals had their own separate cemeteries.

This had not always been the case, since excavation of Late
Roman and Anglo-Saxon cemeteries has revealed lepers
buried in the community burial grounds.[3] Indeed, one
seventh-century woman buried at Edix Hill, Barrington
(Cambridgeshire) was clearly a member of the elite. She was
buried on a bed and accompanied by items indicating she came
from a wealthy family. The fact that her face would have been
marked by nodules and copious discharge from her nose did
not mean she was denied high-status burial in the communal
cemetery. However, this would not have been the case later in
the Middle Ages.

But leper hospitals, although usually sited outside town
walls, were not always as isolated as one might expect. That at
Brough (Yorkshire), for example, was a pilgrim hospice, a
general hospital and a leper hospital. The bodies of women and
children appear in surprisingly large numbers in leper
hospitals. This contrasts with the usual picture from urban
hospitals, where younger men occur in greater numbers. This
may be because a widespread medieval belief blamed leprosy
on sexual sin. So, at least some of the women buried at leper
hospitals might have been prostitutes, or other women
considered to have broken medieval sexual codes of conduct.
This idea is supported by the fact that as leprosy declined in the
later Middle Ages these same hospitals extended their care to
others labelled as deviants or outcasts, such as the mentally ill,
epileptics and unmarried pregnant women.[4] Clearly, this belief
contrasted with the association of lepers with Nazirites.

The anxiety about leprosy grew during the thirteenth
century as its incidence increased. At the same time its disfiguring effects came to be described in some sources as a physical
uncleanliness which reflected a spiritual state, and this
sharpened attitudes towards lepers and strengthened the association between leprosy and supposed sin. In this way the
image of the 'holy leper' faced increasing competition from the
image of the 'condemned leper'. The fact that lepers were one
of three groups forced to wear distinctive clothing (the others

being Jews and prostitutes) supports the view that the groups were, by this point, regarded as being in some way comparable. The physical separation from the rest of society was another common feature of all three groups, as was the accusation of sexual deviancy. Again, this demonstrates the very strange ambiguity in attitudes towards leprosy in the Middle Ages. On one hand it was a horrific disfigurement which was considered to be a judgement on sin and which put lepers firmly amongst those most 'on the edge' in medieval England. And yet on the other hand, 'the leper had been granted the special grace of entering upon payment for his sins in this life, and could therefore look forward to earlier redemption in the next.'[5]

Flemings and the Hanseatic League: economic rivals

In June 1381 during the Peasants' Revolt, rebels allied with discontented townspeople murdered members of London's Flemish community. Thirty-five Flemings were beheaded one after the other on a block set up outside the church of St Martin-in-Vintry, inside which they had vainly sought sanctuary. Why did this atrocity occur? Under Edward III, Flemish weavers were allowed to settle in England to contribute to the English woollen trade. Colonies were soon established in Norwich (Norfolk), York and Cranbrook (Kent). It was a Fleming – Thomas Blanket – who founded the first recorded factory in Bristol and gave his name to this form of warm cloth. Other Flemings settled in London. In all these places their weaving skills stimulated growth in the small English cloth-manufacturing industry. However, resentment at the skills and economic prosperity of these foreigners boiled over into violence when royal authority was weakened. During 1381, the Flemings butchered at St Martin-in-Vintry were not alone in facing the violence of racist attacks. Other Flemings were murdered at Colchester (Essex), at Yarmouth (Norfolk), at St John's, Clerkenwell (where they had sought sanctuary) and in many places across London.

Racist resentment towards 'outsiders' who were accused of taking English jobs was not restricted to the Flemings. The relationship with German merchants from the Hanseatic League could also be very tense at times, since they too were considered an economic threat. For English merchants the opportunity to trade in the Baltic opened up large areas to the sale of goods such as English cloth and allowed them access to attractive commodities such as amber, beeswax and furs from Russia (referred to exotically in some fourteenth-century accounts as 'The land of darkness'). After a successful English penetration of the Baltic trade in the late fourteenth century, hostilities between English and German traders broke out in the early fifteenth century. Treaties in 1409 and 1437 allowed reciprocal arrangements again, whereby merchants from Lübeck, Hamburg and the other Hanseatic ports could trade in English ports and English east-coast merchants could do the same in the Baltic ports. However, relations remained strained. In 1450 English ships attacked a large fleet of Dutch, Flemish and Hanseatic ships returning from collecting salt from the French Bay of Bourgneuf, on the coast of the Vendée. These ships were forced in to the Isle of Wight, from where all but the Hanseatic ships were soon released. The event aggravated an already-difficult relationship with these north German trading cities. More general hostilities broke out in 1468–74, which were not resolved. By 1500 English ships were excluded from the valuable Baltic trade. This breakdown in trade with the Baltic and northern Europe had a damaging effect on a number of eastern English ports.

Racially motivated violence was prone to periodic outbursts and targets varied. On May Day 1517, unemployed London youths attacked foreigners and smashed their premises along Fenchurch Street and in Leadenhall. At a time of economic depression there was suspicion of foreigners who appeared to have favourable relationships with the royal authorities and who were apparently prospering in a number of different business areas. Led by a broker named John Lincoln, a large group of apprentices and others met in the churchyard of Old St Paul's on 1 May, where their high state of agitation was further inflamed by a preacher named Dr Beal. Thomas More, who was at that time the under-sheriff of London, tried unsuccessfully to disperse the increasingly violent crowd, and gangs entered the eastern quarters of the city hunting for foreigners. This was despite the guns at the Tower of London being fired to deter them. It was not until the early hours of 2 May that armed troops finally restored order. Fortunately no foreigners were killed but, for leading the riot, John Lincoln was hanged, drawn and quartered and 13 others were executed. During the trial, which took place at Westminster Hall, Queen Katherine herself pleaded for mercy for the defendants and Henry VIII granted pardons to 400 of those involved in the riots. Within London the event became known as 'Evil May Day'. It was a vivid demonstration of the level of racial and ethnic distrust which lay beneath the surface of life in the capital and the way in which economic hardship could bring it to the surface in violent expressions of hatred.

The following conclusion on medieval developments regarding minority groups, by Robert Moore, offers a disturbing view of the Middle Ages: 'The period 950–1250 witnessed a fundamental and irreversible change in Europe. A persecuting society formed that may be seen as the origin and forerunner of the atrocities of the religious wars, the executions of the Reformation, even the Holocaust of the twentieth century.'[6] This clearly is a controversial viewpoint but, nevertheless, it is one which deserves our attention. Moore argues that in Europe between the tenth and the thirteenth centuries, the persecution of heresy, the establishment of the inquisition, the persecution and mass murder of Jews and the segregation of lepers were not unrelated developments. They were, he believes, part of a pattern of persecution which now appeared for the first time to make Europe 'a persecuting society'. Even if some of these developments did not occur as strongly in England as in other European countries (i.e. the persecution of heresy), the pattern is still comparable. To it we could add the racist violence perpetrated against the Flemings and the grouping of Jews and lepers with prostitutes. Clearly, intolerance of 'outsiders' was a recognizable feature of English society in the Middle Ages and one which would influence behaviour well beyond this period.

The fact that the end of the medieval period coincided with the start of the Great Witch Hunt (which would dominate much of the first two centuries of the Early Modern period) may be relevant to this argument.[7] Although the Great Witch Hunt was a product of its times – and a response to particular religious, social and cultural features – it grew out of a society in which persecution of 'outsiders' was already a significant cultural trend. Consequently, it was both a legacy of the Middle Ages and part of a new and emerging post-medieval Europe. Clearly the uncertainty inherent in 'living on the edge' in medieval England was one of the negative contributions medieval society made to later history.

Chapter 10

SIGNS AND MARVELS:
THE MEDIEVAL COSMIC ORDER

Many aspects of life in the Middle Ages may puzzle the modern reader, but some are stranger than others. What can possibly explain the following event reported from Orford Castle, in Suffolk? This is an amazing tale and was told by Ralph of Coggeshall in about 1205. Ralph reports an incident that happened about 40 years earlier.

> Men fishing in the sea caught in their nets a wild man. He was naked and was like a man in all his members, covered with hair and with a long shaggy beard. He eagerly ate whatever was brought to him, but if it was raw he pressed it between his hands until all the juice was expelled. He would not talk, even when tortured and hung up by his feet. Brought into church, he showed no signs of reverence or belief. He sought his bed at sunset and always remained there until sunrise. He was allowed to go into the sea, strongly guarded with three lines of nets, but he dived under the nets and came up again and again. Eventually he came back of his own free will. But later on he escaped and was never seen again.

Parts of this story are really shocking. The guards at Orford castle were curious: what language did the strange man speak? So they tortured him just to satisfy their curiosity. It is disturbing to note how Ralph reports this atrocity without any negative comment, in the same way that Walter Map (as we shall shortly see) reported the sexual abuse of a supposed fairy-woman.

'As to whether this was a mortal man, or some fish pretending human shape, or was an evil spirit hiding in the body of a drowned man', Ralph could not say. And neither can we. Whatever was going on at Orford, if anything at all, is now lost to us. But what Ralph commented next is particularly interesting. He then casually remarked: '. . . so many wonderful things of this kind are told by many to whom they happened.' So, apparently, Ralph was getting news of events like this all the time. For him it was just an everyday story of mermen and monsters.

Monks, like Ralph of Coggeshall, who wrote the great medieval chronicles occupied a position midway between historians and journalists, and their position on that line depended on their personal interest and inclination. As well as recording events from the past up to their own time (using whatever sources of information were available to them and often simply copying existing histories), their other main objective was to record the news and events of their own day. These events were frequently written down as a fairly contemporary record. But before this causes anyone to assume their reliability, it must be remembered that these medieval chroniclers interpreted and judged, gossiped and condemned and were often highly selective in both their choice of events to record and the interpretation they placed on them. This was particularly the case if the event in some way affected the religious house of which they were a member. Surviving chronicles range from sober – if at times biased – accounts of political and religious developments through to more sensational records of signs and marvels. It is this latter type of document which forms the basis of this chapter. We frequently do not know the sources of the wilder tales but, nevertheless, they offer us a view into the mindset, world view and cosmic view of the Middle Ages. They need to be set alongside the evidence on town trade, church building and manor court judgements if we really want to get the 'full flavour' of living in medieval England.

Signs and marvels in the sky

As the location of heaven in the medieval world view, it is not surprising that unusual events which occurred in the sky were held to be of particular importance. Some of these, as recorded in medieval chronicles, are inexplicable as natural phenomena. One of these would be that recorded in the *Anglo-Saxon Chronicle* for the year 685: 'In this year in Britain it rained blood, and milk and butter were turned into blood'. Some are more easily imagined as unusual arrangements of clouds, such as this account, again from the *Anglo-Saxon Chronicle* for the year 773: 'In this year a red cross appeared in the sky after sunset. This same year the Mercians and the Kentishmen fought at Otford; and strange adders were seen in Sussex.' What is revealed in this description is the belief that such an event must signify something – it was a *sign*. While the chronicler does not actually say there was a link between the red cross and the battle, a connection is implied. Occasionally a marvellous event is noted but no link made, such as in the *Anglo-Saxon Chronicle* for 806: 'On 4 June the sign of the holy cross appeared in the moon one Wednesday at dawn'. However, more usually such a sign would be seen as a portent of some kind. A clear combination of natural events and supernatural signs comes from 793 in the *Anglo-Saxon Chronicle*. It refers to the sacking of the monastery of Lindisfarne in a Viking raid.

> In this year terrible portents appeared over Northumbria, and miserably frightened the inhabitants: these were exceptional flashes of lightning ['exceptional high winds and flashes of lightning' in manuscript D], and fiery dragons were seen flying in the air. A great famine soon followed these signs; and a little after that in the same year on 8 January the harrying of the heathen miserably destroyed God's church in Lindisfarne.

Strange sights in the sky are found in a great many chronicler's accounts. In *The Chronicle of John of Worcester*, under the year 1048, is a reference which may refer to severe lightning: 'A great earthquake occurred on Sunday, 1 May at Worcester, Droitwich, Derby and many other places. Sudden death for man and beast swept many regions of England, and fire in the air, commonly called wildfire, burnt many townships and cornfields in Derbyshire and several other regions.' The same chronicler records a series of events which may be references to a comet, under the year 1106.

> On Friday, 16 February, in the first week of Lent, a strange star appeared in the evening, and shone in the same shape and at the same time between the south and the west for twenty-five days. It seemed small and dark, but the lustre which shone from it was extremely bright, and darts of light, like huge beams, flashed into the same star from east and the north. Many said that they saw several unusual stars at the same time. On the night of Maundy Thursday [22 March], two moons were seen, a little before dawn, one in the east and the other in the west, and both were full, for this moon was fourteen days old.

What is unusual in this account is that John of Worcester was content to leave it as a simple observation. A more usual approach would have been to consider it a sign of some kind. A good example of this is the *Anglo-Saxon Chronicle* for 1107: 'Many declared that they saw various portents in the moon during the year, and its light waxing and waning contrary to nature.' A similar entry survives from 1122: 'On the Tuesday after Palm Sunday, 22 March, there was a very violent wind; after which numerous portents appeared far and wide in England, and many illusions were seen and heard.' While the writer of these entries was not able to decode the 'portents', Henry of Huntingdon, in *The History of the English People*, saw a clear connection between bad government and signs in the sky. 'In this year [1117], due to the king's pressing needs, England was squeezed by repeated gelds [taxes] and various exactions. Then there were storms of thunder and hail on 1 December, and in the same month the sky appeared red, as if on fire.' Similarly, Ralph of Coggeshall, in his *English Chronicle*, was prepared to trace a political connection at the end of the twelfth century: 'It is said, the appearance of a comet, visible even in daylight, prefigured the death of King Richard I.' And for 1194: 'Two strange circles in the sky presaged storms and famine.' The same approach is found in a number of other chronicles, such as in the *Chronicles of Edward I and Edward II*: 'In 1233 there appeared in the sky four suns, in addition to the true one, beyond the boundaries of Herefordshire and Worcestershire. This was a sure portent of the slaughter to follow in the Marches [in the Marshall Rebellion].'

At other times the accounts are simply impossible to decipher and we do not know if we are reading an elaborated description of a natural event or a tale which has grown hugely in the telling so that it bears little resemblance to any real occurrence. These – less *signs* and more *marvels* – are accounts of strange and striking events which embellish many medieval records and which are often recorded alongside straight-forward accounts of Church and government. They clearly appealed to a sense of the supernatural, even when the events described did not have any apparent spiritual meaning. John of Worcester, for example, claims – in a very long and complex account – that in 1130 a bright light in the sky moved in and out of a cloud and that: 'In shape and size it was like a small pyramid, broad at the bottom, and narrow at the top.' Furthermore, something like a plank seemed to balance on the cloud. The description is hard to follow and even harder to visualize. However, John was determined to defend the accuracy of his account, claiming that: 'This was seen by the clerks of St Guthlac in Hereford castle. It was also seen by the watchmen in Brecon castle as well as in Herefordshire by the shepherds watching their flocks that same night. I have written down what I have heard. May Christ's mercy save us!' A simi-larly puzzling event at Dunstable (Bedfordshire) is recorded by William of Newburgh, in *The History*, under the year 1188. According to William, observers one afternoon saw: 'in the clear atmosphere the form of the banner of the Lord, conspicuous by its milky whiteness, and joined to it the figure of a man crucified, such as is painted in the church in remembrance of the passion of the Lord, and for the devotion of the faithful.' What is particularly interesting in this account is the chronicler's conclusion: 'Let everyone interpret this wonderful sight as he pleases ... What the Divinity may have intended to signify by it, I know not.' Such reticence in interpreting God's will was not always so apparent.

This phenomenon may have been a cloud formation, and this certainly seems the most likely explanation of an event recorded by Matthew Paris, in his *Major Chronicles*, under the year 1254. As witnessed by a group of monks from St Alban's Abbey, staying at Redbourne (Hertfordshire), 'there appeared in the sky, wonderful to relate, the form of a large ship, well shaped, and of remarkable design and colour'. A similar explanation seems likely to explain the 'battle formation of warriors' which appeared in the sky in Suffolk in 1285, according to John of Oxenedes, and the red and blue banners which seemed to clash with each other according to *Knighton's Chronicle, 1337–1396*, for the summer of 1355. However, this may be better explained as an example of the Aurora Borealis, but seen particularly far south. When the same chronicler records night fires which appeared to follow travellers in 1388, he was possibly describing static electricity, or St Elmo's fire.

Signs and marvels on (and in) the Earth

The sky was not the only place in which it was thought signs of divine origin might be seen; the Earth too was a place of portents. Henry of Huntingdon recounted events from 1144 in which churches were fortified against King Stephen by Robert Marmion and by Earl Geoffrey de Mandeville. As a result, 'blood bubbled out of the walls of the church and the adjacent cloister, clearly demonstrating the divine wrath and prophesying the destruction of the wrongdoers.' Henry went on to catalogue the way in which this judgement of God was seen in the lives of those involved in this outrage. Robert Marmion was killed; Earl Geoffrey died excommunicated; his son was captured and exiled; the commander of the earl's knights fell from his horse and died with his brains pouring out; the commander of the earl's foot soldiers was becalmed at sea, placed in a boat with his wife and some stolen money and sucked down by a whirlpool. Henry of Huntingdon was not alone in interpreting such 'signs' as portents. Thomas Walsingham, in *The St Albans Chronicle, 1376–1394*, also felt he discerned a message in unusual events which occurred in 1385: 'Four days after this storm [thunder and lightning in 1385] an earthquake occurred around nine o'clock in the evening, portending perhaps the pointless trouble between the two kings of England and France, who had now assembled enormous armies.'

However, as with the signs in the sky, some of those recorded on Earth are marvels designed to astonish. William of Newburgh, for example, has a story of two dogs which were discovered 'On splitting a vast rock, with wedges, in a certain quarry'. The animals were, he claims, actually inside the rock. As if to support the reality of the claim he added that, while one of these dogs died, the other was 'for many days fondled by Henry, Bishop of Winchester' [Henry of Blois, bishop 1129–71]. In another quarry William claimed that 'there was found a beautiful double stone, that is, a stone composed of two stones, joined with some very adhesive matter'. And inside this stone was 'a toad, having a small golden chain around its neck'. On the bishop's order the stone and toad were reburied. William himself believed these were made by evil angels to puzzle mankind and to capture their attention.

A related kind of marvel of secrets from within the Earth is recorded by Matthew Paris. He claimed that in 1236, near Roche Abbey (Yorkshire), 'bands of well-armed knights, riding on valuable horses, with standards and shields, coats of mail and helmets, and decorated with other military equipments' appeared from out of the ground and vanished back into it again. With this, though, we may be entering into a long tradition of other worlds existing beneath the ground. This, no doubt, had featured in pre-Christian beliefs and continued – adapted – into the Middle Ages. Sometimes this shows itself in beliefs in fairy worlds. At other times it appears in traditions of parallel universes existing under the ground. Sometimes the hidden realms are hostile; sometimes friendly; at other times neutral. While these accounts were recorded by literate Churchmen it seems clear that, in many cases, the Christian concepts of heaven and hell, realms of being and spiritual worlds were stretched by medieval folklore to accept 'other worlds' which had no relationship with Biblical concepts.

This idea of fairy realms appears strongly in the account, by Walter Map, of a legendary Saxon named Edric 'the Wild'. In a collection of wondrous and engaging stories, called, appropriately, *Courtiers' Trifles*, Walter recounted how Edric was travelling by night through 'wild country, uncertain of his path' when he chanced on a house within which were dancing women, 'most comely to look upon, and finely clad in fair habits of linen only, and were greater and taller than our women.' Edric is attracted to one and tries to seize her – despite, according to Map, being aware of tales of vengeance being done to men who disturb such groups of beings described as 'nightly squadrons of devils'. Despite being injured by the other women, he succeeded in capturing this dancer. 'He took her with him, and for three days and nights used her as he would, yet could not wring a word from her.' It is remarkable how calmly Walter retells this tale of what is clearly the kidnapping, rape and sex slavery of this unfortunate 'fairy woman'. This in itself tells us a lot about medieval male attitudes towards women and sex. In the story, the fairy woman finally agrees to marry Edric so long as he never mentions her fairy origins, or the women with whom she was dancing. However, when some time later he returns and she is not at home he forgets his promise and '. . . called her and bade her be summoned, and because she was slow to come said, with an angry look: "Was it your sisters that kept you so long?" The rest of his abuse was addressed to the air, for when her sisters were named she vanished.' Edric then pined away and died. Incidentally, Edric was an Anglo-Saxon thegn who held manors in Shropshire and Herefordshire in 1066 and lived until about 1072. He revolted against Norman rule but eventually made peace with William the Conqueror. Attacks from the woodland gave him his nickname *silvaticus* ('woodman, wildman'). He was mentioned by the Norman historian Orderic Vitalis as living 'wild in the woods'.

Walter Map does not explicitly refer to a fairy world under the ground, but this was its usual location in such folklore. William of Newburgh claimed that at Woolpits (Suffolk):

> two children, a boy and a girl, completely green in their persons, and clad in garments of a strange colour, and unknown materials, emerged from these excavations [wolf pits]. While wandering through the fields in astonishment, they were seized by the reapers, and conducted to the village, and many persons coming to see so novel a sight, they were kept some days without food.

The children refused to eat anything until offered raw beans, which they eagerly ate. They ate this for many months until they got used to bread. Slowly their colour changed, 'through the natural effect of our food' and they learnt English. They were baptized but the boy soon died; however the girl survived and was soon indistinguishable from a local girl. Later she married at King's Lynn and lived in the area. They claimed they came from 'the land of St Martin'. This appearance was supposed to have happened in the reign of Stephen. Ralph of Coggeshall, who places the appearance in the reign of Henry II, also told this tale. He claimed he gained his information from Sir Richard de Calne, in whose household the children lived. William himself wrote that he did not believe the story but that 'I have been compelled to believe, and wonder over a matter, which I was unable to comprehend, or unravel, by any powers of intellect'. What compelled him was the supposedly large number of witnesses of this event. What is particularly interesting in this story is that the two children were supposed to have come out of pits dug to catch wolves. This connection with 'the wild' and with a way into the earth puts the story firmly into the category of fairy folklore.

William of Newburgh collected more than one such story, and another was set in Yorkshire. A peasant returning home one night heard singing which seemed to come from inside a hill. Investigating an open doorway into the hill, he found a room inside where men and women were feasting. Offered a drink, he poured out the contents but left with the cup. He was pursued but escaped with a cup 'of unknown material, unusual colour, and strange form'. It was, claims William later, 'offered as a great present to Henry the elder, king of England [Henry I], and then handed over to the queen's brother, David, king of Scotland, and deposited for many years among the treasures of his kingdom.'

A similar and traditional association of a fairy hill and an other-wordly drink is found in the collection of stories *Recreation for An Emperor*, written by Gervase of Tilbury. The location of his fairy hill appears to have been in the Forest of Dean (Gloucestershire). There:

> In a leafy glade of this forest was a hillock, which rose to a man's height . . . if anyone strayed a long way from his companions and climbed it alone, and then, though alone, said 'I'm thirsty', as if he were speaking to someone else, at once to his surprise, there would be a cupbearer standing at his side, in rich attire, with a merry face, and holding in his outstretched hand a large horn, adorned with gold and jewels.

According to Gervase the drink was delicious – but strange – and refreshed the weary. Once more the motif emerges of theft of a fairy drinking vessel. In this case a knight steals the horn. However, his overlord condemned the thief, confiscated the horn and presented it to Henry I. Why this particular king is singled out by both William of Newburgh and Gervase of Tilbury is difficult to say.

Gervase of Tilbury also collected a story of a swineherd who pursued a pig into a cave at Peak Castle, near Castleton (Derbyshire) and:

> came out from the darkness into a light place, and found that he had emerged into wide open fields; advancing into the countryside, which was cultivated all round, he found harvesters gathering in crops, and in the midst of the hanging ears of corn he recognised the sow, which had dropped its litter of several piglets.

The story was told to Gervase by Robert, Prior of Kenilworth [Warwickshire], who was a native of the Castleton area. He was prior 1160–86. In the story the swineherd was received in a friendly manner and allowed to go home with his pigs. On returning home he found it was still winter, although it had been summer in 'the other world'.

The idea of a person vanishing into another world and then returning is also found in the *Chronicles of the reigns of Edward I and II*, although in this case there is no hint of what this 'other place' was like:

> In the summer of 1315 a boy of fourteen was taken, completely naked, in the parish of St Botolph outside Bishopgate in London. No one knew what had become of him. A day later he was returned to the place from which he had vanished, to tell of many marvels.

Other supernatural beings occur in medieval accounts and show the persistence of pre-Christian beliefs in fairy folk, goblins and other similar creatures. Gervase of Tilbury records a belief in creatures that he names as 'portunes', which appear in peasants' houses at night:

> warming themselves at the fire and eating little frogs which they bring out of their pockets and roast on the coals. They have an

aged appearance, and a wrinkled face; they are very small in stature, measuring less than half a thumb, and they wear tiny rags sewn together.

Gervase believed these creatures were not dangerous, but this was not the case with creatures he named as 'grants':

It is like a yearling colt, prancing on its hind legs, with sparkling eyes. This kind of demon very often appears in the streets in the heat of the day or at about sunset, and whenever it is seen, it gives warning of an imminent fire in that city or neighbourhood.

Gervase clearly had a great interest in such traditions, as he also gives an account of an event he believed occurred in Inglewood forest, near Penrith (Cumbria). While hunting there, a knight was caught in a violent thunderstorm and suddenly caught sight of a 'huge dog running with fire darting from its jaws'. This creature, Gervase explains:

entered the house of a priest on the outskirts of the same town, passing through the doors though they were shut against it, and it set fire to the house together with the unlawfully begotten family.

In this one account the chronicler brings together two medieval intellectual strands. The first is a widespread belief in other-world beings. The second is an assumption that misfortune indicates punishment for sin. In this case the offence is in the form of a married priest, who has resisted the Church pressure (which was increasing from the twelfth century onwards) for celibacy.

Signs and marvels in the water

The idea that natural events reflected problems in society was a common medieval belief. This could show itself in a number of ways, and pools 'bubbling blood' was a striking one. There are a number of examples; the most famous ones are linked with Finchampstead, in Berkshire. The first time this claim appears is in the *Anglo-Saxon Chronicle* for the year 1098.

In the summer of this year, in Berkshire at Finchampstead, a pool bubbled up blood, as many faithful witnesses reported who were said to have seen it. Before Michaelmas the sky appeared almost the whole night as if it were on fire. This was a very disastrous year because of excessive taxation, and on account of the heavy rains which did not leave off throughout the whole year.

This event made a deep impression on medieval writers. Henry of Huntingdon, in an entry written by 1154, recorded the same phenomenon. '1098. In summer blood was seen to bubble up from a certain pool at Finchampstead in Berkshire. After this the heaven appeared to burn nearly all night.' In Henry's record this follows a description of William II fighting rebellions and demanding heavy taxes.

Bad king . . . high taxes . . . pools bubbling blood. Henry does not make the link explicitly but the connection is clear: William II was a bad king because his rule caused rebellions and led to high taxes, and the natural world protested (the blood-red spring). If anybody had missed the connection, Henry recorded another outpouring of the spring in 1100: 'A little earlier [Henry has just described the death of William II in the New Forest] blood was seen to bubble up from the ground in Berkshire.' So, the spring which had protested at William II's bad government now sent out another signal when he was murdered. Clearly, royal murder upset the natural world even when the king was bad.

The same connection between bad government and springs flowing with blood was made by William of Malmesbury, in *The History of the English Kings*, written in about 1126.

In the thirteenth year of William's reign [1100], which was the year of his death, there were many sinister occurrences; among others, this was the most terrifying, that the Devil visibly appeared to men in woods and byways, and spoke to passers by. Besides which, in the village of Hampstead in Berkshire for fifteen days on end a spring ran blood so abundantly that a nearby pool was stained with it. The king heard of these things and laughed, caring nothing either for his own dreams about himself, or for what other people saw.

For William of Malmesbury it was important to show how the king reacted. It revealed what a bad king he was and this made it clear that the bloody spring was making a point about his bad rule and his bad attitude.

But this was not the end of the Finchampstead spring. In 1103 it was active again and once more the *Anglo-Saxon Chronicle* linked it to problems in the land:

> In this year too, at Finchampstead in Berkshire, blood was seen coming from the ground. It was a very disastrous year here in this country by reason of numerous taxes and also as a result of murrain [cattle disease] and the ruin of the harvest . . .

Again, Henry of Huntingdon – writing about 50 years after this event – was sure that the event was once more linked to bad politics. 'Blood was seen to bubble up from the ground at Finchampstead. In the course of the next year the king and his brother were at odds over several matters.'

It is clear that pools 'bubbling with blood' were a major event at Finchampstead – so much so that the reports of it were picked up by so many medieval chroniclers. The connection with some kind of national disaster was made by every one of them (high taxes, rebellions, death of the king, cattle diseases, poor harvests). A pool bubbling blood just had to be a sign of trouble in the land. It had to be some kind of pointer to just how bad a state the country was in. It was as if the natural world had to respond to problems in the human world; to act like a mirror. This is hardly surprising since red-coloured water suggests that the earth is bleeding.

In addition, to the Biblically aware medieval writers the springs flowing with blood-coloured water would have reminded them of the first plague of Egypt, when the river Nile turned to blood (*Exodus*, chapter 7, verses 14–24). Pools bubbling with 'blood' would suggest God's judgement on human sins. In the same way, the *Book of Revelation* (chapter 16, verse 4),[1] talks of one of God's judgements just before the end of the world as being '. . . on the rivers and springs of water, and they became blood.'

The coincidence of political unrest, an unpopular ruler, poor harvests and 'blood-red' springs will have meant only one thing to medieval writers. It was a sign of the anger of God. So, what was going on in Finchampstead? There is probably a very simple explanation for what was happening. There are 4,000 known species of red algae in the world and, though they are often present in tropical marine waters, they can also be found in fresh water. Their colour is due to a red pigment reflecting red light and absorbing blue light. The most likely explanation for the events at Finchampstead is red algae bloom in the water. The fact that two records clearly describe it as a summer event support this likelihood. Increased summer temperatures, along with excess nutrients, encourages the growth of algae. In the same way, modern summer heat has led to related blue-green algae in lakes, poisoning dogs who drank from it. The presence of red (and possibly semi-toxic) water will have been a very striking occurrence; especially at a time of political, or social, unrest. Sadly, the spring in question was destroyed by road widening in the early twentieth century.

The *Westminster Chronicle, 1381–1394*, records another way in which strange water phenomena were thought to be portents of great events:

On 1 February [1388] near Abingdon the bed of the river Thames was empty of water for the length of a bowshot; and remained so for an hour, conveying a striking omen of events that were to follow [The crisis at the Westminster Parliament between Richard II and earls accused of plotting against him].

John of Worcester records a similarly strange event which happened in 1110:

Amazing things occurred all over England. At Shrewsbury there was a large earthquake. At Nottingham, from dawn right up to the third hour, a mile of the Trent dried up so that men walked along its channel dryshod. A comet appeared on 8 June and was visible for three weeks.

The clue here probably lies in the earthquake. It is not at all unusual for earthquakes to disturb springs and rivers. Unlike the Westminster chronicler, John of Worcester does not speculate as to the possible meaning of the event, although his tone suggests he felt something significant was happening.

As with other medieval records of wondrous events, some chroniclers also record accounts of marvellous creatures whose activities are not interpreted as portents but who form part of the medieval fascination with strange animals. In this fascination real creatures mix with mythological beasts but both are treated with the same level of seriousness. It is this absence of observational criticism which most clearly differentiates the medieval from the modern study of nature. However, it has to be remembered that popular modern interest still focuses on such things as the Loch Ness Monster, Big Foot and the Abominable Snowman. In this respect there is little difference between some modern and medieval outlooks. And some cases – such as the Big Cat sightings in England – may occupy the mysterious twilight zone of possibly being based on real animals.

Gervase of Tilbury reports without comment on the existence of *sirens* off the British coast.

> They have a female head, long, shining hair, a woman's breasts, and all the limbs of the female form down to the navel; the rest of their body tails off as a fish. With the immense sweetness of their singing these creatures so penetrate the hearts of passing sailors that they succumb utterly to the sensuous enticement of their ears; they become forgetful of their duty, and very often suffer shipwreck through carelessness.

In this report, Gervase was giving a British location for something he would have known about from his reading of classical sources. However, classical sirens, such as those described by the Roman poet Ovid (born 43 BC), were half bird/half woman. By about AD 700 descriptions of mermaid forms first appear. However, a beautiful woman with a fish's tail had earlier appeared in the Latin writings of Horace (born 65 BC). By the mid-twelfth century the idea of the fish-woman was well established, though the bird-woman still sometimes appeared in some accounts. The location of sirens in English waters may simply have occurred due to a desire to link classical creatures with a familiar location. On the other hand, it may have been stimulated by the presence of seals on sandbanks. Nothing so simple, though, would seem to explain the Merman of Orford Castle described at the start of this chapter, and this fascinating claim must stand as an example of one of the strangest reports of marvels from the Middle Ages.

Another curious claim – given the ease of testing it as being false – is found in the mid-thirteenth-century *Bestiary MS Bodley 764*, which contains a strange tale about a bird which sounds like a confused combination of a kingfisher and a dipper. But the most amazing things about this bird, according to this writer, are that 'If, after they have died, they are kept in a dry place, they never putrefy.' As if this was not strange enough: 'what is even more extraordinary, if they are hung by the beak in a dry place, they renew their plumage each year, as if some part of the living spirit was dormant in the remains.' This astonishing claim refers to birds in Ireland, but the description of the birds and their natural habits would clearly have applied to kingfishers in England too. Perhaps the fact that the Irish birds were in another land seemed to justify them having particularly strange characteristics.

More easily understood is the medieval tradition regarding barnacle geese. When is a bird a fish? This was a serious question, according to Gervase of Tilbury. He wrote about an odd tradition near Faversham Abbey in Kent:

> Small trees grow on the sea-shore, about the size of willows. From them nodes sprout but when they have grown for the time allotted in creation, they take on the shape of little birds.

Now this might seem odd enough, but:

At the end of the number of days required by nature, these birds hang down by their beaks and come to life with a light fluttering of their wings; then they drop into the sea. Sometimes they are caught by the locals, but sometimes they go free on the ocean-waves, escaping human grasp. These birds grow to the size of small geese.

The intriguing thing is that this is not the first time this claim was made. This legend was first recorded by an Arab writer in the tenth century AD. Similar descriptions are found in other medieval writings. But the reason why medieval monks were so interested was because:

In the season of Lent they are roasted and eaten, their manner of birth being taken into consideration for this rather than the fact that they taste of meat. The people call this bird the barnacle-goose.

This was not an isolated record of this impact of the supposed origin of barnacle geese on medieval fasting habits. The *Bestiary MS Bodley 764* claimed that: 'In some parts of Ireland, bishops and men of religion eat them during times of fasting without committing a sin, because they are neither flesh, nor born of flesh.' Ranulf Higden, in *The Universal Chronicle* (written in about 1320), also knew about this belief:

The barnacle geese grew from trees, and hung by their beaks like the shellfish that clings to timber. When they were covered with feathers, they either fell into the water, or else flew away. They were eaten on fasting-days because . . .

At which point Ranulf reveals that he's not convinced, because 'they were *supposed* not to be born from animals, but none the less these birds were flesh'.

The reasons for this tale of an animal-wonder are fairly obvious. Barnacle geese flock on the sea shore when on migration. Now, large barnacles look a bit like eggs, plus the egg cases of fish such as ray, dogfish and skate are often found on the sea shore. Those produced by dogfish have tendrils used to attach the egg case to seaweed. They actually look like seaweed. This clearly encouraged the idea that these eggs were in some way connected to the flocking geese. The attraction of this belief, for some, clearly lay in the fact that it made it acceptable to eat roast goose in Lent. How far this was followed is impossible to know, and it may be that it only occurred in isolated incidents.

The walking dead

There was a very strong medieval fear of *revenants*, or the walking dead. The popularity of these stories may reflect the strength of Church teaching on making a good death through being confessed and absolved, receiving the Last Rites and being in a good relationship with the Church. What had its roots in common folklore tales of ghosts soon became an educational tool to encourage the correct attitude towards preparation for death. Interestingly, while clerical writers explained the walking dead as being re-animated by demons, more popular accounts stressed that they were those who had experienced a bad death coming back to life to harm the living. The 30 days after death were seen as particularly important in assisting the dead through purgatory by prayers and the saying of Masses. Prayers over new graves, for a period after death, both assisted the dead and protected the living as the buried body experienced decomposition.

One of the most striking accounts of revenants is found in the *Life and Miracles of St Modwenna*, written by Geoffrey of Burton. It involved two villeins living in Stapenhill (Derbyshire, now Staffordshire) under the jurisdiction of the Abbot of Burton. These villeins, seeking to escape their servile status, ran away to a nearby village called Drakelow – as Geoffrey put it, in a defence of the social status quo, 'wrongfully leaving their lords, the monks'. The next day – on their first day of illicit freedom – the two men dropped dead and their bodies were returned to Stapenhill for burial. However, this was not the end, as:

> they appeared at evening, while the sun was still up, at Drakelow, carrying on their shoulders the wooden coffins in which they had been buried. The whole following night they walked through the paths and fields of the village, now in the shape of men carrying wooden coffins on their shoulders, now in the likeness of bears or dogs or other animals. They spoke to the other peasants, banging on the walls of their houses and shouting.

This horrific visitation took place every evening and night for some time, until a terrible disease broke out in the village of Drakelow and killed all its inhabitants except three. The manorial lord of the village, who earlier had been willing to accept the runaway villains, was Count Roger the Poitevin. In desperation he paid compensation to the abbey, via the reeve of the village, one of the three survivors. The local bishop then gave permission to exhume the bodies of these walking dead from their graves.

> They found them intact, but the linen cloths over their faces were stained with blood. They cut off the men's heads and placed them in the graves between their legs, tore out the hearts from their corpses, and covered the bodies with earth again. They brought the hearts to the place called Dodecrossefora/Dodefreseford and there burned them from morning until evening. When they had at last been burned up, they cracked with a great sound and everyone there saw an evil spirit in the form of a crow fly from the flames. Soon after this was done both the disease and the phantoms ceased.

Two sick villagers recovered and gave thanks to St Modwenna, and thereafter Drakelow became a deserted medieval village. This account is a concise piece of theological and social engineering. It combines warnings about dying with unconfessed sins with defence of the Church's rights to demand villein service from its tenants (who should accept their lot). It also warns neighbouring lords not to poach labourers from Church-run manors. Furthermore, it was accounted to the credit of St Modwenna, the saint that Geoffrey particularly venerated.

There are many such stories. Walter Map retells one in which:

> ... in the time of Roger, bishop of Worcester [bishop 1164–79], a man, reported to have died unChristianly, for a month or more wandered about in his shroud both at night and also in open day, till the whole population of the neighbourhood laid siege to him in an orchard, and there he remained exposed to view, it is said, for three days. I know further that this Roger ordered a cross to be laid upon the grave of the wretch, and the man himself to be let go. When, followed by the people, he came to the grave, he started back, apparently at the sight of the cross, and ran in another direction. Whereupon they wisely removed the cross: he sank into the grave, the earth closed over him, the cross was laid upon it and he remained quiet.

This is a classic of the revenant genre of stories. The episode opens with a 'bad death' and is resolved when the bishop excommunicates the walking corpse.

Walter's book contained a number of these warning tales. One, set in Northumberland, is similar to the Stapenhill/Drakelow story in its relatively crude defence of Church manorial rights and worldly power. In this next story, a knight is shocked by the appearance of his dead father. The walking dead asked for a priest to be called. The priest duly arrived and:

> ... falling at his feet the ghost said: 'I am that wretch who long ago you excommunicated unnamed, with many others, for unrighteous withholding of tithes; but the common prayers of the Church and the alms of the faithful have by God's grace so helped me that I am permitted to ask for absolution.' So being absolved he went, with a great train of people following, to his grave and sank into it, and it closed over him of its own accord.

At other times such stories betray their links to older traditions of fairies and other worlds. Such a story is that recounted by

Walter Map, which is without the social and theological content of Geoffrey of Burton's account of the dead villeins, or Walter's own account of the dead father of the knight:

> What are we to say of those cases of 'fantasy' which endure and propagate themselves in a good succession, as this of Alnoth . . . in which a knight is said to have buried his wife, who was really dead, and to have recovered her by snatching her out of a dance and after that to have got sons and grandsons by her, and that the line lasts to this day, and those who come of it have grown to a great number and are in consequence called 'sons of the dead mother'.

William of Newburgh combines the two themes – the walking dead and Church authority – in an event said to have occurred in Buckinghamshire. In this account a dead man 'entered the bed where his wife was reposing, he not only terrified her on awaking, but nearly crushed her by the insupportable weight of his body'. This horrible event, for which William offered no explanation, continued every night for several days and then the dead man took to haunting others and appearing in the daytime too. At last the bishop of Lincoln became involved and wrote a letter of absolution – since he thought that the 'usual' response of digging up and burning the dead person's body was improper. The letter was to be placed on the dead man's body. When the grave was opened:

> the corpse was found as it had been placed there, and the charter of absolution having been deposited upon its breast, and the tomb once more closed, he was thenceforth never more seen to wander.

Cross-species monsters

From the twelfth century onwards *bestiaries* became very popular, with their illustrated accounts of strange and exotic animals. Many of these were purely mythological fantasies, while others are clearly based on garbled travellers' tales of unusual animals, such as giraffes and rhinos. Mixed in with this was an intellectual trend which was relatively new in the twelfth century. This change in learned thinking reveals itself in some very unusual tales of marvels regarding cross-breeding, both animal and human.

Gerald of Wales recorded claims of human–animal cross-breeds in Wales and in Ireland and had a particular interest in horror stories connected with sex. Furthermore, he wrote 'there was a beautiful woman', but things were not as they appeared because she 'turned into a hairy creature, rough and shaggy while in the embrace of a man.' The message is a mixture of belief in werewolves (half wolf, half human) and fear of women. Gervase of Tilbury, who wrote in about 1200, also claimed: 'I have known at least two werewolves, one of whom devoured infants.' Though he doesn't actually claim these were-wolves were cross-breeds, his story is part of the same fear of mixed animals and people. Exactly who these 'werewolves' were is unknown. They might have been psychopathic child killers for whom the only suitable description was 'werewolf'. Unfortunately, Gervase does not give us any more clues.

We now know that Gerald's and Gervase's ideas were part of a changing view of animals. We can see it in the writings of a number of chroniclers from the twelfth century onwards. Before this time, animals and people were thought of as being totally different. Cross-breeding between animals and people was not thought possible. However, it was thought possible that animals might in rather strange ways influence human reproduction, though not through actually cross-breeding. The *Bestiary MS Bodley 764*, written in about 1250 but based on manuscripts dating from the late Roman period and earlier, suggested that:

> many people think that pregnant women should not look at ugly beasts such as apes and monkeys, in case they bring children into the world who resemble these caricatures. For women's nature is such that they produce offspring according to the image they see or have in mind at the moment of ecstasy as they conceive.

However, from the time of Gerald of Wales onwards, writers began to think that maybe it *was* possible that humans and animals might breed and produce cross-breeds. This made fears about bestiality even more terrifying. It was no longer seen only as a sin affecting the sinful person. The fear grew that it might also create monsters. Gerald believed that in Ireland there already existed monsters which were half human and half animal. In fact, Gerald had an interest in cross-species monsters even when no human being was involved.

> 'In our own days,' he wrote in 1188 about the English/Welsh border country, 'there was born a deer-cow. A stag mated with a cow. From this union there was born a deer-cow. All its fore-quarters as far back as the groin were bovine; but its rump, tail, legs and hoofs were like those of a deer, and it had a deer's colouring and shaggy hair. It stayed with the herds, for it was more of a domestic animal than a wild one.'

Gerald also had another similar story. 'Again in our time a bitch near here had a litter by a monkey and produced puppies which were ape-like in front but more like a dog behind.' But in case anyone asked to see these amazing monkey-dogs, Gerald had an answer as to where the evidence had gone: 'When the warden of the soldiers' quarters [in the castle] saw them, he was amazed at these prodigies of nature. Their deformed and hybrid bodies revolted this country bumpkin.' And so the 'evidence' vanished because: 'He killed the whole lot of them out of hand with a stick. His master was very annoyed when he learned what had happened and the man was punished.' Gerald was not alone in his beliefs. Medieval bestiaries claimed there were five types of monkey, or ape. One, called the cynocephalus, had the face of a dog and a long tail. It is possible that Gerald had heard of this and then, when he later heard local stories of deformed puppies, he concluded they were these monstrous animals.

Strange and unusual people

In a world in which disabilities were not subject to modern sensitivities and belief in equal opportunities, Matthew Paris recorded the occurrence on the Isle of Wight, in 1249, of a boy with greatly restricted height. 'He was not a dwarf, for his limbs were of just proportions; he was hardly three feet tall but had ceased to grow'. What is disturbing is how he was treated because he 'deviated' from the accepted norm. 'The queen ordered him to be taken around with her as a freak of nature to arouse the astonishment of onlookers.' An even more negative assessment of difference was meted out to a child born in Hereford. Matthew asserts that: 'Within half a year his teeth were fully grown and he was as tall as a youth of seventeen.' We may reject the exaggerated height but we are clearly here dealing with an unusually accelerated development, which is not unknown in certain rare cases. What is most revealing is Matthew's verdict on the cause of this unusual growth. He reports the belief, without qualification, that the child was 'begotten it was said by a demon' and, as a result, the 'mother was taken ill after the birth, pined away, and died miserably. Both of these were freaks of nature, the latter exceeding man's natural size, the former not attaining it.'

Matthew also combines condemnation of lesbianism with the idea that a hidden sin cannot remain hidden, in a report that:

> A woman of gentle origins, free and unmarried, made another woman pregnant. Their names were Hawisia and Lucia and they had two sons. The third pregnancy horrified the mother who confessed.

This, of course, went against all medieval ideas concerning pregnancy, which held that the male was solely responsible and the woman entirely passive in the act of conception. Clearly Matthew was prepared to accept that, in exceptional circumstances, this process might be overturned in order to reveal sin. In reality, the event might have resulted from an elicit heterosexual relationship which, on discovery through pregnancy, was for some reason blamed on a lesbian relationship as a way of shielding the father. This, though, is speculation.

Strange as the above account is, some stories of medieval marvels are so astonishing that they defy any possible modern rational explanation. They simply stand as testimony to a non-scientific mindset and a fascination with the bizarre. How else are we to explain the following report from Friar Roger Bacon? He claimed: 'A woman in Norwich, stout and of good stature, did not eat or excrete for twenty years. A fact proven in front of the bishop.' It would be interesting to see the nature of the 'proof'.

But perhaps the last word should go to the *Chronicle of Adam Usk, 1377–1421.* In a type of reporting which might be found in some modern tabloid newspapers, he claimed that:

> During this parliament [1399], two valets of the king who were dining in London found, in five eggs which were served up to them, the exact likeness of men's faces in every detail, the white having congealed and separated from the faces above the forehead in place of hair before passing down the jowls to the chin; one of which I saw.

Which suggests that there is a capacity to be entertained by the bizarre which is timeless.

Chapter 11

THE CYCLE OF THE YEAR

The Church in the Middle Ages structured the year to create different time periods in which the core beliefs of the Christian faith were celebrated. Today many Christian denominations continue to do this, and Christian liturgical calendars of Western Christians (as opposed to Eastern Orthodox Christians) – such as Lutheran, Anglican and other Protestant churches – to some extent follow the cycle of the Roman, or Latin, Rite of the Catholic Church. This cycle pre-dates the Reformation and developed through the Middle Ages. The so-called 'liturgical seasons' of the year in Western Christianity are: Advent, Christmas, Ordinary Time (Time after Epiphany), Lent, Easter and Ordinary Time (Time after Pentecost, or after Trinity). The phrase 'ordinary time' sounds strange and needs a little explanation. The word 'ordinary' comes from the same root as 'ordinal', and in the liturgical calendar means 'the counted weeks'. These are weeks which do not belong to an identified season; as such they act as a kind of bridge between major festivals. The greatest concentration of medieval ritual events occurred between Christmas and midsummer, and this has led some commentators to talk of a 'ritual half of the year' and a 'secular half of the year'. However, this is misleading because the whole of the year was affected by ritual and communal activities; this division of the year is really one of emphasis and not of striking contrast.[1]

This cycle of the year guided people in the Middle Ages through the calendar. It gave a purpose and a meaning to the passage of the seasons as they revealed truths about the Christian faith. The celebrations, feasts, fasts, vigils and processions gave structure, colour and texture to people's lives. They added to the sense of being part of a comprehensive world view and, in a period where many could not read or write, they served to educate people in central aspects of the Catholic Christian faith. Over time these developed, and occasionally there were new rituals added to the cycle, or new ways in which established celebrations were expressed. Other, more secular, festivities were also woven into this yearly calendar and played a part in marking the passage of time. A great deal of the study of this seasonal structure, its origins, development and the impact on it of the sixteenth-century Reformation has been carried out by Ronald Hutton,[2] and this overview of the medieval year, though also assisted by the work of other historians, is greatly indebted to the evidence he has presented.

In this overview only those festivities carried out in the Middle Ages will be discussed and there will be no attempt to account for their development since the mid-1550s, since that lies outside the scope of this book. In exploring this theme the structure of the Western Christian liturgical year will be followed, although some of the events discussed were secular in origin and will be identified as such.

Advent: preparing for the birth of Christ

Advent Sunday is the fourth Sunday before Christmas. As such it starts the liturgical year as it looks forward to the birth (*Nativity*) of Christ. Between Advent Sunday and Christmas Day was a four-week period of fasting. Of these fast days the holiest was Christmas Eve, when all meat, cheese and eggs were forbidden. The kinds of fast experienced at Advent, in Lent and at many other times of the Christian year were not times of abstaining from all food. Instead, they were times of reduced diet in which richer food was not eaten and in which fish replaced meat.

Christmas: The birth of Christ and the Twelve Days of Christmas

By the Middle Ages the celebration of Christ's birth on 25 December had become part of a twelve-day celebration – the *Twelve Days of Christmas*. The block of time between 26 December and 6 January was regarded as one interlinked sequence of festivities in which there were three fast days in the middle, surrounded by celebrations. The *Sarum Rite* (a form of service compiled at Salisbury Cathedral, Wiltshire) indicates that Christmas Day should start with a Mass. This was followed by reciting the genealogy of Christ, which was accompanied by lighting of candles and tapers in the darkened church. The largest of these was the candle burning on the *rood loft*, the wooden screen dividing the chancel from the nave and surmounted by statues of Jesus, St John and the Virgin Mary. The rest of Christmas Day was a celebration which ended the Advent Fast. As such it began the Christmas Season, rather than featuring as its climax. Many lords provided feasts for their tenants as well as for their immediate household.

In addition to celebrations on 25 December there were other important festivities associated with this period of the year. On 26 December, St Stephen the first Christian martyr was remembered. 27 December became the day of St John the Evangelist. 28 December was Holy Innocents' Day, which recalled the children of Bethlehem murdered by Herod's soldiers. This day linked back to Christmas Day and forward to 6 January, Epiphany. 1 January, already significant as New Year's Day, became the feast of Christ's Circumcision. Older traditions concerning New Year's Day continued to cause concern to Church leaders. In northern England it was influenced by activities whose roots went back to pagan Viking times and to which has become attached the Scandinavian word *Yule*. This word was not known in England before the eleventh century, though it may have had an earlier form to describe midwinter events which were pagan in origin. Sometime before 1008 Archbishop Wulfstan condemned superstitious activities associated with this period, and in the late twelfth century the bishop of Exeter identified a specific act of penance for those involved in 'heathen rites' on this day. Fourteenth- and fifteenth-century comments have also survived which condemn attempts to tell the fortune of the year on this day. At Torksey (Lincolnshire), an amnesty for disputes was called *Yule-girth*: at York this ran for 12 days from St Thomas' Day on 21 December and apparently attracted many undesirable characters to the city to make the most of this permissive period. The fact that 1 January was tainted with activities linked to pre-Christian festivals may explain why, in 1155, New Year's Day was shifted to 25 March, which was the Christian feast of the Annunciation. This way of calculating the start and end of the year lasted until 1752. Despite this, New Year's Eve and New Year's Day continued to be a time of community events.

The Twelve Days were times of community celebration. Villeins did not have to work on the demesne land of the lord of the manor during this period. Lords provided a feast, though on a number of manors it was more a bring-and-share lunch, since villeins were expected to bring foodstuffs as gifts for their manorial lord! The feasts given by royal, episcopal and aristocratic households could be enormous. Party games were also enjoyed and the record of the keeping of Christmas by the bishop of Salisbury in 1406 refers to 'games' and 'disguisings'. During the fifteenth century manor accounts also record money paid to travelling entertainers. While we do not know the content of these plays, it is likely that many focused on the theme of the Nativity itself. These festivities were accompanied by singing carols. A large number of these survive from the decades either side of 1500, although the first are recorded from 1300. They are songs which accompanied a dance and which often had lyrics concerned with the Nativity, or a saint, although some had secular themes. Card and board games, it can be surmised, also played a part in these times.

Late Medieval records also refer to decorating churches with evergreen plants such as holly and ivy. Houses seem to have been decorated in the same way. There are hints that holly decorated the inside and ivy the porches. There are no medieval references to mistletoe being used in these decorations, and no sense whatsoever that anything remotely pagan was associated with this foliage. The record of laying mistletoe on the altar at York Minster dates from no earlier than the seventeenth century and, while this clearly goes back to a pre-Christian past, it had long been stripped of any pagan belief system and was assimilated into the Christian world/cosmic view of life continuing within a period of darkness and death.

Despite many claims to the contrary there are few medieval records of any other midwinter celebrations, apart from a suggestion that, in about the 1520s, the Abbots Bromley Horn Dance (in Staffordshire) was already in operation. Here it seems that a Christmas-time celebration involved some use of a *hobby horse* and probably the reindeer horns later used by dancers. The horns themselves have been dated to the eleventh century. There is, however, no evidence for anything else like it elsewhere in England.[3] Other hobby horses are known from the northern Midlands in the early sixteenth century and were part of events designed to raise money for the parish.

The tone of an aristocratic Christmas is provided in the late fourteenth-century poem *Sir Gawain and the Green Knight*, which describes the seasonal festivities at the legendary court of King Arthur:

> The king lay at Camelot at Christmas-tide
> with many a lovely lord, lieges most noble . . .
> and jousted full joyously these gentle lords;
> then to the court they came at carols to play.
> For there the feast was unfailing fifteen days.[4]

The importance of New Year festivities is also apparent in this poem, along with seasonal games and the giving of gifts. Indeed it was New Year which appears to have been the main focus for gift giving:

> then nobles ran anon with New Year gifts…
> Competed for those presents in playful debate;
> ladies laughed loudly, though they lost the game.[4]

Another form of seasonal entertainment which appears in the English records from the thirteenth century is *momerie*, or *mumming*. In 1347 it is recorded at the court of Edward III and involved the wearing of elaborate masks. What started as a kind of disguised fancy dress event could – sadly – become a cloak for crime. In 1405 the city authorities in London banned mumming on the streets and similar restrictions were put into force in Bristol and Chester in the fifteenth century. What is very interesting is that there is absolutely no evidence at all from the Middle Ages of the kinds of plays about combat and resurrection later associated with mummers, and it seems clear that this was not an ancient custom which can be traced back to this time.

A more constructive activity was that of *hogglers*, who first appear in local records in the 1450s and who seem to have toured the parish raising money for parish projects and at times paying for candles lit in the local church. This collecting of money was perhaps linked to the New Year's Day tradition of gift giving, and lower down the social scale this – like hoggling – probably involved pressure exerted on reluctant givers in some instances. In London in 1419 a prohibition was passed against threats being used by members of the households of city officials to get New Year's Day gifts from local traders!

Holy Innocents' Day appears in England to have been associated with processions and events involving young people – often choirboys – from the 1220s. In 1222 at Salisbury it was described as the 'Feast of Boys'. The event seems to have involved the election of one choirboy as the 'Boy Bishop' and in 1225 there is evidence from London of a small bishop's mitre being purchased for use. By the early fourteenth century the idea seems to have spread from the cathedrals down to local parishes. From 1263 the clergy at St Paul's in London revised the procedures so that they chose which boy had the honour. (This attempt to control the event and keep it more orderly lay behind a rule introduced at Salisbury, in 1443, banning the carrying of staves.) At Winchester and York the Boy Bishop had the honour of saying Mass. Some nunneries in the thirteenth century allowed girls to lead the services on Holy Innocents' Day. At Bristol, in the 1480s, the city's mayor and corporation attended services at St Nicholas' church, led by the Boy Bishop. This linking of the Boy Bishops with St Nicholas was not unique and begins a long tradition of associating this saint with children at Christmas time.

Linked with the idea of Boy Bishops was the idea of a 'Lord of Misrule'. This was another role-reversal custom and involved a member of a household being chosen by lot to be 'lord for the day'. The position was sometimes called 'Bean King', as a bean cooked into a cake was the way by which the person was selected, depending on who got the bean. Bean Kings are recorded at the English royal court in 1315 and 1335. During the fifteenth century 'midwinter kings' appear at Oxford and Norwich. A 'Lord of Misrule' and an 'Abbot of Unreason' were set up in the royal court in 1489, and a Lord of Misrule continued to be a feature of royal Christmas-tide celebrations until 1553 and the start of the reign of Mary Tudor. The idea was not confined to the royal court, as the examples of the Oxford colleges and the city of Norwich demonstrate, and such 'Lords' were found in many well-off households. The day after Twelfth Night was called Distaff Day and signalled a return to normal behaviour and the usual social order.

From the 1320s descriptions increase of a communal gathering, sharing drink from a *wassail* cup and wishing each other well. The word 'wassail' was derived from the Old English for 'good health to you'. Earlier thirteenth-century accounts refer to the dipping of cakes or bread in a common bowl, which appears to be a variant of this tradition.

Epiphany: the revealing of Christ
6 January was the Feast of Epiphany. The theme celebrated was the revealing of the nature of Jesus through events in His life as recorded in the New Testament. The earliest of these was the visit of the Magi and the later baptism of Jesus by John the Baptist in the river Jordan. Other revealings also came to be celebrated on this day, including the miracle of turning water into wine at the wedding at Cana and the Feeding of the Five Thousand. The one which came to be particularly associated with this date was the visit of the Magi to the young Jesus. Although not numbered or named in Matthew's gospel they soon became so associated with their gifts of gold, frankincense and myrrh that it was assumed they had been three in number and were kings.

Twelfth Night was sometimes associated with the raising of gilded Stars of Bethlehem in some churches to celebrate the Wise Men. In wealthier households, in the late fifteenth and early sixteenth centuries, there are records again of feasting and of gift giving during this time.

Plough Monday: the breaking of the soil of winter
Between Christmas and Lent ploughing started. January, February and March saw villagers engaged in this wet and exhausting work. And yet the survival of the community rested on the success of the crop which lay at the end of this process. As a result the start of ploughing attracted a great deal of concern and villagers marked it in many different ways. By 1450 the practice had been long established of setting aside the first Sunday after Epiphany as 'Plough Sunday' and the first Monday after Twelfth Night as 'Plough Monday'. Plough races might be held and there are critical mentions of villagers hauling their plough around a fire, in order (presumably) to

'purify' it and prepare it for the work ahead. Candles, called 'plough lights', were set up in churches and are mentioned in the church accounts of a number of parishes in East Anglia and the eastern Midlands of England. In some parishes the ploughs were kept in the churches prior to the start of ploughing, and in the period 1547–53 the practice was condemned as 'conjuring of ploughs'. From the mid-fifteenth century there are mentions in church records of ploughs dragged around villages, of collections of money to pay for the plough lights and of village feasts.

Candlemas

On 2 February the Feast of the Purification of the Blessed Virgin Mary recalled and celebrated the presentation of the baby Jesus in the Temple (recorded in Luke 2: 22–35). Simeon's response to the baby Jesus included these words:

> For my eyes have seen your salvation, which you have prepared in the sight of all people, a light for revelation to the Gentiles and for glory to your people Israel.[5]

This gave the event its particular focus on light and on candlelit processions, and from this came its traditional name in England of *Candlemas*. Parishioners brought candles to church to be blessed. Afterwards in some parishes these were paraded around the church; in others they were burnt before statues of the Virgin Mary; in others they were taken home to be lit in times of crisis. In a number of towns the services and processions were followed by feasting. It is clear though that the candles were starting to be venerated themselves, in a process which characterizes a large number of Catholic festivals and celebrations in the Middle Ages: starting as symbols, objects came to be invested with attributions of holiness themselves. It was this and the strong focus on the Virgin Mary which made the event the target of Protestant reformers in the 1540s and early 1550s.

St Valentine's Day: 14 February

In the 1440s the English poet John Lydgate refers to an English custom at the royal court of sending romantic gifts to the person they loved of the opposite sex. The same event is mentioned in the *Paston Letters* from the 1470s. In some cases the person selected was chosen by lot within the household. Whether this custom was only practised by the wealthy, or whether it was supported by ordinary people, is impossible to tell from the surviving evidence. The actual feast day of St Valentine was abolished under Edward VI but the romantic fun continued, now disconnected from any religious context.

Lent

The 40 days prior to Easter were marked by a time of fasting, referred to as Lent. This time both recalled Jesus's time in the wilderness prior to the start of His earthly ministry, and also prepared believers for the celebration of Easter, which marked the climax of His time on earth. All of the feasts, fasts and celebrations related to Easter are 'movable feasts' because Easter itself moves, being celebrated on the first Sunday after the first full moon after the Spring equinox. As a result Easter-related events can occur as early as 4 February and as late as 24 June.

Lent was preceded by Shrove-tide. This covered 'Collop Monday' and 'Shrove Tuesday'. The names preserve the dual characteristics of this time – preparing for Lent (*shrove* coming from the word for confession) and feasting before the start of the time of fasting (*collop* being a piece of cooked meat). The period was a time of active celebration and feasting. Pancakes are not actually recorded until about 1586 but may have been present a lot earlier. Other – more active and rowdy – entertainments also marked Shrove Tuesday: cockfighting, football and boisterous collection of money. In 1314 the playing of football was banned in London on this day, and in 1409 the money collections were similarly outlawed. A traditional entertainment was 'cock threshing'. This involved hurling missiles at a cock to kill it, or burying one up to its neck in the ground and striking at it blindfolded until the head came off. The brutal nature of this activity offers a shocking glimpse into life in the Middle Ages – which may be set against the illuminated manuscripts and magnificent Church architecture of the time. The same society which produced these was quite capable of the most shocking cruelty towards animals, and this is a feature of many societies prior to the modern period. The football games could be equally violent. The game appeared to have had no rules (apart from getting control of the ball at all costs), no limits on numbers of players, and a reputation for damage and injury.

And after this – the fast. During Lent the following were prohibited: butter, cheese, eggs, meat, milk, marriage and sexual intercourse. In some areas the fast was encouraged to be absolute during daylight hours, with acceptable foodstuffs being consumed in the evening. Fish would have been consumed in very large quantities as it was on all usual fast days, principally Fridays. However, some people were prepared to eat barnacle geese since it was popularly believed that these were hatched from barnacles and were therefore more fish than fowl (see Chapter 10). The period of fasting started on the morning of 'Ash Wednesday' with a service characterized by confession and the marking of ash crosses on the foreheads of those attending. At the same time the altar, the lectern and images of Christ, the Virgin Mary and saints were covered in white cloths decorated with red crosses.

Easter

The climax of the period of Lent was the great Christian celebration of the death and Resurrection of Christ. The week before Easter was known as Holy Week and started with Palm Sunday. This Sunday celebrates Christ's triumphant entry into Jerusalem in the week before His death and Resurrection. The celebrations on this Sunday varied but the central theme was the reading of New Testament accounts of Christ's entry into Jerusalem and the blessing of branches and processions – headed by the consecrated host – from the church into the churchyard and back again. In some churches people dressed as Old Testament prophets read Bible passages in the churchyard, and flowers and cakes were thrown to those processing as they re-entered the church. At the end of the service small crosses were made from the branches and taken home. As with so many medieval customs the slide from symbol to superstition meant that these 'Palm Crosses' were regarded by many as being good-luck charms and as a consequence would later be banned under Edward VI.

During Holy Week the Church events moved day by day towards Easter and at each point prepared people for the events at the end of this special week. In a service on Wednesday the cloth covering the altar was either torn or removed. In the evening occurred the first of the Services of Shadows (the *Tenebrae*), a very powerful and moving service which recalled the desertion of Jesus by His disciples and his abandonment by the world as He alone carried the sins of the world in His crucified body. Candles were set up in church and, one by one, snuffed out until only the candle representing Christ stood burning in the dark.

On Maundy Thursday English rulers had, since John in 1210, followed the tradition of washing the feet of selected (and presumably well-cleaned) poor people and presenting them with gifts. This was in memory of Jesus washing the feet of his disciples on the evening before His crucifixion. From 1361 (in the reign of Edward III) the monarch washed the feet of the number of poor people corresponding to his age. The same procedure was followed at a number of cathedrals and abbeys. In the Middle Ages the day was called *Sharp Thursday* and this was probably derived from the cutting of hair in preparation for Easter. In churches altars and their cloths were washed and parishioners attended confession. Bells were not rung on this day. In the evening, in a number of churches, the Tenebrae was followed once more.

On Good Friday altars were again washed. Some people emphasized their sense of repentance by subjecting themselves to scourging by their priest. On the same day monarchs since Edward II blessed rings which it was then thought would have healing power against epilepsy. This survived the reign of Edward VI and eventually stopped only during the reign of Elizabeth I. During the Good Friday service a crucifix was laid on the steps leading up to the altar and clergy and laity crawled to it to kiss it in a ceremony known as 'Creeping to the Cross'. After the service the cross and a piece of the host consecrated on Maundy Thursday were wrapped in cloth and laid in a specially made tomb on the northern side of the chancel. This was the 'Easter Sepulchre'. It was covered with a richly embroidered cloth and often surrounded with candles. In many churches these candles were paid for by the Corpus Christi guilds of the parish (see 'Corpus Christi', below). In some churches members of the parish kept watch beside the tomb, and bread and ale was provided from local collections. That night the final Tenebrae was sung.

On Holy Saturday all candles in the church were put out according to the Sarum Rite and then relit from a new fire started by the priest. This relighting included the Paschal Candle, which was the largest candle used in any church service or event. By 1500 the next great step in the Easter celebration was the opening of the Easter Sepulchre early on Easter morning, while it was still dark. The cross was carried around the church and the bells – which had not been rung since the Wednesday of Holy Week – pealed out. Afterwards, the cross was laid on the altar and Creeping to the Cross took place once more. The empty sepulchre had candles lit before it and this continued until the Friday following Easter. Statues which had been covered for the whole of Lent were again uncovered. This was followed by gifts being given to the local church. Easter Day was a popular day for baptisms, as it was so central to Christian faith and to the hope of Eternal Life. Feasting followed the Easter Mass and the giving of painted eggs often occurred at this time as symbols of new life. This is documented as early as 1290 in the royal court of Edward I.

The Mass at Easter was the centre point of the year, as far as the involvement of laity in the Eucharist was concerned, because this was normally the only time that they partook of the *host*. Following its consecration at the high point of the Mass it was distributed to all the parishioners present on Easter morning. So holy was the host that parishioners often held a linen cloth under their chin – the *houselling towel* – to prevent any crumbs of the host from falling to the ground. Usually, on other Sundays throughout the year, as a substitute for the host, those present at Mass shared a piece of the *holy loaf*. This was a loaf of bread presented to the priest at the start of the service; later blessed and distributed amongst the congregation as a sign of their unity. (Though often the size of the pieces received reflected the social hierarchy of the local community!) The wine of the Mass was only ever consumed by the priest, and the shift to receiving the Eucharist in 'both kinds' was one of the major changes brought about by the Protestant Reformation of the sixteenth century.

Easter Monday was often accompanied by local feasts called 'church ales' in which money was collected for parish funds, especially the support of the poor. This was sometimes associated with the return of the wassail cup – last used following Christmas – and Lords of Misrule in some areas. This continued during *Hocktide* or the *Hokkedays*, which fell on the second Monday and Tuesday after Easter. First recorded in London in 1406, this was traditionally claimed to recall either the massacre of the Danes in England under Ethelred II, in 1002, or the death of the last Danish king to rule England, Harthacnut, in 1042. There is, however, no evidence connecting the Hocktide activities with these ancient events and the origin of the activity is obscure. Traditionally the events consisted of the men of the parish, on the Monday, capturing and tying up the women and demanding a kiss for their release. On the Tuesday the women returned the favour by capturing the men and demanding payment before freeing them. The cash collected went to parish funds and very large sums of money were raised. Hocktide activities were made illegal under Edward VI as they were associated with disorder.

St George's Day

23 April was the feast day of St George, a celebration which first appeared in England in 1222. A large number of town guilds were set up to celebrate the fame of this very popular saint through 'ridings' on his feast day. This took the form of a procession with a model dragon and people dressed as St George. It was nationally supported and had come to have a patriotic character as well as a religious one. Despite this St George would not survive the Reformation dismissal of cults of saints.

May Day and May Games

Activities linked to the first day of May are recorded as early as the middle of the thirteenth century. The events centred on the cutting of flowers and green branches, often flowering hawthorn, with which houses were decorated to mark the coming of summer. This was the famous 'bringing in the May'. By 1350 maypoles (with their attendant dancing) were central features of the day. From the fifteenth century there is evidence of young women making and selling May garlands.

One of the most striking of later medieval events were the May Games. These were often held on the two days after Whitsunday but could occur on a number of occasions during the month of May. These were often associated with 'church ales' called 'Whitsun Ales', where church wardens would arrange a communal meal to raise money for parish funds. These May Games became very popular during the fifteenth century. They often involved dancing and the crowning of a mock king and queen to oversee the events. Brief references to these mock coronations date from as early as 1240. In a number of parishes after the 1450s this position was taken by Robin Hood. This very popular outlaw was usually accompanied by the young men of the village and toured the local area raising money for parish funds. From the earliest records of these May Games he is associated with another character named Little John, and from later (after about 1500) with Friar Tuck and Maid Marian. It seems that the 'Queen of May' and 'the friar' were earlier and separate characters associated together with early Morris Dancing. The original friar may not even have been the same character as the later Friar Tuck. As early as about 1283 a French play by Adam de la Halle linked a Robin with a shepherdess named Marion and the two became part of the French version of the May Games. The two first appeared in England in a poem, written by the English poet John Gower between 1376–9. They seem to be part of a quite different tradition from that of Robin Hood, and their role developed alongside his legends in the fifteenth century until Robin Hood and the Robin of the May Games became one character. This clearly seems to have occurred by 1500. In this way Marian became the Queen and Robin Hood the King of the May Games.[6]

Morris Dancing was also associated with these May-time revels. A great deal of fanciful speculation has centred on the origins of Morris Dancing but Ronald Hutton has reviewed the evidence, alongside the rival interpretations, to convincingly demonstrate that in England it began life as a mid-fifteenth-century energetic dance which was popular in royal and aristocratic circles and, though royal interest declined in the 1520s, it had by then become popular amongst commoners.[7]

Rogationtide

This event took place on the Monday, Tuesday and Wednesday before Ascension Day and involved asking God's blessing on the growing crops as parishioners processed around the parish preceded by a cross. The name is derived from the Latin word for 'asking' and the processions were also known as Cross Days. Places where prayers were said on these processions gave rise to local minor names and field names such as 'Amen Corner', still found in English country areas today. Sadly, these processions could sometimes lead to violence as processions from rival parishes met in the fields and lanes. At Durham three processions made a circuit of the priory precinct accompanied by portable shrines and the banner of St Cuthbert. This was one day within a cycle of processions which occurred at Durham between St Mark's Day (on 25 April) and Corpus Christi.

Ascension Day
Celebrated on the sixth Thursday after Easter, this event recalled the Ascension of Jesus into heaven. Church bells were rung and the Easter Paschal Candle was lit for the last time. When it was taken out of the church it was symbolic of Christ now being in heaven. In some areas there were processions around the parish led by crosses and, if a church possessed any, carrying relics of a saint.

Whitsunday, or Pentecost
The Christian celebration of Pentecost (on the seventh Sunday after Easter) recalls the pouring of God's Holy Spirit upon the assembled disciples in Jerusalem following Ascension Day. In England Pentecost was also known as *Whitsunday*, probably after the white baptismal robes worn by those baptized on this day. Whitsunday was often the occasion of more parades and, where a church was a daughter church of a larger one or under the control of a monastery, visits to these might take place with gifts, known as 'Pentecostals'. Church ales and May Games often followed for the next two days. At Chester and Norwich there were parades and pageants and plays more usually associated with Corpus Christi Day.

Trinity Sunday
Pope Alexander II (1061–73) refused a request for a special feast to honour the Holy Trinity on the grounds that such a feast was not a tradition within the Catholic Church and that every day the Church honoured the Holy Trinity. However, he did not

forbid continuing the celebration in churches where it already existed. Later, Pope John XXII (1316–34) revised this decision. He ordered that there should be a special feast day dedicated to the Holy Trinity, for the entire Church, and that it should take place on the first Sunday after Pentecost. A new form of service for this day had earlier been written by the Franciscan John Peckham (died in 1292), who was later archbishop of Canterbury. The Sundays until Advent then became counted either from Pentecost, or from Trinity Sunday. In time, Trinity Sunday marked the end of a three-week period (starting on Rogation Sunday) when weddings were forbidden. At All Saints' church, South Lynn (Norfolk) the Holy Trinity Guild of the parish paid for the candles which burnt before the image of the Holy Trinity there, and such guilds (which, along with Corpus Christi guilds and those dedicated to the Virgin Mary, were very popular) would have placed particular emphasis on supporting devotions on Trinity Sunday.

Corpus Christi

This medieval celebration took place on the second Thursday after Pentecost and was a late addition to the yearly cycle of Church events, as it did not appear until 1317. It was formally started to draw greater attention to the Catholic under-standing of the Mass. This held that Christ was actually present in the bread and wine of the Eucharist; the term used to describe this is 'the Real Presence'. It was encouraged by the developing theology of *Transubstantiation* – an idea that had been growing for centuries within the Catholic Church, although it was not until 1215 and the Fourth Lateran Council that the word 'transubstantiation' was used in a profession of faith, when describing the change that was believed to take place in the Eucharist.

In 1318 the celebration of Corpus Christi is first recorded at Gloucester and at Wells. The theme of the day was a statement of the unity of the whole community and centred on the cele-bration of Christ's sacrifice and presence in the Catholic Mass.

This increased its popularity right across the social spectrum: from the Church hierarchy (for whom it became a central feature of Church authority, since priests were believed to be the only ones capable of channelling this presence of Christ), through secular authorities (for whom it provided a focal point for community unity), to ordinary men and women (because they believed it provided a way by which they could come into the very presence of God, in the Mass). There is a great deal of evidence which points to the fact that Catholic beliefs about the Mass were well understood and were loyally followed by most of the community. It was, in the words of John Bossy, the 'social miracle' which brought together all communities – even those which in other ways were economically and socially divided.[8] As Corpus Christi became a target for Lollard criticism (see Chapter 4), after 1390, its importance as a way of stating traditional and orthodox belief increased in the fifteenth century.

Despite this focus on community unity, Corpus Christi Day could be interpreted in a revolutionary sense in certain circumstances. It was surely no coincidence that the Peasants' Revolt broke out on 13 June – Corpus Christi Day – 1381. At a time when many people felt that high taxes and corrupt government threatened community life, the day became a platform for protest. It was also an opportunity to declare a new social order, in which the end of villeinage, the removal of worldly priests and the sharing out of Church lands would create a new community of the 'true commons'.[9] At St Albans those in revolt particularly resented the abbot's insistence on locals being forced to pay to use his mill. An early abbot had confiscated the millstones of tenants and had set them into the floor of the parlour of the monastery as a sign of his power over them. In 1381 the rebels dug up these millstones, broke them up and gave pieces to each present to take home. This was a deliberate re-enactment of the theme of Corpus Christi and that of the 'holy loaf' (see 'Easter', above). It reminds us how deep Christian belief and devotion to Corpus Christi ran in the hearts, minds and popular culture of England in the Middle Ages, and that it did not always take the form that those in authority wished it to! The chronicler, Thomas Walsingham, who described the events at St Albans on that Corpus Christi day, knew exactly what was going on – and did not approve.

The occasion itself was marked by processions of the host through the streets, and by 1400 it had become the third most popular focus of attention by religious guilds, after the Virgin Mary and The Trinity. These guilds existed to channel activities towards a particular form of Christian devotion: meeting for Mass on the day that was particularly special to them, paying for candles and services, and asking God's blessing on the groups responsible. They often held a feast on these days, and both men and women could be members, although women were rarely officers.[10] These religious guilds grew to increasing prominence in the second half of the fourteenth century. In many towns the Corpus Christi processions were very elaborate and included shrines to house the host and a canopy to protect the shrine from rain. Crosses and candles were carried and town dignitaries followed the priests. As the host passed, those on the street were expected to remove their hats and stand bare-headed in reverence. Churches were decorated with flowers, bells were rung and parish accounts refer to the purchase of wine for those taking part in the procession.

After the procession, dramatic presentations often took place. These dramas had as their focus key Biblical themes relating to Creation, the Fall, God's Salvation for believers in Christ and the Last Judgement. In larger towns huge pageants on carts were pulled through the streets – these appeared at York from 1376, and by 1415 the actors on their carts were part of an elaborate display. The same development occurred across England, and from this arose the *Mystery Plays* (see Chapter 8). The name derives from the guilds or 'mysteries' (i.e. skilled craftsmen who guarded the secrets of their trade) who paid for and organized different aspects of these plays. The Mystery Plays were made up of a cycle of different plays which had the same themes as earlier tableaux. They are known in Coventry from the 1440s, York by 1460 and Chester, where a developed cycle of plays was in operation by the 1520s. In the last case the cycle of plays was moved to Whitsun. The guilds spent huge amounts of money on costumes and scenery and usually took a theme appropriate to their trade, such as fishmongers presenting scenes on the Sea of Galilee, or shipwrights constructing Noah's ark. It has been suggested that the reason why some towns produced these elaborate events while others did not was because they had particular reasons for needing large-scale community projects designed to encourage unity, perhaps because of particular stresses or conflicts between groups.[11] Whether this was true or not is unclear, but certainly many major towns did not produce such cycles of plays, or even the less demanding pageants.

Summer events

Some seasonal events and customs had no place within the calendar of the Christian Church, not even as pre-Christian events which had been incorporated into Christian activities or adapted to Christian teaching. The most obvious of these took place at midsummer, at a time when there were relatively few Church feasts and celebrations. Many of these community activities involved fire. In the fourteenth century, at Winchcombe (Gloucestershire), a flaming wheel was rolled down a steep slope of the Cotswolds. Something similar happened at Buckfastleigh (Devon), only there it was thought lucky if the wheel could be guided into a stream to extinguish it. Both these took place on Midsummer's Eve (23 June) which was also the evening before the feast of St John the Baptist. At Whitby (Yorkshire) fire celebrations occurred on the eves of the Nativity of St John the Baptist (23 June), Saints Peter and Paul (28 June) and the Translation of St Thomas Becket (of his body from its first burial place) (6 July). Other fire ceremonies involved carrying lighted torches around cornfields; these events were associated with village feasts. Examples of such fire ceremonies date from the thirteenth century, and the fires were sometimes referred to as 'St John's Fire'. Bonfire parties also occurred in many villages, and in some towns there were processions, such as those which took place in London from 1378. In London, Chester, Coventry and many other towns these processions developed into major pageants, with burning torches, musicians, hobby horses and models of fabulous animals.

First fruits, harvest and the turning of the year

1 August was generally regarded as the start to the harvest and was called Lammas Day (from the Old English word *hlafmaesse*, meaning 'loaf-mass'). In a number of areas it was the custom to cut the first sheaf, bake the flour into bread and dedicate it to God. In this way the 'first fruits' of the harvest were consecrated and God's blessing was sought for the whole harvest. Lammas was also an important day for fairs and rent payments.

Early September saw the harvest gathered in. On some manors the custom grew up of the lord of the manor providing food and drink for the reapers during harvest. At others a Harvest Supper was held, with food and drink provided by the lord. Shortly after harvest was Michaelmas, on 29 September, which was the feast of St Michael the Archangel. Like Lammas, it was a day on which a number of the organizational aspects of rural life were brought together: courts were held, rent was paid and a Michaelmas goose was traditionally consumed.

This time of the year was also the traditional time for dedication feasts, or *wakes*, in honour of the saint after whom the local church was named. There was no fixed date for these church services and communal meals. Parishes often invited neighbouring parishes to join them, and the mutual partying could go on for days – with harvest safely in and winter approaching many people clearly felt the need for an extended period of festivity.

Some of the feast days of saintly patrons could attract rather unusual activities. At Bury St Edmunds (Suffolk) a white bull, garlanded with flowers, was led to the abbey accompanied by barren wives who stroked its flanks and – once the abbey was reached – prayed that they might conceive. The oblique link between this symbol of sexual potency and a saint who was a 'glorious king, virgin and martyr' (to quote his titles publicized at Bury) is only a thin veneer over a blatantly superstitious activity. While this example is fairly extreme, it helps explain why Protestant reformers were very antagonistic to the cult of saints and some of the highly questionable – and at times non-Christian – activities which had become associated with some of them during the Middle Ages.[12] At St Paul's cathedral, London, on the feast day of St Paul a fallow buck was delivered from the Essex hunting chase of one of its manors and carried through the cathedral to the high altar. From there it was sent for cooking, except for the head and antlers which were paraded back through the cathedral before the cross, to the west door. Here a hunting horn was sounded and other horns replied from around the city.[13]

Autumn and the coming of winter

In November the dark days of autumn turning to winter were alleviated by the twin festivals of All Saints' Day, or All Hallows' Day, on 1 November, and All Souls' Day on 2 November. On All Saints' Day prayers were said to speed the souls of the dead through purgatory (a Catholic belief in the refining of souls prior to the Final Judgement to heaven, or to hell). Following this, the church bells were rung to comfort these souls. In some parishes the bells rang until midnight. Sometimes these ceremonies were transferred to the following night – the evening of All Souls' Day.

The final November event was that of Martinmas, on 11 November, the feast of St Martin. This took place at the time of the slaughtering of surplus farm animals for whom there was insufficient of the valuable hay supplies to feed them over the winter. As a result this date became closely associated with community feasts as the last fresh meat of the year was eaten; the remainder being salted or smoked to preserve it.

In some parishes St Catherine's Day (the saint associated with the 'Catherine Wheel'), on 25 November, was marked with feasts. Some celebrated St Clement's Day, on 23 November, in the same way. More parishes elected Boy Bishops (otherwise associated with the Twelve Days of Christmas) on St Nicholas's Day on 6 December and allowed these to perform the role of priest. However, for most English Christians in the Middle Ages, Martinmas was the last major celebration until the cycle of the year started again with the First Sunday in Advent.

The impact of the Reformation on the cycle of the year

The Reformation had a tremendous impact on the cycle of seasonal events. The new Protestant Prayer Book under Edward VI (1547–53) put an end to the traditional services held on Christmas Morning and at Epiphany. Not only the traditional services were banished; in many churches the rood lofts themselves were physically demolished at this time. However, the fact that so many of the celebrations at this time were based on events recorded in the Bible meant that the Twelve Days of Christmas survived from the Middle Ages into the Early Modern period more intact than many other medieval celebrations. In this way the celebrations of Christmas, St Stephen, St John the Evangelist, Holy Innocents, Christ's Circumcision and Epiphany survived. Decorating with holly and ivy, however, appears to have gone out of fashion at about the time of these changes; probably because it was disapproved of as unbiblical. In 1541 Henry VIII banned the tradition of Boy Bishops on Holy Innocents' Day.

With the coming of the reign of Mary Tudor in 1553 the Lords of Misrule vanished from the royal court, though there seems to have been no theological reason for this. It was probably simply that they were too closely associated with the previous regime's Christmas celebrations.

In 1538, under Henry VIII, all 'holy candles' were banned and in one action this put an end to plough lights and Candlemas. In 1547, under Edward VI, the guilds which set up and paid for these candles were banned. Some revived under Mary Tudor but then slowly declined thereafter; the momentum of continuous custom had been disrupted. In 1539 Candlemas came under scrutiny in regulations which did not abolish it but which banned any superstitious actions thought to invest objects with holiness, or with what was condemned as magical powers. In 1548 it was banned outright. The same ban stopped religious celebration of St Valentine.

In 1538 Henry VIII ordered that it was acceptable to eat dairy products during Lent. He did this with his new authority as Head of the Church in England. However, Lent continued as a fast from meat and survived the reign of Edward VI and so out of the period covered by this book. Other features of Lent suffered more negative attention. In 1548 the blessing of ashes on Ash Wednesday was banned, as was the veiling of images (since images themselves were banned).

Henry VIII allowed Palm Sunday celebrations, so long as they did not involve any hint of superstitious belief about the crosses themselves, but both processions and making crosses were banned in 1547. In 1548 the blessing of branches was banned, as was Creeping to the Cross and ash crosses on Ash Wednesday. Similarly banned was the Service of Shadows on the Wednesday of Holy Week. In the same year Easter Sepulchres were attacked by Archbishop Cranmer and swiftly stopped. Revived under Mary, these finally ceased under Elizabeth I. The same occurred with the Easter Paschal Candle. Linked to disorderly conduct, the Hockday celebrations vanished during the reign of Edward VI, along with other disorderly events such as hoggling. The same thinking probably lay behind the condemnation of Whitsun Ales, which, though not banned, rapidly went into decline from the late 1540s.

It was not disorder but opposition to what were considered Catholic practices which caused the decline of the tremendously popular St George's Day celebrations. The banning of statues of saints and the dissolving of guilds dedicated to them in the first year of the reign of Edward VI saw the collapse of St George's Day. In 1552 it was omitted from the calendar of religious events, as St George had no Biblical backing. No official banning took place of Rogationtide marches and Whitsunday processions, but they declined during the reign of Edward VI through disapproval of carrying saints' images and of crosses set up around parish boundaries, which some reformers considered attracted superstitious attention. Under Elizabeth I the Rogationtide processions reappeared as a way of establishing local boundaries, but with a minimum of ceremonies.

In 1547 the suppression of religious guilds removed the main means by which Corpus Christi plays were performed and organized. When the new Prayer Book of 1549 removed all reference to Corpus Christi, as a Catholic doctrine, it put an end to the processions, pageants and plays dedicated to its celebration. This celebration had long been disapproved of by those critical of Catholic doctrine, and from the 1390s it had been a target for Lollard criticism.[14] The Midsummer Processions too declined in the late 1540s. The possibly magical perception of the fires and the fear of public disorder meant that, though never formally abolished, a sense of official disapproval signalled their end.

It seems to have been a reaction to over-extended holidays which caused Henry VIII to stop the traditional wakes and instead, in 1532, directed all churches to hold their dedication day on the first Sunday in October. Prior to this, the feasting and partying could go on for days. However, it was a straight-forward collision between Reformed Protestant beliefs and medieval Catholicism which led to the ending of the ceremonies associated with All Saints and All Souls. There was an attempt to abolish ringing bells for the dead in 1546 and, although never actually formally abolished, this was heavily criticized by royal inspectors and quickly ceased.

The end of the medieval ritual year – or the 'fall of Merry England' to quote Ronald Hutton[15] – was brought about by many factors. The two most significant were changing religious ideas and changing economic structures, which broke existing social relationships and encouraged employers to try to force a new discipline on their workers. As such it was not only a 'Reformation of religion' but also a 'Reformation of manners' which happened after 1530. Together they broke the cycle of the year which had turned for almost a millennium.

Chapter 12

THE SHAPE OF
ENGLISH SOCIETY BY 1553

It was under Henry VIII and his son, Edward VI, that the greatest assaults took place on the Catholic Church which had been such a focal point of national and local community life throughout the Middle Ages. This accompanied a complex process of reorganization within the English Church – already some of the more questionable arrangements of the Church structure of the Middle Ages were being addressed. In 1200 there had been about 9,500 parishes in England, and by 1535 this had been rationalized to somewhere in the region of 8,800. But this was as nothing when compared with the changes that were coming.

In 1531 Thomas Cromwell launched an attack on papal authority in England. The fine of £100,000 levied on the clergy in return for a pardon for accepting foreign jurisdiction both contributed to depleted royal finances and tapped into popular resentment against worldly clergy. In 1532 (temporarily) and 1534 (permanently) the pope's right to tax the English clergy was removed. At the same time Convocation (the ruling body of the English Church) was forced to accept royal authority over its decisions. In 1543 the Act of Supremacy finally recognized Henry as 'supreme head' of the Church in England. But it can be argued that 'The Act of Supremacy represents not an attack on Catholicism as such, but a consolidation of royal authority, in effect, a nationalisation of the Church in England . . .'[1] This process started in 1531, continued in 1536 with the suppression of the lesser religious houses and in 1538 with an all-out assault on the larger religious houses, until, by 1540, all the religious houses in England and Wales had been dissolved. The Crown gained over £1 million from this campaign. The dissolution of the monasteries put an end to institutions which had dominated much of the life of the Middle Ages. It is clear though that, by the early sixteenth century, monasticism as an idea was in decline. Recruitment had been reduced to a trickle and bequests of land had all but stopped. The wealth of many monasteries meant that a large number could have continued for many years even in this condition, but it is important to realize that Henry's dissolution struck at an already ailing institution. Even so, the dissolution removed important features of the medieval world, since many monasteries had become the focal points of pilgrimages and the veneration of relics and of saints. It is not surprising, then, that within a decade these two areas of devotion had also come under sustained attack. Furthermore, the distribution of monastic land meant that a large number of local landowners had a vested interest in ensuring that there would be no return to the world of the great religious houses, even if the destruction had not already made such a development impossible to imagine.

Nevertheless, there remained a deep-seated commitment to the Catholic faith in Lincolnshire and in much of the north and the south-west of England. The Middle Ages would not vanish overnight. Indeed, in the later years of Henry's reign the 'Middle Ages' were fighting back at the very centre of government. In the same year as the Pilgrimage of Grace failed in its attempt to defend the traditional Catholic faith, the passing of The Ten Articles by Convocation established the basic beliefs of the English Church. However, apart from listing only three sacraments (baptism, penance and the Eucharist) and describing the Eucharist in terms whose ambiguity could give comfort to both Catholics and Protestants, the articles were very conservative. Henry had certainly not launched a 'Protestant Reformation'. But more radical measures were to follow. In 1538 laws were passed banning the burning of candles before images of saints, burning candles in commemoration of the dead, statues and images which were objects of veneration. Aspects of medieval practice which had survived for centuries were ended in a matter of months. After 1539 not a single will recorded in the diocese of Salisbury left money for 'lights' (the burning of candles), whereas in the previous eight years about 50 per cent of all wills had included such requests.[2] In addition, an English Bible was to be placed in every parish church.

But the world of the Middle Ages was not yet gone. Resistance by more conservative elements – allied to the king's own conservative outlook in religious matters – led, in 1539, to the passing of The Act of Six Articles. These reasserted Catholic beliefs in such key areas as transubstantiation and clerical celibacy. In 1543 the publication of *The King's Book* asserted the continuation of prayers for the dead and, by implication, the idea of purgatory. In addition, the Mass remained in Latin, although Cranmer had succeeded in publishing his *English Litany* in 1544, which would later be the forerunner of the *Book of Common Prayer*. The mindset of 'the Middle Ages' and that of 'the Early Modern World' were wrestling for control of the character of England.

Henry VIII's break with Rome had allowed significant inroads of Protestantism and Lollardy into London and the south-east, where it already had some support. Not that Henry had intended any of this – he died in all his essential beliefs a Catholic who no longer accepted the authority of the pope. It was the Protestant policies of Edward VI's government which really ended the Catholic ritual year of the Middle Ages and changed the texture of life for most English people. As Diarmaid MacCulloch has argued: 'The Edwardian adventure was a religious revolution, demolishing the traditional Church in order to rebuild another'.[3] Arguably it was in these later changes that the feel, the colour and the rhythm of the Middle Ages was truly dislocated and replaced by a new experience. During the young king's short reign (1547–53) the widespread removal and destruction of religious images occurred, the Act of Six Articles was repealed, chantries were dissolved (their continuation was in question anyway because of their cost), clerical celibacy was no longer required and all religious orders were banned. The revolutionary intent of the new government was apparent in the fact that the ordinance requiring the removal of religious images came only a few weeks into the new regime and went well beyond earlier decrees. This time not only statues but two-dimensional images, such as stained glass, were included in the prohibition. All over the country statues, ancient rood screens, 'Jesse Trees' and stained-glass windows were smashed or removed. Much of the internal fabric of churches, which had grown up over the previous millennium, vanished in a reign which only lasted six and a half years.

While the Catholic belief in transubstantiation was not officially rejected, both the bread and wine were now to be received in the Eucharist, instead of bread only, as in previous Catholic practice. In addition, the 1549 Act of Uniformity insisted on the use of the new English *Book of Common Prayer* in churches. In 1552 a second edition of the Prayer Book was issued. The radical nature of these changes was clearly recognized at the time. Those who approved of the changes described Edward VI as a young Josiah, a reference to the eight-year-old king of Judah in the Old Testament who had purged his nation of idolatry. Edward himself was just nine years old when he became king and, having been brought up to support the Protestant reformed religion, his actions stemmed as much from his personal sincerity as from his regency council. And, although this end to the community traditions of the Middle Ages was in many ways a government-driven revolution, it nevertheless was in alliance with a significant minority of the population, particularly in London and the south-east. Once in place (and given the brevity of the counter-reformation reign of Edward's half-sister Mary and the moderate Protestant policies of Elizabeth), the changes soon became part of national culture. The evidence for this reveals itself in curious ways. Despite earlier developments, the great majority of wills in London during the last years of Henry VIII's reign were still worded in the terminology of the Catholic faith. But in the short reign of Edward VI the proportion expressing themselves in the vocabulary of the new reformed religion rose to 44 per cent.[4] A way of looking at and understanding death – and life – had changed. If there is an 'end to the Middle Ages', then the period 1547 to 1553 is as reasonable a time to choose for it as any.

This 'end' revealed itself in building as well as in destruction. After the relative stagnation in church architectural styles in the fifteenth century, the early sixteenth saw a return to increased elaboration and decoration. But this did not last. Renaissance ideas, with their focus on classical forms, diverted fashions and funds from church building into the mansions of the elite. At the same time, the Reformation swept away monasteries and the national framework of huge church building projects (with their coordinated community of craftspeople) which had made the great medieval churches possible. By 1550 medieval styles seemed compromisingly Catholic. When medieval style became acceptable again, after 1600, it was no longer innovative and would soon be challenged by classical forms.[5]

Population, land and economic change
The sixteenth century saw other major changes in English society. Of these, one of the most significant was an increase in

population. In 1520 the population stood at about 2.5 million, by 1541 it had risen to 2.7 million and by 1551 it reached about 3 million – and the upward trend continued. This created social and economic stresses. Firstly, prices and rents soared as there was increased demand for land and accommodation. As a result investors began to buy land not as an end in itself but for profit, which created a speculation boom in land prices. While this benefited a small number of investors and property speculators, it also resulted in a large number of tenants, or copyholders, being forced out of the market as they could not afford the increased rents. Many migrated into towns in search of work. In addition, food prices increased yet further as speculators attempted to sell foodstuffs in the dearest markets in order to offset the rising cost of purchasing land. This in turn depressed the living standards of the poorest members of society.

In order to maximize profits from land which was now more expensive to buy or rent, a number of larger landowners attempted to increase their profits by enclosing land for sheep farming. The attraction of this lay in the reduction of the cost of wages paid for the running of sheep farms (which required relatively few workers) compared with arable farming, which was more labour intensive. This development hit poorer members of rural communities as it frequently involved the enclosure of common land, or the amalgamation of smaller farms into larger, more efficient and therefore more profitable land units.

This increased drive to maximize profit from land was manifested in many ways. One of the most unusual was in a virtual declaration of war on animals which were not part of the rural economy (and especially those accused of consuming crops). Henry VIII's first Vermin Act of 1532 put a price on the head of birds and animals which damaged agriculture and 'ordeyned to dystroye Choughes, Crowes and Rookes'. But it did not end there. The list of animals to be exterminated included foxes, kingfishers, bullfinches, golden eagles, woodpeckers, owls, pine martens, badgers, otters, choughs and hedgehogs. Hedgehogs were thought to suck milk from cows – though quite what the economic consequences were considered to be is a puzzle. Choughs were thought to carry embers which might set fire to houses. These accusations are clearly bizarre, but the hard-headed economics which drove these exterminatory drives waged war on the fauna of the medieval landscape. Churchwardens were charged with keeping a record of kills and for paying bounties for severed heads or tails. Elizabeth I's Vermin Act of 1566, passed for 'the preservation of Grayne', laid down the rewards of a penny for three crows' heads or twelve starlings' heads, rising to a shilling each for foxes and badgers. Even ospreys (fourpence), kingfishers (a penny) and otters (twopence) were considered a threat to 'Grayne', though in what sense is hard to imagine. These accounts tell a terrible story of destruction: for example, 498 hedgehogs killed in one year in the Cheshire parish of Bunbury, at 2d a head, and 380 red kites killed in a 13-year period at Tenterden in Kent, for a penny a time.[6]

The problems of increasing population were slightly softened (though not permanently) by a warmer fluctuation in the climate. Although the 'Little Ice Age' lasted from about 1450 to 1850, the period in the middle of the sixteenth century – according to tree-ring analysis – was one of the warmest before 1900. This needs to be set against contemporary records, which can give an unbalanced picture through focusing on unusual climatic events such as the Thames freezing over three times, severe rainfall in 1526–7 and 1535, and severe drought in 1536. Incidentally, the Thames freezing was not in itself unusual since, before the later dredging and embanking of the river, it was much shallower than today and therefore more prone to a dramatic response both to very cold weather and to summer droughts.

Accompanying these developments, the sixteenth-century changes in economic relationships ended many features of medieval social networks. This was the latest chapter in a process which had started in the thirteenth century. In the century after 1200 English landlords were aggressively expanding their control. They demanded more work on their demesne land, increased control over villeins, reduced wages and increased rent. In the 150 years after 1350 much of this trend was reversed. Demesne land was rented out for cash payments, villeinage vanished, wages went up and rents went down. All of this altered the traditional relationships in rural communities. However, after 1500, rising population altered this pattern yet again, with some wealthier farmers – the *yeoman* class – increasing their wealth at the expense of a growing population of the landless and dispossessed. A new rural gentry class was emerging. This was subdivided hierarchically, even as it held itself distinct from those below it on the social scale. In addition, lords were no longer actively engaged in agricultural production and tenant farmers were now the 'locomotive of change' in the developing countryside. Clothiers and yeoman farmers had stepped into the positions left vacant by the retreating influence of feudal lords.

The increasing tendency of landowners to enclose their land was both a symptom and a cause of this break with the past. It went hand in hand with a lessening of communal cooperation and an increase in a more private and exclusive use of land. This was especially striking when the land involved had once been 'common land', used by the whole local community. The newly hedged fields were mostly designed to control sheep and livestock and these in turn reduced the demand for agricultural workers and drove many from the land. In addition, the hedges were also barriers aimed at excluding the poor and their animals from the pastures in question. As one recent study put it, they were 'organic barbed wire', which even at the time was regarded as being as divisive socially as it was agriculturally. Not for nothing would revolutionaries of the next century be called *Levellers*. We interpret this term as coming from their demands for social equality but the name itself was inspired by 'hedge-levelling', a common way in which popular unrest and resentment expressed itself. Hedges then were symbols of an emerging and privatized Early Modern World and the end of the more communal world of the Middle Ages.[7]

However, if this drive for agricultural efficiency in a money economy sounds like modern capitalism, we must pause before we make an assumption too far. If something like the cash-driven economy of the modern world was emerging around 1500, it still had a long way to go before it dominated life. As late as 1525 as many as 60 per cent of households were effectively self-employed; a proportion similar to the situation in 1300.[8] It would be a long time before a wage-earning majority created a social and economic situation comparable to modern capitalist economies and societies. The social structure of England in the sixteenth century, although changing, was still largely medieval.

The drive for increased profit by successful landowners was accompanied, in the late 1530s, by the dissolution of the monasteries, which led to major changes in wealth distribution and church patronage. This actually had less impact on agri-culture than might be supposed, since many monastic estates were already leased to local gentry, who now bought them and converted their tenancies into outright ownership. Nevertheless, the sixteenth century saw a steady growth in the number of local gentry, from a baseline of about 4,500 in 1524. Appearing in the sixteenth-century records under such imprecise terms as 'gentleman' and 'esquire', their exact numbers can be difficult to calculate with any precision, but it is clear that they were growing as a class. What is evident is that these new social groupings emerged in a time of increasing economic turbulence.

By the time Henry VIII came to the throne, in 1509, inflation was eating away at the economic stability which had begun to emerge in the final decades of the fifteenth century. One reason for this was recovering population growth, which pushed up food prices; another was a flooding of the European silver market due to the discovery of new supplies in the Tyrol, Saxony and Bohemia in the 1460s and 1490s. But a more serious cause lay in government policy. Warlike foreign policy drained national resources through heavy taxation. It was a drive to increase the liquid assets at the disposal of the Crown which led to the dissolution of the abbeys and the sale of their property in the 1530s. This was accompanied by ten debasements of the currency between 1542 and 1551, each of which reduced the silver content of the English coinage further and lowered its value. So thin was the silver wash on pennies that, when used, it quickly wore off the highest points of Henry VIII's portrait, earning him the nickname of 'Old Copper-nose'. By 1550 the spending power of the average English worker had fallen by about 33 per cent compared with 1500. The result – when combined with rising population – was increasing levels of underemployment, unemployment and vagrancy.

It is clear, from the issues just explored, that many apparent certainties of the later Middle Ages faced serious challenges by the middle years of the sixteenth century. A notable casualty was the cloth trade. In 1550 cloth exports reached their peak. In this market London led the way, but other ports also bene-fited from this boom in the cloth trade. However, there was a corresponding decline in the export of raw wool, which had once been one of the main export trades of the later Middle Ages. After 1550, even finished cloth would face a slow decline, in the face of competition from the continent and as a result of exchange-rate fluctuations after 1544.

But the picture was not solely one of decline. Merchant Venturers, such as those of Bristol, were leading the search for a north-west passage to Asia. While they failed in this, their journeys to the north-east coast of North America led to an expansion in the fishing industries based in Bristol, which processed the fish products of Newfoundland. While Tudor exploration of the new world was limited and small scale compared with that of the Spanish, it was a tentative sign of things to come – though few can have guessed its importance at the time. However, it is significant that, as the Middle Ages drew to a close, this contact was beginning – pointing as it did to future developments of immense importance that would have a profound impact on the economy of England and of Europe as a whole.

The 'new world'

Other tentative evidence exists from the sixteenth century of increased international connections. Travellers, who became known in England as *Egyptians* or *Gypsies* (but who called themselves *Roma*) were, it is claimed, first recorded in Scotland in 1505. However, an entry in the Book of the Lord High Treasurer in 1492, in the reign of the Scots king James IV, referring to someone titled '*King of Rowmais*' may actually be the earliest record. This title sounds like the kind often used by leaders of early travelling groups of Roma. Other titles in sixteenth-century British sources include 'Earl of Little Egypt' and 'Earl of Greece'. In England this community of travellers was first recorded in about 1515. The first discriminatory law against them, expelling Gypsies from England, dates from 1530, by which it was forbidden to transport Gypsies into England. The punishment for doing so was the considerable fine of £40 for a ship's owner or captain. The Gypsies themselves, if identified, were to be hanged by a law of 1554. They were regarded as aliens and became the objects of mistrust: it was the start of a long history of persecution which would extend into modern times. Gypsies became another group living on the edge of society, and their persecution adds to the argument that discrimination against minorities was, sadly, well established by the sixteenth century.

At the same time, other newcomers to England seem to have been the first recorded Africans in the country since the Roman Empire. In 1501 Katherine of Aragon landed at Deptford with a multicultural retinue including Moors, as well as Muslims and Jews. In 1507 a black African trumpeter named John Blanc was paid by Henry VII for playing at royal events. In a painting of the Westminster Tournament of 1511 he became the first black Londoner ever to be portrayed. Documents from the High Court of Admiralty reveal that in 1547 a black slave named Jacques Francis, from Guinea, in West Africa, was employed by an Italian salvage operator as a diver recovering items from a ship which had sunk in the Solent. In 1555 a group of West Africans, who were cooperating in opening up African markets to Tudor traders, were brought to England. But it was in 1562 that John Hawkins began a more terrible connection with Africa, which pointed to greater atrocities to come. In that year he transported African slaves for the first time in English ships. It was another indication of the Early Modern period which was emerging from the end of the Middle Ages.

The complex mixture of social tension for some and increased wealth for others means it is hard to generalize regarding the life experiences and mental outlook of English men and women at the end of the Middle Ages. For some it was a time of lessening independence and falling living standards, accompanied by the loosening of the spiritual anchors which had provided stability throughout the Middle Ages. For others, a 'new world' was opening up of increased wealth at home, new global markets and a new dynamic and individual religious experience. For many people in 1553, the jury would have been out on whether these changes were going to be a positive or a negative experience overall. But that things were changing could not be denied.

Accompanying the other great currents of religious, economic and social change which were sweeping England in the first half of the sixteenth century was one of increasing intellectual awareness driven by the greater availability of books – a 'revolution in the mind'. This was due to the arrival of printing in the second half of the fifteenth century. In the 1530s it was printing presses which took the debates of Thomas More and William Tyndale to a wider audience: one disseminating, the other countering Reformation ideas. More people could engage with the arguments because of the new technology. And, of course, it was the availability of printing which made it possible to place the English-language Great Bible in every parish church in 1539.

While regional identities remained strong, the newly invented printing press and the associated increase in literacy meant that more of a 'national culture' was beginning to emerge. This particularly benefited the spread of the English language into the northern and western areas of the British Isles. Not a single book was printed in Cornish, or Irish or Scots Gaelic in this period (there was in fact no printer in Ireland before 1551). The first book in Welsh was printed in only 1546. As a result, the prolific printing houses of London and Edinburgh meant that it was the southern – London – version of English which was the dominant form of the language in England, and Lowland Scots (a form of English) which was becoming the dominant language of Scotland. Soon even this Scots form of English (sometimes called *Inglis*) would give way to the London-based form amongst educated Scots. Bibles in Scotland, as in England, were printed in the southern (London) form of English. Indeed, it would not be until 1983 that a Scots translation of the Bible appeared. In the face of this advance of English, Welsh, Cornish and Gaelic began an uphill struggle to survive. The linguistic landscape of the Middle Ages – and with it the cultural and social fabric – was being transformed.

From a modern perspective it is easy to see the fourteenth and fifteenth centuries as disastrous, and therefore the end of the Middle Ages in the sixteenth century as something of an anti-climax. It is as if the dynamism of the medieval period had slowly collapsed in disorder and eventual dissolution. Yet by 1500 England – like Europe as a whole – had survived and was recovering from its demographic upheavals. Large building projects continued (although those connected with the Church would lose impetus after the 1530s) and voyages of exploration had begun, even if the early English ones were modest compared with those of the Spanish and Portuguese. The strength and resilience of medieval civilization is revealed in the fact that England and Europe by the 1550s, for all the trauma and turmoil that would follow in the next century, were not in terminal decline but instead stood at the start of a process of world domination. Whatever our modern verdict on this may be, it says a great deal about the achievements of the Middle Ages that it was possible.

NOTES

Introduction

1   Bailey, Mark, *The English Manor, c.1200–1500*, Manchester University Press, 2002, p.216.

2   Ibid., pp.220–1.

Chapter 1

1   Wood, Michael, *Domesday: A Search for the Roots of England*, BBC Publications, 1986, pp.149–50.

2   Hodges, Richard, *The Anglo-Saxon Achievement*, Duckworth, 1989, p.150.

3   *Coin News*, Jan. 2003, p.43.

4   Leahy, K., 'Detecting the Vikings in Lincolnshire', *Current Archaeology*, no.190, vol.XVI, no.10, Feb. 2004, pp.462–8.

5   Mays, Simon, 'Wharram Percy: The Skeletons', *Current Archaeology*, no.193, Aug./Sept. 2004, pp.45–9.

6   Richards, J., *Viking Age England*, Batsford, 1991.

7   Smith, L. (ed.), *The Making of Britain: The Dark Ages*, Macmillan, 1984.

8   Barnes, M., 'The Scandinavian languages in the British Isles: The Runic Evidence', in: Adams, J. & Holman, K. (eds), *Scandinavia*

and Europe, 800–1350: Contact, Conflict and Coexistence, Brepols, 2004.

9   Redmond, Angela, *Viking Burial in the North of England*, BAR British Series, 429, 2007, p.28.

10   Hadley, D.M., *The Vikings in England: Settlement, Society and Culture*, Manchester University Press, 2006, p.70.

11   Ibid., p.128.

12   Ibid., p.130.

13   Carver, Martin, 'Why that? Why there? Why then? The politics of early medieval monumentality', in: Hamerow, H. & MacGregor, A., *Image and Power in the Archaeology of Early Medieval Britain*, Oxford University Press, 2001.

14   Turner, S., 'Converting the British Landscape', *British Archaeology*, no.84, Sept.–Oct. 2005.

15   Blair, John, *The Church in Anglo-Saxon Society*, Oxford University Press, 2005, p.228.

16   Ibid., p.498.

17   McNeill, Tom, *Faith, Pride and Works: Medieval Church Building*, Tempus, 2006, p.25.

18   Ibid., pp.30–3.

19   Ibid., pp.37–9.

20   Jesch, Judith, 'Scandinavians and "Cultural Paganism" in Late Anglo-Saxon England', in: Cavill, P. (ed.), *The Christian Tradition in Anglo-Saxon England*, D.S. Brewer, 2004.

21   Fowler, P., 'Farming in early Medieval England: some fields for thought', in: Hines, J. (ed.), *The Anglo-Saxons From The Migration Period to the Eighth Century. An Ethnographic Perspective*, Boydell Press, 1997.

22   Hooke, D., *The Landscape of Anglo-Saxon England*, Leicester University Press, 1998.

23   Fyfe, Ralph; Rippon, Stephen & Brown, Tony, 'Pollen, farming and history in Greater Exmoor', *Current Archaeology*, no.192, vol.XVI, no.12, June 2004, pp.564–7.

24   Hey, G., *Yarnton: Saxon and Medieval Settlement and Landscape*, Thames Valley Landscapes Monograph, 2004.

25   Fellows-Jensen, G., 'Scandinavian Settlement in the British Isles and Normandy: What the Place-Names Reveal', in: Adams, J. & Holman, K. (eds), *Scandinavia and Europe, 800–1350: Contact, Conflict and Coexistence*, Brepols, 2004.

26   Hadley, D., *The Northern Danelaw. Its Social Structure, c.800–1100*, Leicester University Press, 2000.

27   Selkirk, Andrew, 'The Saxons', *Current Archaeology*, no.200, Nov. 2005, pp.416–23.

28   Miles, David, *The Tribes of Britain*, Phoenix, 2006, p.251.

29   Oosthuizen, Susan, *Landscapes Decoded: The Origins and Development of Cambridge's Medieval Fields*, University of Herts Press, 2006.

30   Pestell, T. & Ulmschneider, K. (eds), *Markets in Early Medieval Europe: Trading and 'Productive' Sites, 650–850*, Windgather Press, 2003.

31   Scull, C., 'Urban centres in pre-Viking England?' in: Hines, J. (ed.), *The Anglo-Saxons From The Migration Period to the Eighth Century. An Ethnographic Perspective*, Boydell Press, 1997.

32   Wickham, C., *Framing the Early Middle Ages. Europe and the Mediterranean, 400–800*, Oxford University Press, 2005.

33   Blair, op. cit., p.290.

34   Ibid., p.282.

35   Hinton, D., *Gold and Gilt, Pots and Pins. Possessions and People in Medieval Britain*, Oxford University Press, 2005, p.170.

36   Kopke, N. & Baten, J., 'The Biological Standard of Living in Europe During the Last Two Millennia', *European Review of Economic History*, vol.9, no.1, Cambridge University Press, 2005.

37   Payne, Sebastian, 'Ancestral Myth', *British Archaeology*, Sept. 2005, p.51.

38   Fell, Christine, *Women in Anglo-Saxon England*, British Museum Publications, 1984, p.57.

39   Laing, Lloyd & Jennifer, *Anglo-Saxon England*, Routledge and Kegan Paul, 1979, pp.167–179; *Early English Art and Architecture*, Sutton, 1996, pp.169–91.

40   Laing, 1996, op. cit., p.203.

Chapter 2

1   Rigby, S.H., *English Society in the Later Middle Ages: Class, Status and Gender*, Macmillan, 1995, p.28.

2   Meager, David, 'Slavery in Europe from the End of the Roman Empire', *Cross†Way*, Winter 2007, no.103.

3   Dyer, Christopher, *The Origins of the Medieval Economy, c.850–c.1100*, Yale University Press, 2002, pp.92–4.
4   Rigby, op. cit., p.22.
5   Jones, E.D., 'The Medieval Leyrwite: A Historical Note on Female Fornication', *The English Historical Review*, vol.107, no.425 (Oct. 1992), pp.945–53.
6   Dyer, Christopher, *Standards of Living in the Later Middle Ages, Social Change in England c.1200–1520*, Cambridge University Press, 1989, pp.110–40.
7   Rigby, op. cit., pp.105–7.
8   Ibid., p.24.
9   Wood, Michael, *Domesday: A Search for the Roots of England*, BBC Publications, 1986, pp.191–2.
10 Miller, E. & Hatcher, J., *Medieval England: rural society and economic change 1086–1348*, Longman, 1985 edn, pp.28–9.
11 Jones, Richard & Page, Mark, *Medieval Villages in an English Landscape: Beginnings and Ends*, Windgather Press, 2006, p.137, Fig.50.
12 Bathe, Graham & Greenaway, Dick, 'A Lye Pit in Savernake', *Wiltshire Archaeological and Natural History Magazine*, vol.100, 2007, pp.207–10.
13 Knight, David & Vyner, Blaise, 'Quarry harvest,' *British Archaeology*, May–June 2007, no.94, pp.16–19.
14 Dix, J., Bull, J. & Lenham J., 'Saxon Fish Weirs in the Blackwater Estuary, Essex', www.arch.soton.ac.uk/ Research/ justin/ saxon%20fisheries.html, 1999.
15 Parfitt, Keith & Corke, Barry, 'Excavating Dover's Medieval Seafarers', *British Archaeology*, May–June 2007, no.94, pp.32–7.
16 Jones, Richard & Page, Mark, op. cit, pp.192–3.
17 Ibid., p.183.
18 Ibid., p.204.
19 Rigby, op. cit., p.115.
20 Dobson, R.B., *The Peasants revolt of 1381*, Pitman, 1970, pp.373–5.
21 More, Thomas, *Utopia*, translated by Turner, Paul, Penguin Books, 1965, p.46.

Chapter 3
1   Dyer, Christopher, *Making a Living in the Middle Ages: The People of Britain 850–1520*, Yale University Press, 2002, pp.192–3.

2 Ibid., p.194.
3 www.bristol.ac.uk/researchreview/2002/1112697846.
4 Dyer, op. cit., p.207.
5 Ibid., p.212.
6 Calendar of Fine Rolls, vol.V, 1337–1347, HMSO 1915.
7 Rigby, S.H., *English Society in the Later Middle Ages: Class, Status and Gender*, Macmillan,1995, p.151.
8 'Cambridge historic city centre revealed', *Current Archaeology* 208, vol.XVIII, no.4, Mar./Apr. 2007, pp.22–31.
9 Rigby, op cit, p.148.
10 Shaw, Mike; Chapman, Andy & Soden, Iain, 'Northampton', *Current Archaeology*, no.155, vol.XIII, no.11, Dec. 1997, pp.408–15.
11 Longcroft, Adam, 'The avant-garde architects of late medieval Norfolk', *Current Archaeology*, 211, vol.XVIII, no.7, Sept. 2007, pp.40–3.

Chapter 4

1 The Holy Bible, New International Version, Hodder and Stoughton, 1979.
2 Moorman, J.H., *Church Life in England in the Thirteenth Century*, Cambridge University Press, 1945, pp.4–5, 52–6, 67, 410–13.
3 Lawrence, C.H, *Medieval Monasticism*, Longman, 1989, p.254.
4 Mittuch, Sally, 'The Norwich Book of the Dead', *British Archaeology*, no.92, Jan./Feb. 2007, pp.46–9.
5 McNeill, Tom, *Faith, Pride and Works: Medieval Church Building*, Tempus, 2006, p.14.
6 Ibid., p. 227.
7 Calendar of Patent Rolls, Henry V, 1413–1416, HMSO 1910.
8 Williams, Howard, *Death and Memory in Early Medieval Britain*, Cambridge University Press, 2006, p.103.
9 Boddington, Andy, *Raunds Furnells: The Anglo-Saxon Church and Churchyard*, English Heritage Archaeological Report 7, 1996.
10 Carver, Martin, 'Burial as Poetry: The Context of Treasure in Anglo-Saxon Graves', in: Tyler, E. (ed.), *Treasure in the Medieval West*, York Medieval Press, 2000, p.37.
11 Goldberg, P.J.P., *Medieval England: A Social History, 1250–1550*, Hodder Headline, 2004, p.281.

12   Gilchrist, Roberta & Sloane, Barney, *Requiem: The Medieval Monastic Cemetery in Britain*, Museum of London Archaeology Service, 2005, pp.214–30.

13   Ariès, Philippe, *The Hour of Our Death*, translated by Helen Weaver, Alfred A. Knopf, 1981; Binski, Paul, *Medieval Death: Ritual and Representation*, Cornell University Press,1996.

14   Calendar of Close Rolls, Edward III, 1330–1333, HMSO 1898.

15   Calendar of Patent Rolls, Edward III, 1370–1374, HMSO 1914.

16   Bellerby, Rachel, 'Society and Solitude: The Reaction against Monasticism', *Medieval History*, Issue 11, July 2004, pp.26–31.

17   Watson-Brown, Martha, 'Marks of Faith: Pilgrims at the Shrine of Saint Richard of Chichester', *Medieval History*, Issue 12, Aug. 2004, pp.48–55.

18   *Council for British Archaeology Wessex News*, Apr. 2007, p.24.

19   Weaver, F.W., 'Keynsham Abbey, Part 2', *Somerset Archaeological and Natural History Society*, vol.53, 1907, pp.15–63.

Chapter 5

1   Ziegler, Philip, *The Black Death*, Penguin Books,1982, pp.158–9.

2   Goldberg, P.J.P., *Medieval England, A Social History, 1250–1550*, Hodder Headline, 2004, pp.71–5.

3   Patrick, P., 'In search of Friar Tuck', *Current Archaeology*, 198, July/Aug. 2005, pp.306–7.

4   Gilchrist, Roberta & Sloane, Barney, *Requiem: The Medieval Monastic Cemetery in Britain*, Museum of London Archaeology Service, 2005, p.307.

5   Ibid., p.212.

6   Ameen, S., Staub, L., Ulrich, S., Vock, P., Ballmer, F. & Anderson, S.E., 'Harris lines of the tibia across centuries: a comparison of two populations, medieval and contemporary in Central Europe', *Skeletal Radiology*, vol.34, no.5, May 2005.

7   Roberts, Charlotte & Cox, Margaret, *Health and Disease in Britain: from prehistory to the present day*, Alan Sutton, 2003, pp.244–6.

8   Dyer, Christopher, *Making a Living in the Middle Ages, The People of Britain 850–1520*, Yale University Press, 2002, p.357.

9   Mays, Simon, 'Wharram Percy: the Skeletons', *Current Archaeology*, 193, Aug./Sept. 2004, pp.45–9.

10 Wilson, R.L., *Soap Through The Ages* (4th edn), London: Unilever Ltd, 1955.

11 Somerville, J., *Christopher Thomas – Soapmaker of Bristol*, Redcliffe Press, 1991. This information on soap is from: Hunt, John A., PhD, FRPharmS, 'A short history of soap', *The Pharmaceutical Journal*, vol.263, no.7076, Dec. 18/25 1999, pp.985–9.

12 http: //www.channel4.com/history/microsites/H/history/i-m/london2.html.

13 Ibid.

14 Ibid.

15 Dimbleby, David, *BBC History Magazine*, vol.8, no.6, June 2007, p.69.

16 Ziegler, Philip, *The Black Death*, Penguin Books, 1982, p.128.

17 www.stmarysashwell.org.uk/church/graffiti/decode.htm.

18 Quoted in Fryde, E.B., *Later Medieval England*, Alan Sutton, 1996, p.2.

19 Hatcher, John, 'Mortality in the fifteenth century: some new evidence', *Economic History Review*, 39, 1986, pp.19–38.

20 http: //www.british-history.ac.uk/report.asp?compid=33639, '*Introduction*', *Calendar of letter-books of the city of London: L: Edward IV-Henry VII* (1912), pp.I–XLIV.

21 Dormandy, Thomas, *The White Death: A History of Tuberculosis*, Hambledon Press, 1999.

22 Travis, John, reporting in *Science News*, June 3, 1995, vol.147, no.22, p.346, on www.sciencenews.org.

23 Knighton, Henry, *Knighton's Chronicle, 1337–1396*, edited and translated by G. Martin, Clarendon Press, 1995.

24 Brothwell, Don, 'Studies on Skeletal and Dental Variation: a View Across Two Centuries', in: Cox, Margaret & Mays, Simon (eds), *Human Osteology in Archaeology and Forensic Science*, Greenwich Medical Media Ltd, 2000, p.5.

25 'London's Monasteries', *Current Archaeology*, no.162, vol.XIV, no.6, Apr./May 1999, pp.204–14.

26 Waldron, Tony, *St Peter's, Barton-upon-Humber, Lincolnshire. A Parish Church & its Community: Vol 2, the Human Remains*, Oxbow, 2007.

Chapter 6

1 Whittock, Martyn (ed.), *The Pastons in Medieval Britain*, Heinemann, 1993, p.25.
2 Bailey, Mark, *The English Manor, c.1200–1500*, Manchester University Press, 2002, p.213.
3 Ibid., pp.202, 211.
4 Ibid., p.233.
5 Karras, Ruth Mazo, *Sexuality in Medieval Europe: Doing Unto Others*, University of Minnesota, New York: Routledge, 2005.
6 Salih, Sarah, *Versions of Virginity in Late Medieval England*, Boydell & Brewer, 2001.
7 Bernau, Anke; Salih, Sarah & Evans, Ruth (eds), *Medieval Virginities*, Toronto University Press, 2003.
8 Gilchrist, Roberta, *Gender and Material Culture: the Archaeology of Religious Women*, Routledge, 1994.
9 Razi, Zvi, 'The Myth of the Immutable English Family', *Past and Present*, 140, 1993, pp.3–44.
10 Goldberg, P.J.P., *Medieval England, A Social History, 1250–1550*, Hodder Headline, 2004, pp.17–18.
11 Ariès, Philippe, *Centuries of Childhood: a Social History of Family Life*, Alfred A. Knopf, 1962.
12 Ibid., p.33.
13 Classen, Albrecht (ed.), *Childhood in the Middle Ages and the Renaissance: The Results of a Paradigm Shift in the History of Mentality*, Walter de Gruyter, 2005.
14 Peters Auslander, Diane, 'Victims or Martyrs: Children, Anti-Judaism and the Stress of Change in Medieval England', in: Classen, Albrecht (ed.), *Childhood in the Middle Ages and the Renaissance: The Results of a Paradigm Shift in the History of Mentality*, Walter de Gruyter, 2005, p.108.
15 William Langland, *Piers the Ploughman*, translated by Goodridge, J.F., Penguin Books, 1966, p.62.
16 Aston, Margaret, 'Segregation in Church', in: Sheils, W.J. & Wood, D. (eds), 'Women in the Church', *Studies in Church History*, 27, 1990, pp.237–94.
17 Goldberg, op. cit., p.57.
18 Ibid., p.284.
19 Watt, Diane, *Medieval Women's Writing: Works by and for Women in England, 1100–1500*, Polity, 2007.

20 Childs, Jessie, 'The Monstrous Regiment', *BBC History Magazine*, vol.8, no.1, Jan. 2007, pp.33–5.

Chapter 7

1   Bailey, Mark, *The English Manor, c.1200–1500*, Manchester University Press, 2002, pp.223–6.
2   Ibid., pp.203, 211.
3   Hamilton, Derek; Pitts, Mike & Reynolds, Andrew, 'A revised date for the early medieval execution at Stonehenge', *Wiltshire Archaeological and Natural History Magazine*, vol.100, 2007, p.202.
4   Williams, Howard, *Death and Memory in Early Medieval Britain*, Cambridge University Press, 2006, pp.89–90.
5   Ibid., p.186. The reinterpretation of 'heathen burials' was made by Andrew Reynolds, 'Beheadings, burials and boundaries: the landscape of execution in Anglo-Saxon Wiltshire', Wiltshire Archaeological and Natural History Society lecture, March 2008.
6   Gilchrist, Roberta & Sloane, Barney, *Requiem: The Medieval Monastic Cemetery in Britain*, Museum of London Archaeology Service, 2005, pp.73–4.
7   Hanawalt, Barbara, *Crime and Conflict in English Communities, 1300–1348*, London & Cambridge, Massachusetts, 1979, pp.261–73.
8   Campbell, Bruce M.S., 'The Land', in: Horrox, Rosemary & Ormrod, W. Mark (eds), *A Social History of England, 1200–1500*, Cambridge University Press, 2006, p.227.
9   Dyer, Christopher, *Everyday Life in Medieval England*, Hambledon, 2000, p.9.
10 Campbell, op. cit., p.228.
11 Prestwich, Michael, 'The enterprise of war', in: Horrox, Rosemary & Ormrod, W. Mark (eds), *A Social History of England, 1200–1500*, Cambridge University Press, 2006, p.89. Note also: warfare gave increased status to the members of the professional armies of the fifteenth century and the term 'esquire' became interchangeable with 'man-at-arms'; the term 'yeoman' with 'archer': Bell, Adrian; Chapman, Adam; Curry, Anne; King, Andy & Simpkin, David, 'What did you do in the Hundred Years' War, Daddy?' *The Historian*, no.96, Winter 2007–2008, p.8.

12 Harvey, B.F., 'Introduction: the 'crisis' of the early fourteenth century', in: Campbell, B.M.S., *Before the Black Death: studies in the 'crisis' of the early fourteenth century*, Manchester, 1991, p.15.

13 Hanawalt, Barbara, 'The female felon in fourteenth century England', in: Stuard, S.M., (ed.), *Women in Medieval Society*, University of Pennsylvania Press, 1993.

14 Bellamy, J.G., 'The Coterel Gang: An Anatomy of a Band of Fourteenth-Century Criminals', *The English Historical Review*, vol.79, no.313 (Oct. 1964), pp.698–717.

15 Hanawalt, Barbara, 'The Peasant Family and Crime in Fourteenth-Century England', *The Journal of British Studies*, vol.13, no.2 (May 1974), pp.1–18.

16 Bailey, op. cit., pp.231–5.

17 Whittock, Martyn (ed.), *The Pastons in Medieval Britain*, Heinemann, 1995, pp.14–15.

18 Post, John, 'The King's Peace', in: Smith, Lesley (ed.), *The Making of Britain: The Middle Ages*, Channel Four/Macmillan, 1985, pp.153–4.

19 Bailey, op. cit., p.228.

20 Carpenter, David, 'Working the Land', in: Smith, Lesley (ed.), *The Making of Britain: The Middle Ages*, Channel Four/Macmillan, 1985, p.99.

21 www.bl.uk/treasures/magnacarta/translation/mc_trans.html.

22 Reported in *The Week*, 31 Mar. 2007, Issue 607, p.46.

23 www.robinhoodministries.org.

24 Holt, James, *Robin Hood*, Thames and Hudson, 1989.

25 Ibid., pp.187–8.

26 Ibid., p.190.

27 Ibid., p.16.

28 Ibid., p.40. This reference also applies to the Andrew de Wyntoun rhyme in the previous lines.

29 Ibid., p.69.

Chapter 8

1 McLaren, Mary-Rose, *The London Chronicles of the Fifteenth Century. A Revolution in English Writing. With an annotated edition of Bradford, West Yorkshire Archives MS 32D86/42*, Boydell & Brewer, 2002.

2 Miles, David, *The Tribes of Britain*, Phoenix, 2006, p.238.

3   Orme, Nicholas, *Medieval Children*, Yale University Press, 2001. Niles, Philip, 'Baptism and the Naming of Children in Late Medieval England', *Medieval Prosography*, 3, 1982, pp.95–107.

4   Reaney, P.H., *A Dictionary of English Surnames*, revised 3rd edn, with corrections and additions by R.M. Wilson, Oxford University Press, 1997, p.xxiii.

5   Harrison, Julian, 'Whatever happened to our medieval manuscripts?', *Medieval History*, vol.2, no.4, Issue 16, Dec. 2004, pp.40–7.

6   Ibid., p.43.

7   Cherry, John, 'Images of power: medieval seals', *Medieval History*, Issue 8, Apr. 2004, pp.34–41.

8   Black, Maggie, *Medieval Cookery: Recipes and History*, English Heritage, 2003;'Knowing Your Place. Table etiquette in medieval society', *Medieval History*, Issue 12, Aug. 2004, pp.56–9.

9   Blackbourne, Matthew, 'Mystery Plays', *Medieval History*, Issue 11, July 2004, pp.22–5.

10 Northall, Philip, 'Worts and Ale: Ale, Inns, Taverns and Alehouses in Merrie England', *Medieval History*, Issue 14, Oct. 2004, pp.48–55. This reference also applies to the lines from the John Skelton poem of 1517 (*The Tunning of Elynour Rummyng*) and from Andrew Boorde's *The Fyrste Boke of the Introduction of Knowlegde*, in the previous paragraphs.

11 Jackson, Sophie, 'The Ancient History of Backgammon', *Medieval History*, Issue 11, July 2004, pp.40–9. See also Bell, R.C., *Board and Table Games from Many Civilisations*, Dover Publications, New York, 1979.

12 Bailey, Mark, *The English Manor, c.1200–1500*, Manchester University Press, 2002, p.1.

13 Holland, William, 'The Medieval Menagerie', *BBC History Magazine*, vol.8, no.1, Jan. 2007, pp.30–1.

Chapter 9

1   'The Milk Street Mikveh', *Current Archaeology*, 190, vol.XVI, no.10, Feb. 2004, pp.456–61.

2   Karras, Ruth Mazo, *Sexuality in Medieval Europe: Doing Unto Others*, University of Minnesota, New York: Routledge, 2005.

3   Manchester, K., 'Medieval Leprosy: The Disease and its Management', in: Deegan, M. & Scragg, D.G. (eds), *Medicine in*

Early Medieval England, Manchester Centre for Anglo-Saxon Studies, 1987, pp.27–32.

4   Gilchrist, Roberta & Sloane, Barney, *Requiem: The Medieval Monastic Cemetery in Britain*, Museum of London Archaeology Service, 2005, pp.205–7.

5   Moore, R.I., *The Formation of a Persecuting Society. Authority and Deviance in Western Europe, 950–1250*, Blackwell Publishing, 2006 (2nd revised edn).

6   Ibid.

7   Cohn, Norman, *The Great Witch-Hunt*, Chatto-Heinemann, 1975. Provides a detailed analysis of both the origins and the course of the Great Witch Hunts.

Chapter 10

1   The Holy Bible, New International Version, op cit.

Primary sources

The quotations in this chapter taken from medieval chronicles are from these following excellent modern translations. In each case the name of the chronicler and his principal work is followed by details of the modern edition.

Adam Usk. The Chronicle of Adam Usk, 1377–1421
The Chronicle of Adam Usk, 1377–1421. Edited and translated by C. Given-Wilson, Clarendon Press, 1997.

Anglo-Saxon Chronicle
The Anglo-Saxon Chronicle. Translated by G. Garmonsway, Everyman's University Library, 1972.

Bestiary MS Bodley 764
Bestiary MS Bodley 764, translated by R. Barber, The Boydell Press, 1999.

Geoffrey of Burton. Life and Miracles of St Modwenna
Geoffrey of Burton. Life and Miracles of St Modwenna. Translated and edited by Robert Bartlett, Clarendon Press, 2002.

Gerald of Wales. The Journey Through Wales and The Description of Wales
Gerald of Wales. The Journey Through Wales/The Description of Wales, Translated and introduced by Lewis Thorpe, Penguin Books, 1978.

Gervase of Tilbury. Recreation for An Emperor
Gervase of Tilbury, Otia Imperialia, Recreation for an Emperor, edited
and translated by S. Banks & J. Binns, Clarendon Press, 2002.

Henry of Huntingdon. The History of the English People
*Henry, Archdeacon of Huntingdon. Historia Anglorum. The History
of the English People*. Edited and translated by Diana Greenway,
Clarendon Press, 1996.

Henry Knighton. Chronicle (sometimes called *Chronica de Eventibus
Anglia*)
Knighton's Chronicle, 1337–1396, Edited and translated by G. Martin,
Clarendon Press, 1995.

John of Worcester. The Chronicle of John of Worcester
*The Chronicle of John of Worcester. Volume II, The Annals from 450
to 1066*, edited by R. Darlington & P. McGurk, translated by J. Bray
& P. McGurk, Clarendon Press, Oxford, 1995. And *Volume III, The
Annals from 1067 to 1140 with The Gloucester Interpolations and The
Continuation to 1141*, edited and translated by P. McGurk,
Clarendon Press, 1998.

Matthew Paris. Chronica majora (the '*Major Chronicles*')
*The Illustrated Chronicles of Matthew Paris, Observations of
Thirteenth Century Life*, translated, edited and introduced by Richard
Vaughan, Allan Sutton, 1993. This anthology covers the period 1247–50.
And *Matthew Paris's English History From the Year 1235 to 1273*, trans-
lated by Rev. J. Giles, London, 1852, volume I (years 1235–44).
Published in three volumes.

Ralph of Coggeshall. Chronicon Anglicanum ('*English Chronicle*')
The translation of the Orford Merman is from: www.castles-
abbeys.co.uk/Orford-Castle.html, and at http: //norfolkcoast.co.uk/
myths/ml_orfordmerman.htm.

Ranulf Higden. The Universal Chronicle
The Universal Chronicle of Ranulf Higden, by John Taylor, Clarendon
Press, 1966.

Thomas Walsingham. The St Albans Chronicle, 1376–1394
*The St Albans Chronicle, The Chronica maiora of Thomas Walsingham,
I, 1376–1394*, edited and translated by J. Taylor, W. Childs & L.
Watkiss, Clarendon Press, 2003.

Walter Map. Courtiers' Trifles
Walter Map, De Nugis Curialium, Courtiers' Trifles, edited and translated by M. James, revised by C. Brooke & R. Mynors, Clarendon Press, 1983.

Westminster Chronicle, 1381–1394
The Westminster Chronicle, 1381–1394. Edited and translated by L. Hector and B. Harvey, Clarendon Press, 1982.

William of Malmesbury. The History of the English Kings
William of Malmesbury, Gesta Regum Anglorum, The History of the English Kings, volume I. Edited and translated by R. Mynors, completed by R. Thomson & M. Winterbottom, Clarendon Press, 1998.

William of Newburgh. The History
The History of William of Newburgh, translated from the Latin by Joseph Stevenson (1856 edn), based on Herne's text of 1719. Facsimile reprint by Llanerch Publishers, 1996.

Secondary Sources
The following secondary sources also provide excerpts from medieval chronicles and thought-provoking commentaries.

- Prestwich, Michael, 'The "Wonderful Life" of the Thirteenth Century', in: *Thirteenth Century England VII, Proceedings of the Durham Conference, 1997*, Woodbridge, 1999. This very useful essay explores a number of signs and marvels, including ones quoted by John of Oxenedes, Ralph of Coggeshall and Friar Roger Bacon, and those found in the Chronicles of Edward I and Edward II.
- Salisbury, J., *The Beast Within. Animals in the Middle Ages*, Routledge, 1994.
- Wilson, D., *Signs and Portents, Monstrous births from the Middle Ages to the Enlightenment*, Routledge, 1993.

Chapter 11
1   Phythian-Adams, Charles, *Local History and Folklore*, Bedford Square Press, 1975, pp.23–4.
2   Hutton, Ronald, *The Rise and Fall of Merry England, The Ritual Year 1400–1700*, Oxford University Press, 1994 and *The Stations of the Sun*, Oxford University Press, 1996.
3   Hutton, 1996, op cit, pp.90–1.

4   *Sir Gawain and the Green Knight*, translated by Tolkien, J.R.R., George Allen & Unwin Limited, 1975, p.26.

5   Luke 2: 30–32, The Holy Bible, New International Version, op cit.

6   Holt, Professor James, *Robin Hood*, Thames and Hudson, 1989, p.160.

7   Hutton, 1996, op. cit., pp.262–8.

8   Bossy, John, *Christianity in the West, 1400–1700*, Oxford University Press, 1985, pp.57–75.

9   Aston, M., 'Corpus Christi and Corpus Regni: heresy and the Peasants' Revolt', *Past and Present*, 143 (1994), pp.3–47.

10 Duffy, Eamon, 'Religious belief', in: Horrox, Rosemary & Ormrod, W. Mark (eds), *A Social History of England, 1200–1500*, Cambridge University Press, 2006, p.306.

11 James, Mervyn, 'Ritual, Drama and Social Body in the Medieval English Town', in: *Society, Politics and Culture*, Cambridge University Press, 1986, pp.17–41.

12 Hazlitt, W.C., *Tenures of Land and Customs of Manors*, 1874, p.54, referred to in Phythian-Adams, Charles, 'Ritual reconstructions of society', in: Horrox, Rosemary & Ormrod, W. Mark (eds), *A Social History of England, 1200–1500*, Cambridge University Press, 2006, p.369.

13 Phythian-Adams, 2006, op. cit., pp.376–7.

14 Duffy, op. cit., p.332.

15 Hutton, 1994, op. cit.

Chapter 12

1   Goldberg, P.J.P., *Medieval England, A Social History, 1250–1550*, Hodder Headline, 2004, p.239.

2   Ibid, p.240.

3   MacCulloch, Diarmaid, *Tudor Church Militant: Edward VI and the Protestant Reformation*, Allen Lane, 1999.

4   Brigden, Susan, *London and the Reformation*, Oxford, 1989.

5   McNeill, Tom, *Faith, Pride and Works: Medieval Church Building*, Tempus, 2006, pp.236, 242.

6   Lovegrove, Roger, *Silent Fields. The long decline of a nation's wildlife*, Oxford University Press, 2007.

7   Blomley, Nicholas, 'Making Private Property: Enclosure, Common Right and the Work of Hedges', *Rural History:*

Economy, Society, Culture, vol.18, no.1, Cambridge University Press, 2007.

8   Dyer, Christopher, *Making a Living in the Middle Ages, The People of Britain 850–1520,* Yale University Press, 2002, p.364.

BIBLIOGRAPHY

Ameen, S., Staub, L., Ulrich, S., Vock, P., Ballmer, F. & Anderson, S.E., 'Harris lines of the tibia across centuries: a comparison of two populations, medieval and contemporary in Central Europe', *Skeletal Radiology*, vol.34, no.5, May 2005.

Ariès, Philippe, *Centuries of Childhood: a Social History of Family Life*, Alfred A. Knopf, 1962.

Bailey, Mark, *The English Manor, c.1200–1500*, Manchester University Press, 2002.

Barnes, M., 'The Scandinavian languages in the British Isles: The Runic Evidence', in: Adams, J. & Holman, K. (eds), *Scandinavia and Europe, 800–1350: Contact, Conflict and Coexistence*, Brepols, 2004.

Bell, R.C., *Board and Table Games from Many Civilisations*, Dover Publications, 1979.

Bellerby, Rachel, 'Society and Solitude: The Reaction against Monasticism', *Medieval History*, Issue 11, July 2004, pp.26–31.

Bernau, Anke, Salih, Sarah & Evans, Ruth (eds), *Medieval Virginities*, Toronto University Press, 2003.

Black, Maggie, *Medieval Cookery: Recipes and History*, English Heritage, 2003.

Black, Maggie,'Knowing Your Place. Table etiquette in medieval society', *Medieval History*, Issue 12, Aug. 2004, pp.56–9.

Blackbourne, Matthew, 'Mystery Plays', *Medieval History*, Issue 11, July 2004, pp.22–5.

Blair, J., *The Church in Anglo-Saxon Society*, Oxford University Press, 2005.

Burton, Janet, *Monastic and Religious Orders in Britain, 1000–1300*, Cambridge University Press, 1994.

Cannon, Jon, *Cathedral: the great English cathedrals and the world that made them*, Constable, 2007.

Capelli, C., et al., 'A Y Chromosome Census of the British Isles', *Current Biology*, 13, May 2003, pp.979–84.

Carver, Martin, 'Why that? Why there? Why then? The politics of early medieval monumentality', in: Hamerow, H. & MacGregor, A., *Image and Power in the Archaeology of Early Medieval Britain*, Oxford University Press, 2001.

Cherry, John, 'Images of power: medieval seals', *Medieval History*, Issue 8, Apr. 2004, pp.34–41.

Childs, Jessie, 'The Monstrous Regiment', *BBC History Magazine*, vol.8, no.1, Jan. 2007, pp.33–5.

Classen, Albrecht (ed), *Childhood in the Middle Ages and the Renaissance: The Results of a Paradigm Shift in the History of Mentality*, Walter de Gruyter, 2005.

Cox, Margaret & Mays, Simon (eds), *Human Osteology in Archaeology and Forensic Science*, Greenwich Medical Media Ltd, 2000.

Cubitt, Catherine, 'Images of St Peter: The Clergy and the Religious Life in Anglo-Saxon England', in: Cavill, Paul (ed), *The Christian Tradition in Anglo-Saxon England*, D.S. Brewer, 2004.

Danziger, Danny & Gillingham, John, *1250: The Year of Magna Carta*, Hodder & Stoughton, 2003.

Duffy, Eamon, *Marking the Hours: English People and their prayers, 1240–1570*, Yale University Press, 2006.

Dyer, Christopher, *Standards of Living in the Later Middle Ages, Social Change in England c.1200–1520*, Cambridge University Press, 1989.

Dyer, Christopher, *Everyday Life in Medieval England*, Hambledon, 2000.

Dyer, Christopher, *Making a Living in the Middle Ages: The People of Britain 850–1520*, Yale University Press, 2002.

Dyer, Christopher, *An Age of Transition? Economy and Society in England in the Later Middle Ages*, Oxford University Press, 2005.

Fell, Christine, *Women in Anglo-Saxon England*, British Museum Publications, 1984.

Fellows-Jensen, G., 'Scandinavian Settlement in the British Isles and Normandy: What the Place-Names Reveal', in: Adams, J. & Holman, K. (eds), *Scandinavia and Europe, 800–1350: Contact, Conflict and Coexistence*, Brepols, 2004.

Fletcher, R., *Bloodfeud: Murder and Revenge in Anglo-Saxon England*, Oxford University Press, 2003.

Fowler, P., 'Farming in early Medieval England: some fields for thought', in: Hines, J. (ed), *The Anglo-Saxons From The Migration Period to the Eighth Century. An Ethnographic Perspective*, Boydell Press, 1997.

Fryde, E.B., *Later Medieval England*, Alan Sutton, 1996.

Gilchrist, Roberta & Sloane, Barney, *Requiem: The Medieval Monastic Cemetery in Britain*, Museum of London Archaeology Service, 2005.

Goldberg, P.J.P., *Medieval England, a Social History, 1250–1550*, Hodder Headline, 2004.

Hadley, D, *The Northern Danelaw. Its Social Structure, c800–1100*, Leicester University Press, 2000.

Happe, Peter, *English Mystery Plays*, Penguin, 1975.

Harrison, Julian, 'Whatever happened to our medieval manuscripts?' *Medieval History*, vol.2, no.4, Issue 16, Dec. 2004, pp.40–7.

Hart, Cyril, *The Danelaw*, Hambledon & London, 2003.

Harvey, P.D.A. & McGuiness, Andrew, *A Guide to British Medieval Seals*, University of Toronto Press, 1996.

Hey, G., *Yarnton: Saxon and Medieval Settlement and Landscape*, Thames Valley Landscapes Monograph, 2004.

Hinton, D., *Gold and Gilt, Pots and Pins. Possessions and People in Medieval Britain*, Oxford University Press, 2005.

Hodges, R., *The Anglo-Saxon Achievement*, Duckworth, 1989.

Holland, William, 'The Medieval Menagerie', *BBC History Magazine*, vol.8, no.1, Jan. 2007, pp.30–1.

Holt, James, *Robin Hood*, Thames and Hudson, 1989.

Hooke, D., *The Landscape of Anglo-Saxon England*, Leicester University Press, 1998.

Horrox, Rosemary & Ormrod, W. Mark (eds), *A Social History of England, 1200–1500*, Cambridge University Press, 2006.

Howard, I., *Swein Forkbeard's Invasions and the Danish Conquest of England, 991–1017*, Boydell Press, 2003.

Hunt, John A., PhD, FRPharmS, 'A short history of soap', *The Pharmaceutical Journal*, vol.263, no.7076, Dec. 18/25 1999, pp.985–9.

Hutton, Ronald, *The Pagan Religions of the Ancient British Isles*, Basil Blackwell, 1991.

Hutton, Ronald, *The Rise and Fall of Merry England, The Ritual Year 1400–1700*, Oxford University Press, 1994.

Hutton, Ronald, *The Stations of the Sun*, Oxford University Press, 1996.

Jackson, Sophie, 'The Ancient History of Backgammon', *Medieval History*, Issue 11, July 2004, pp.40–9

Jesch, Judith, 'Scandinavians and "Cultural Paganism" in Late Anglo-Saxon England', in: Cavill, P. (ed), *The Christian Tradition in Anglo-Saxon England*, D.S. Brewer, 2004.

Jones, E. D., 'The Medieval Leyrwite: A Historical Note on Female Fornication', *The English Historical Review*, vol.107, no.425 (Oct. 1992), pp.945–53.

Jones, Richard & Page, Mark, *Medieval Villages in an English Landscape: Beginnings and Ends*, Windgather Press, 2006.

Kopke, N. & Baten, J., 'The Biological Standard of Living in Europe During the Last Two Millennia', *European Review of Economic History*, vol. 9, no.1, Cambridge University Press, 2005.

Laing, Lloyd & Jennifer, *Anglo-Saxon England*, Routledge and Kegan Paul, 1979.

Laing, Lloyd & Jennifer, *Early English Art and Architecture*, Sutton, 1996.

Lawrence, C.H., *Medieval Monasticism*, 2nd edn, Longman, 1989.

Leahy, K., 'Detecting the Vikings in Lincolnshire', *Current Archaeology*, no.190, Vol.XVI, no.10, Feb. 2004, pp.462–8.

Lovegrove, Roger, *Silent Fields. The Long Decline of a Nation's Wildlife*, Oxford University Press, 2007.

Loveluck, C., 'Wealth, waste and conspicuous consumption. Flixborough and its importance for mid and late Saxon settlement studies', in: Hamerow, H. & MacGregor, A., *Image and Power in the Archaeology of Early Medieval Britain*, Oxford University Press, 2001.

Mays, Simon, 'Wharram Percy: The Skeletons', *Current Archaeology*, no.193, Aug./Sept. 2004, pp.45–9.

McLaren, Mary-Rose, *The London Chronicles of the Fifteenth Century, A Revolution in English Writing. With an annotated edition of Bradford, West Yorkshire Archives MS 32D86/42*, Boydell & Brewer, 2002.

Meager, David, 'Slavery in Europe from the End of the Roman Empire', *Cross†Way*, Winter 2007, no.103.

Miles, David, *The Tribes of Britain*, Phoenix, 2006.

Miller, E. & Hatcher, J., *Medieval England: rural society and economic change 1086–1348*, Longman, 1985 edn.

Mittuch, Sally, 'The Norwich Book of the Dead', *British Archaeology*, no.92, Jan./Feb. 2007, pp.46–9.

Moorman, J.H., *Church Life in England in the Thirteenth Century*, Cambridge University Press, 1945.

Niles, Philip, 'Baptism and the Naming of Children in Late Medieval England', in *Medieval Prosography*, 3, 1982, pp.95–107.

Northall, Philip, 'Worts and Ale: Ale, Inns, Taverns and Alehouses in Merrie England', *Medieval History*, Issue 14, Oct. 2004, pp.48–55.

Orme, Nicholas, *Medieval Children*, Yale University Press, 2001.

Parfitt, Keith & Corke, Barry, 'Excavating Dover's Medieval Seafarers', *British Archaeology*, May–June 2007, no.94, pp.2–37.

Pestell, T. & Ulmschneider, K. (eds), *Markets in Early Medieval Europe: Trading and 'Productive' Sites, 650–850*, Windgather Press, 2003.

Pryor, Francis, *Britain in the Middle Ages: An Archaeological History*, Harper Press, 2006.

Reaney, P.H., *A Dictionary of English Surnames*, revised 3rd edn, with corrections and additions by R.M. Wilson, Oxford University Press, 1997.

Richards, J., *Viking Age England*, Batsford,1991.

Rigby, S.H., *English Society in the Later Middle Ages: Class, Status and Gender*, Macmillan, 1995.

Roberts, Charlotte & Cox, Margaret, *Health and Disease in Britain: From Prehistory to the Present Day*, Alan Sutton, 2003.

Salih, Sarah, *Versions of Virginity in Late Medieval England*, Boydell & Brewer, 2001.

Scull, C., 'Urban centres in pre-Viking England?', in: Hines, J. (ed.), *The Anglo-Saxons From The Migration Period to the Eighth Century. An Ethnographic Perspective*, Boydell Press, 1997.

Smith, Lesley (ed.), *The Making of Britain: The Dark Ages*, Channel Four/Macmillan, 1984.

Smith, Lesley (ed.), *The Making of Britain: The Middle Ages*, Channel Four/Macmillan, 1985.

Staley, Lynn (ed.), *The Book of Margery Kempe, Book I, Part I*, Medieval Institute Publications, 1996.

Watson-Brown, Martha, 'Marks of Faith: Pilgrims at the Shrine of Saint Richard of Chichester', *Medieval History*, Issue 12, Aug. 2004, pp.48–55.

Watt, Diane, *Medieval Women's Writing: Works by and for Women in England, 1100–1500*, Polity, 2007.

Weale, M. et al., 'Y Chromosome Evidence for Anglo-Saxon Mass Migration', *Molecular Biology and Evolution*, 19 (7), 2002, pp.1008–21.

Whittock, Martyn, *The Pastons in Medieval Britain*, Heinemann Educational, 1995.

Wickham, C., *Framing the Early Middle Ages. Europe and the Mediterranean, 400–800*, Oxford University Press, 2005.

Williams, Howard, *Death and Memory in Early Medieval Britain*, Cambridge University Press, 2006.

Woolgar, C.M., Waldron, Tony & Sarjeantson, Dale, *Food in Medieval England: Diet and Nutrition*, Oxford University Press, 2006.

INDEX